REGNUM GLOBAL VOICES

Beyond Integral Mission

Series Preface

The **Global Voices** series takes the missiological work of writers who have written in their own language and makes this accessible to the English-speaking world through translation and republishing. The key principle here is that the translated work reflects the context, experience and thinking of the local context. In so doing, Regnum Books seeks to amplify voices less easily heard outside their own contexts. Work of this nature will make a significant contribution to the development of 'polycentric missiology'; namely, mission thinking and practice that truly reflects the contexts, concerns and contributions of the global church in all its rich diversity.

Series Editors

Paul Bendor-Samuel	Executive Director, Oxford Centre for Mission Studies
Mark Greenwood	BMS Overseas Team Leader for South America and Sub-Saharan Africa
Timóteo Carriker	Mission educator and consultant to the Brazilian Bible Society

REGNUM GLOBAL VOICES

Beyond Integral Mission
Fresh Voices from Latin America

Edited by Daniel Clark

Copyright © Daniel Clark 2022

First published 2022 by Regnum Books International
Originally published in Buenos Aires by: Ediciones KAIROS, 2006
ISBN: 978-978-9403-95-2

Regnum is an imprint of the Oxford Centre for Mission Studies
St. Philip and St. James Church
Woodstock Road
Oxford OX2 6HR, UK
www.regnumbooks.net

09 08 07 06 05 04 03 7 6 5 4 3 2 1

The right of Daniel Clark as the editor of this Work has been asserted by him in accordance with the Copyright, Designs and Patents Act 1988.

All rights reserved. No part of this publication may be reproduced, stored in a retrieval system, or transmitted in any form or by any means, electric, mechanical, photocopying, recording or otherwise, without the prior permission of the publisher or a licence permitting restricted copying. In the UK such licences are issued by the Copyright Licensing Agency, 90 Tottenham Court Road, London W1P 9HE.

British Library Cataloguing in Publication Data
A catalogue record for this book is available from the British Library

ISBN: 978-1-5064-9740-2
eBook ISBN: 978-1-5064-9741-9

Typeset by Words by Design

The publication of this volume is made possible through the financial assistance of **Evangelische Mission Weltweit e.V.**

Distributed by Fortress Press in the US, Canada, India, and Brazil

Contents

Contributors		vii
Acronyms		ix

1. Moving Beyond the Golden Age in Latin American
   Evangelical Theology — 1
   Daniel Clark
2. Integral Mission Theology as a Latin American — 9
   Evangelical Theology
   Regina Fernandes Sanches
3. Integral Mission 'At the Car Wash':
   Facing the Challenges of Post-Odebrecht South America — 19
   Daniel Clark
4. Christianity and Culture in Brazil: A Reformational Approach — 35
   Josué Reichow
5. Economics, Theology and the "Kingdom of God" in
   Latin America — 45
   Martín Ocaña
6. The Ultimate Betrayal: Christianity's Triumph and
   Shame in Power — 57
   Lucas Magnin
7. The Absence of Dialogue in a Technologically Faceless Age:
   An Augustinian Response of Embrace and Confession — 73
   Davi C. Ribeiro Lin
8. Strangers or Friends? A Mexican Perspective on
   Cross-border Relations in Times of Immigration Crisis — 85
   Alejandra Ortiz
9. "Where Do You Come from and Where Are You Going?":
   Refugees in the Pentateuch — 95
   Délnia Bastos
10. "Privileged Is The One Who Reads Aloud":
    An Open Letter from a Visually Impaired Peruvian Theologian — 111
    Julio Gonzáles Ulloa
11. Ultimato: "Talking about Racism" — 117
    *Ziel Machado, Márcio Mendes, Terezinha Candiero,
    Quéfren de Moura, Ana Staut and Atilano Muradas*

12. Redemption for the Land, Justice for Its People:
    A Cry from Peru   131
    Rut Pérez-Saldarriaga
13. The Dawn of the Brazilian Missionary Movement   141
    Felipe Fulanetto
14. Do Christians Have a Place at the Table for Muhammed?
    Separating the "Muhammed of Faith" from the
    "Muhammed of History"   157
    Marcos Amado

Index   171
Bibliography   177

Contributors

Marcos Amado is director of the Centro de Reflexão Missiológica Martureo. He has a Master's degree in Theology from All Nations College in the United Kingdom with specialisation in Islamic Studies and a degree in Advanced Studies in Middle Eastern Religions and Culture from the Institute of Middle East Studies in Beirut, Lebanon.

Délnia Bastos is a director of Interserve Brasil and is a member of the Steering Council for the Vocare Mission Mobilization Movement. She has a master's degree in Missiology from the Centro Evangélico de Missões, Viçosa, Brazil.

Terezinha Candieiro is general coordinator of the International Preschool Programme of the World Missions Board of the Convenção Batista Brasileira. She has a master's degree in Integral Development and degrees in teaching and theology.

Daniel Clark is director of Postgraduate Studies at the Seminario Bautista de Lima, Peru, with BMS World Mission. He has a PhD in Theology and Religious Studies from the University of Wales, Trinity Saint David, and a Master's degree in Aspects of Biblical Interpretation from the London School of Theology.

Felipe Fulanetto is a pastor of the Nazarene Church and theological education coordinator of the Seminario Teológico Nazareno do Brasil Polo Campinas. He is also coordinator of the Hispanic World Missionary Formation of the Centro de Formação Missionária. He has a Master's degree in Missiology from the Centro Evangélico de Missões and a degree in theology from the Seminario Teológico Nazareno do Brasil

Julio Gonzáles Ulloa is principal of the Seminario Bautista de Lima, Peru and pastor of Bethel Baptist Church in Callao, Peru. He has a Master's degree in Theology from the Seminario Bautista de Lima and a degree in Theology from the Seminario Bautista de Trujillo.

Davi C. Ribeiro Lin is a licensed psychologist, a teaching fellow at Seminário Teológico Servo de Cristo, and a pastor at Comunidade Evangélica do Castelo in Belo Horizonte. He holds a joint PhD in Theology from the Katholieke Universiteit of Leuven and Faculdade Jesuíta, and a Master's degree in Theology from Regent College, Vancouver.

Ziel Machado is pastor of Igreja Metodista Livre da Saúde and Vice-Principal of Seminário Servo de Cristo and has also worked with ABUB and IFES. He has a Master's degree in Religious Studies from the Pontifícia Universidade Católica de São Paulo.

Lucas Magnin is a musician and author based in Córdoba, Argentina. He has a Master's degree in Theology from the Universidad Bíblica Latinoamericana, in San José Costa Rica, and a degree in Modern Literature from the Universidad Nacional de Córdoba.

Márcio Mendes is a Major in the Salvation Army.

Quéfren de Moura has worked with the Brazilian Bible Society since 2011, especially in the areas of translation and publishing. She has a Master's degree in Translation from the Universidade de São Paulo and is working on a Doctorate in Critical Studies of the Hebrew Bible at the same institution.

Atilano Muradas is a journalist, pastor, writer, theologian, and composer.

Martín Ocaña Flores is pastor of the Iglesia Evangélica Bautista de Moquegua, Peru. He has a PhD in Theology from the South African Theological Seminary Latin American Doctoral Programme and a Master's degree in Theology from the Universidad Bíblica Latinoamericana, Costa Rica.

Alejandra Ortiz is Latin American Coordinator of the IFES Logos and Cosmos Initiative. She is based in Tijuana, participating in a church which runs a shelter for migrants. She has a Master's degree in Theology from Regent College, Vancouver.

Rut Pérez-Saldarriaga is a Peruvian environmental activist engaging churches with creation care in Peru and Latin America. A toxicologist, she is part of the Peruvian Environmental and Human Health Technical team responsible for monitoring communities affected by heavy metals generated by extractive industries.

Josué Reichow currently works at L'Abri Fellowship in Hampshire, United Kingdom. He has a Master's degree in Theology from the Escola Superior de Teologia, São Leopoldo, Brazil, and a degree in Social Sciences from the Universidad Federal de Pelotas, Brazil.

Regina Fernandes Sanches is editor of Edições Saber Criativo, part of the FTL Board and is involved in theological education in Brazil. She has a Master's degree in Theology and Missiology (Jesuit Faculty) and is a specialist in Afro-Brazilian and Indigenous culture and history.

Ana Staut is a student of journalism and writes on the arts, Christian worldview and behaviour.

Acronyms

ABUB	Aliança Bíblica Universitária do Brasil
AGEUP	Asociación de Grupos Evangélicos Universitarios del Perú
AKET	Associação Kuyper para Estudos Transdisciplinares
AMTB	Associação de Missões Transculturais Brasileiras
CBE	Congresso Brasileiro de Evangelização
CLADE	Congreso Latinoamericano de Evangelización
CLAI	Consejo Latinoamericano de Iglesias
COLEF	Colegio de la Frontera Norte
COMIBAM	Cooperación Misionera Iberoamericana
CONEP	Concilio Nacional Evangélico del Perú
FTL	Fraternidad Teológica Latinoamericana
IFES	International Fellowship of Evangelical Students
ISAL	Iglesia y Sociedad en América Latina
LCWE	Lausanne Committee for World Evangelisation
MEP	Movimento Evangélico Progressista
NAR	New Apostolic Reformation
PT	Partido dos Trabalhadores
RENAS	Rede Evangélica Nacional de Ação Social

1. Moving Beyond the Golden Age in Latin American Evangelical Theology
Daniel Clark

In the year 2000, during my undergraduate studies, I took a module on Contextual Theology. As part of the course, we were assigned Gustavo Gutiérrez's classic, *A Theology of Liberation*.[1] As a Latin American it was hard to recognise the society Gutiérrez was describing, and many of his proposals came across as dated. Years later, my college published a journal with a collection of student essays. The article on Latin America focused on liberation theology, especially what was put forward by Gustavo Gutiérrez.[2] I was left with the question, has nothing new emerged in Latin American theology and missiology since the 1970s?

This volume seeks to provide an affirmative answer to this question. It introduces a series of younger missiological thinkers reflecting on the varied Latin American contexts. Authors write from a diversity of geographical regions, ranging from Mexico to Argentina and a diversity of ecclesial backgrounds, but all broadly write from within the Latin American evangelical theological tradition.

Hence, it is necessary to define what is meant by the term "evangelical" in Latin America. As in post-Reformation Europe, it is generally used to refer to those trinitarian Christians "united in their suspicion and rejection of the Catholic Church."[3] Although it is common in English language scholarship to treat Pentecostals as distinct from evangelicals, in Latin America Pentecostals are considered evangelicals, and thus most evangelicals are Pentecostal. Likewise, all Episcopalians, Lutherans, and Presbyterians are considered evangelicals, irrespective of their theology, especially as the missionaries who founded these denominations usually came from their evangelical wings in North America.

---

[1] G. Gutiérrez, *A Theology of Liberation: History, Politics, and Salvation: Revised Edition with a New Introduction*, Maryknoll: Orbis, 1988.
[2] J. Clarke, 'Friend or foe? An evangelical engaging Latin American liberation theology', *Encounters* 27 (2007). Available online at https://encountersmissionjournal.files.wordpress.com/2011/03/friend_or_foe_27.pdf, accessed 26 April 2021.
[3] W. Shea, *The Lion and the Lamb: Evangelicals and Catholics in America* (New York: Oxford University Press, 2004), p.12. See also M Brinkerhoff and R. Bibby, 'Circulation of the Saints in South America: A Comparative Study', *Journal for the Scientific Study of Religion* 24.1 (1985), p. 44.

Nonetheless, it is hard to move beyond this general statement to provide clear examples of what constitutes evangelical identity in Latin America. In the United Kingdom, the term evangelical is often used to imply a common theological core of "conversionism, activism, biblicism and crucicentrism,"[4] yet this does not apply in Latin America where there is little awareness of having a shared theology. The evangelical scene is diverse and fragmented, with much competition between and within denominations.

Efforts to increase evangelical unity and form representative institutions have had varied levels of success across the continent. Where evangelicals have faced the pressure of hegemonic Catholicism and repressive governments, these institutions have fared better than in contexts of religious freedom. For example, in Peru, the heyday of the National Council of Churches, CONEP, came first in the struggle for religious freedom and then during the persecution of Pentecostal Quechua speaking churches by Marxist guerrillas and the Peruvian armed forces.[5] The transition to democracy and greater religious freedom has led to a weakening of CONEP, with many of the major denominations withdrawing their membership.

Latin American evangelicalism can be better understood in terms of the metaphor of an extended family. Therefore, there are common traits which characterise membership of this family although not all will be possessed by all members. Opposition to the Roman Catholic Church is a key family characteristic. This anti-Roman Catholicism is expressed in opposition to the Pope, Marian spirituality and the cult of the saints and the rejection of any cultural traits or festivals associated with Catholicism. Nonetheless, recent years have seen a thawing of attitudes towards Catholicism, especially in academic circles, and thus, one of our contributors, Davi Lin, seeks to appropriate the theological legacy of Augustine of Hippo.

Latin American evangelicals generally hold the Bible in high esteem. This does not necessarily translate itself into a concern with the literal meaning of the Biblical text, but rather with the use of the Bible as a source of symbols and images and it is a mistake to label Latin Americans as fundamentalists. This repertoire of Biblical images is often expressed in music, which is arguably one of the main sources of a common evangelical identity. Older forms of technology, such as radio stations and CDs combine with newer platforms such as video sharing sites and social media to disseminate the latest worship songs among evangelicals, transcending geographical and denominational boundaries.[6]

---

[4] D. Bebbington, *Evangelicalism in Modern Britain: A History from the 1730s to the 1980s* (London: Routledge, 1989), p. 4.
[5] See for example T. Gutiérrez Sánchez, *Evangélicos, democracia y nueva sociedad: Ensayos de historia política* (Lima: Ediciones AHP, 2005), pp. 175–208.
[6] An example of how music helps form a sense of evangelical identity in the context of a *favela* is narrated in M. Oosterbaan, 'Spiritual Attunement: Pentecostal Radio in the Soundscape of a Favela in Rio de Janeiro', *Social Text* 25.3 (2008), pp. 123–145.

Two main 'clans' can be identified within this diverse evangelical family: the historical churches that arrived in the nineteenth century, and the Pentecostal churches which emerged in the twentieth century. Although there are difficulties in defining Latin American Pentecostalism,[7] key elements include the sense of having experienced the work of the Holy Spirit, especially through the exercise of spiritual gifts such as prophecy, healing and speaking in tongues, the encouragement of a supernatural worldview and the use of music to provide a sense of occasion, even spectacle.[8] Yet, at a congregational level differences between Pentecostals and historical evangelicals are not always clear cut as there have been Pentecostal breakaways from the latter and many historical evangelical churches have taken on features of Pentecostal liturgy. Similarly, some middle-class Pentecostal churches resemble Baptists and Presbyterians in requiring academically trained pastors and a structured liturgy. Freston provides a nuanced perspective in defining historical evangelicals and Pentecostals as "ideal types at the two extremes of a continuum on which most real cases are a highly variable and creative mix."[9] To further complicate matters, since the 1960s there has been an emergence of indigenous Pentecostal churches, with a strong emphasis on prosperity theology, aggressive approaches to spiritual warfare and controversial fundraising methods. These churches are often referred to as Neo-Pentecostal,[10] and have become heavily involved in national media and politics, causing much controversy among evangelicals.

The Golden Age of Latin American Theology

Daniel Salinas defines the 1970s as the "golden decade" of Latin American Evangelical theology.[11] Salinas follows the well-established path of documenting the emergence of the Latin American Theological Fraternity-FTL and its influential role during that decade, in dialogue both with Liberation Theology and more conservative theologians from North America and Europe.

Often, talk about golden ages is a matter of nostalgia and rose-tinted spectacles. For English football fans lamenting over forty years without a major trophy, it is easy to forget that the golden age of English football was heavily indebted to the eyesight of a Russian linesman. Yet, some golden ages did in fact exist. For Brazilian football fans, now accustomed to routine elimination in

---

[7] See K. Westmeier, *Protestant Pentecostalism in Latin America: A Study in the Dynamics of Mission* (Cranbury: Fairleigh Dickinson University Press, 1999), p. 16.
[8] A. Anderson, *An Introduction to Pentecostalism* (Cambridge: Cambridge University Press, 2004), p. 256 and J. Passos, 'Teogonias Urbanas: Os Pentecostais na Passagem do Rural ao Urbano', *São Paulo em Perspectiva* 14.4 (2000), p. 126.
[9] P. Freston 'Neo-Pentecostalism in Brazil: Problems of Definition and the Struggle for Hegemony', *Arch. De Sc. Soc. Des. Rel* 105 (1999), p. 152.
[10] For example, in the chapter by Felipe Fulanetto in this volume.
[11] See D. Salinas, *Latin American Theology in the 1970s: The Golden Decade,* Religion in the Americas Series Volume 9, Leiden; Brill, 2009.

World Cup quarter finals to European opposition, it is galling to remember that Brazilian football had not one golden age, but two, when Pelé, Garrincha and Rivelino (1958–1970) and Romario, Ronaldo and Rivaldo (1994–2002) regularly reduced Europeans to tears.

Likewise, the 1970s can be genuinely considered a golden age of Latin American Evangelical Theology. During this decade luminaries such as Orlando Costas, René Padilla and Samuel Escobar were creatively engaging with the Latin American context and influencing global evangelicalism thereby helping develop the concept of integral mission theology. Aided by their friendship with John Stott, Padilla and Escobar had a profound impact on the Lausanne Covenant, a document which has acquired the status of a missiological creed for many Latin American evangelicals.

The chapter by Regina Fernandes Sanches is written as a continuation of this heritage. Writing as a member of the Fraternity's board, Sanches emphasises that integral mission theology is an example of evangelical mission theology. For Sanches the key to understanding integral mission theology is that it seeks to provide a new way of doing theology in Latin America, combining a commitment to the full scope of the gospel's message with a thorough and holistic understanding of the Latin American context.

Changes Since the Golden Age

Nonetheless, there have been considerable changes to the Latin American context from the golden decade of the 1970s. Politically, there has been a transition from military dictatorships to fragile democracies, plagued by instability and allegations of corruption. Various authors have documented the struggles that liberation theology has had with the transition to democracy, with the transnational Catholic church no longer required as a haven for progressive thought in the face of state sponsored violence.[12] The chapter by Daniel Clark suggests that a similar process is occurring with integral mission theology in the face of the challenges of widespread political corruption, urban violence, and polarisation over issues of sexuality. The chapter ends on a sombre tone, with the author uncertain that integral mission theology will successfully face these challenges.

The last five decades have been a period of sustained evangelical growth throughout Latin America, albeit varying across countries. This growth has led

---

[12] P. Beyer, *Religion and Globalization* (London: Sage, 1994), pp. 153–155, D. Martin, 'Secularisation and the Future of Christianity', *Journal of Contemporary Religion* 20.2 (2005), p. 151, V. Steuernagel, 'The Relevance and Effects of European Academic Theology on Theological Education in the Third World', *The Evangelical Review of Theology* 27.3 (2003), p. 208 and P. Freston, 'Researching the Heartland of Pentecostalism: Latin Americans at Home and Abroad', *Fieldwork in Religion* 3.2 (2008), p. 131.

to a diversity of denominations and a diversity of theological traditions. One consequence has been the decline of the hegemony of the FTL. While the Fraternity continues to be a significant theological actor, it no longer has the role of gatekeeper of evangelical theological production as could be seen in the 1970s. For example, the Reformed theological tradition, with its own network of journals, publishing houses and conferences is increasingly important within Latin America. Although only a small proportion of Latin American evangelicals belong to Reformed denominations, many are seminary teachers and leaders of mission agencies. At times, as the chapter by Clark indicates, Reformed theologians can be hostile in their attitude towards integral mission. Nonetheless, the chapter by Josué Reichow in this volume strikes a more conciliatory tone, discussing how a Reformational approach to culture can provide a positive model for Latin American Christians.

The last fifty years have also witnessed exponential economic growth in Latin America. As such, millions of Latin Americans have been lifted out of extreme poverty. Nonetheless, this has not always led to full social inclusion, and the benefits of this economic growth continue to be unevenly distributed, excluding many indigenous communities and Latin Americans of African heritage. The long-term economic effects of the Covid-19 pandemic are still uncertain, but the economy is undoubtedly going to be a major issue in Latin American societies in the coming years. Thus, in his chapter Martin Ocaña laments the lack of sustained economic reflection by Latin American theologians. Affirming the materiality of life, he emphasises the need for greater dialogue between theologians and economists.

This combination of sustained evangelical and economic growth has led to churches becoming powerful political institutions in many countries. Consequently, evangelical engagement with politics has led to evangelical involvement in numerous political scandals and acrimonious political debates among evangelicals. Lucas Magnin argues in his chapter that this Constantinian turn by many evangelical churches is a betrayal of the kingdom values incarnated by Jesus in the gospels and urges evangelicals to reject using the state to carry out their mission. Davi Lin is concerned with the way technology and social media have reduced the capacity for dialogue among evangelicals. In his chapter, he presents Augustine's theology, especially expressed in *The Confessions* as a resource to enable evangelicals to work for better dialogue and unity.

These recent changes have led to new issues in Latin America and new forms of exclusion. The twenty-first century has seen migration become a major theme in many countries, with the migration of many Latin Americans to the United States and Europe and the mass exodus of Venezuelans towards other Latin American countries. Alejandra Ortiz writes from Tijuana, on the border between Mexico and the United States, where many short-term missions teams arrive as religious tourists seeking to consume a missionary experience, and churches struggle to minister to the many caravans of Central American migrants. Ortiz explores ways in which it is possible to cease to cross borders as strangers and seek, with humility, to become friends. In her chapter, Délnia Bastos turns to the Pentateuch, discerning narratives and principals which can help evangelical churches engage with the refugee crises.

Arguably, one of the most significant migratory movements in Latin American history was the forced migration caused by the slave trade. The legacy of slavery and centuries of oppression against those of African heritage means that racism is a significant problem in Latin American countries. The myth of Latin American countries as new, racially harmonious states has meant that sustained reflection on race has often been avoided, especially among Christians. Nonetheless, globalisation has exposed Latin Americans to the protests against racism in North America in 2020 and the controversies generated by Critical Race Theory and the Black Lives Matter movement. This has encouraged many black South Americans to take a closer look at forms of discrimination in their own societies. *Ultimato*, a leading Brazilian publisher in theology and mission convened a group of authors to reflect on racism in Brazilian society and churches. What emerged was a contextual, biblical reflection, providing fresh insights into a much-discussed topic. *Ultimato* generously granted permission to translate and include this material which urges Christians to recognise and address racism, while celebrating diversity and reconciliation.

Spanish and Portuguese colonial presence in Latin America resulted in death and oppression for indigenous populations and the devastation of the natural environment. Even today, oppression of indigenous peoples and environmental problems are closely related. For example, in Brazil, environmental degradation has grown exponentially under current President Jair Bolsonaro. This often involves lands occupied by indigenous populations. When he was a congressman, Bolsonaro made a parliamentary speech lamenting the incompetence of the Brazilian cavalry in dealing with indigenous populations in the nineteenth century, saying, "the United States cavalry was indeed competent, it killed them in the past and they no longer have this problem in their country."[13] Likewise, in Peru, conflicts between indigenous groups and government authorities often involve the exploitation of natural resources. Writing from the Andean country, Rut Pérez-Saldarriaga pleads for her fellow Christians to no longer ignore the suffering of the environment and indigenous persons.

Disability is a significant, albeit often neglected, form of exclusion in Latin America. Research suggests that up to twelve percent of Latin Americans suffered from at least one form of disability between 2001–2010, a figure of at least sixty-six million people, but possibly more than eighty-five.[14] Julio Gonzáles writes as a representative of the millions of Latin Americans who face visual incapacity. In an open letter he shares the challenges he faces to read and

---

[13] Quoted in C. Rodriguez Garavito and C. Barquero Díaz, *Conflictos socioambientales en América Latina,* digital edition, Buenos Aires: Editores Argentina, 2020.
[14] Economic Commission for Latin America and the Caribbean, *Social Panorama of Latin America 2012* (Santiago: United Nations, 2013), pp. 184–186.

engage in academic research, and the various ways in which he faces exclusion from theological dialogue. He urges his fellow theologians to work towards including others such as himself in the production of theological material.

Samuel Escobar has long championed the need for "mission from everywhere to everywhere." Hence it is encouraging to see the growth of missionary movements within Latin American countries. Felipe Fulanetto provides an update on the surprising growth of the Brazilian missionary movement, which has exceeded both populational growth in Brazil and evangelical growth. Nonetheless, Fulanetto warns that there is no room for triumphalism or complacency, as questions still surround the sustainability of this growth.

This emerging missionary movement needs to face deep missiological issues. One challenge is that Latin Americans have a limited exposure to religious pluralism, as the diversity of religious options in Latin America is predominantly Christian. One major issue is the interaction with the great religious traditions of the world, such as Islam, Hinduism, and Buddhism. Marcos Amado's chapter expresses a desire to move beyond simplistic judgements, which often reduce all non-Christian religions to the category of demonic. He emphasises the need for a fair and balanced assessment of Muhammed, to provide an accurate Christian assessment of the founder of Islam.

Conclusion

A common theme across the different contributions to this volume is that theological labour requires engagement with one's context. There is a strong autobiographical tone in many chapters as, in Latin America, missiology is done on the move. Contributors to this volume are also practitioners, juggling their academic research alongside varied ministerial commitments. Theological reflection takes place on long taxi and bus journeys, while suffering racial discrimination, encountering migrants at the border, or supporting victims of environmental disasters. Rather than missiology being a sub-discipline of theology, theology becomes missionary oriented, serving God's people as they seek to carry out God's mission in the complex Latin American reality.

These chapters together demonstrate the variety and vitality of contemporary Latin American theological and missiological reflection. There is indeed life beyond the golden decade! Nonetheless, the attentive reader will finish reading this volume feeling that they have only scratched the surface of contemporary Latin American reflection. Probably, much of the best missiology and theology in Latin America is taking place in local churches and ministries and remains unpublished and unshared over social media. Hopefully, the coming years will witness an increasing discovery of the wealth that Latin American Christians have to offer to the mission of the global church.

2. Integral Mission Theology as a Latin American Evangelical Theology
Regina Fernandes Sanches

C. René Padilla and Gustavo Gutiérrez both describe "a new way of doing theology", emerging in Latin America in the second half of the twentieth century.[1] Described as "contextual", "Third World" or even "radical", it evolved out of new forms of historical awareness and theological epistemology in the so-called Third World. In these unusual circumstances, theologians such as James Cone, Kosuke Koyama, John Samuel Mbiti, Kazoh Kitamori, Gustavo Gutiérrez, Leonardo Boff, Carlos René Padilla, Orlando Costas, and others sought to address their different socio-historical and cultural contexts. Despite their diversity, these scholars shared the desire to base their theological labour on contextual analysis.

The significance of this epistemological shift is better understood through comparison with classical theology. Classical theologians chose philosophy as their main dialogue partner and mediator for conveying theological knowledge. In contrast, contextual theologians include other forms of knowledge as dialogue partners. For liberation theologians, their concern with context and concrete reality led them to prefer social sciences rather than philosophy. The main innovation lay in subordinating the theoretical task of doctrinal reflection and systematisation of knowledge to the formulation of a new Christian praxis in the world.

Integral mission theology is part of this wider theological shift. It offers an evangelical approach in which the church's presence in the world provides the starting point for a contextual understanding of theology. It focuses on the presence and action of the kingdom of God in the world, providing an alternative to the futuristic and heavenly approach of prevailing eschatological perspectives. This text reflects on this important theological development analysing the historical origins and development of the Latin American integral mission movement.

---

[1] C.R. Padilla, 'My theological pilgrimage', *Journal of Latin American Theology* 4.2 (2009), p. 101 and G. Gutiérrez, *A Theology of Liberation* (Maryknoll: Orbis Books, 1973), p. 15.

Integral Mission Theology as a Latin American Theology

The roots of the integral mission movement lie in theological reflection concerning Latin America's social context in the 1960s. This was often an informal process, as theologians reflected on their diverse pastoral activities, but also involved more deliberate activities such as the organisation of conferences, theological publications, and participation in global conversations. We can, however, consider the formation of the FTL – *Fraternidade Teológica Latinoamericana* (Latin American Theological Fraternity), in the city of Cochabamba, Bolivia in 1970 as the official starting date of the integral mission movement. The FTL's articles of association declare its purpose and express the commitment of its founders:

> 1) To promote reflection on the gospel and its meaning for human beings and society in Latin America and thereby stimulate evangelical reflection on issues which are part of daily life in Latin America. We recognise the Bible as God's normative word for this reflection, listening under the Holy Spirit's guidance to the biblical message with regards to the relative aspects of our concrete situation.
>
> 2) To construct a platform to promote dialogue between thinkers who confess Jesus Christ as Lord and Saviour and who are willing to reflect biblically to communicate the gospel in Latin America's different cultures.
>
> 3) Contribute to the life and mission of evangelical churches in Latin America, without intending to speak in their name or seek to become their voice in the Latin American context.[2]

Integral mission is an example of Latin American theology but, unlike liberation theology, comes from historical evangelicalism's doctrinal and theological tradition. It lies in continuity with traditional protestant missionary efforts in the region, but is also a critical response to this heritage, seeking to engage with the diverse struggles for social transformation. Unlike liberation theology, professionals from a wide variety of fields participated in the foundation of the FTL. Thus, while in liberation theology we encounter an almost exclusive emphasis on social analytic mediation, integral mission is characterised by a multidisciplinary dialogue. This leads integral mission theology to have its own identity, distinct from liberation theology and as an evangelical movement concerned with the nature and practice of the mission of the church.

Liberation theology and integral mission theology were the main Latin American theological currents in the late twentieth century. Both emerged in a regional context where socio-economic problems and government policies accentuated social inequalities and widespread poverty. Their roots lie in the emergence of missiology as a theological discipline in the wake of nineteenth

---

[2] A. Fajardo and D.M. Oliveira, *FTL 45 anos – e as fronteiras teológicas na contemporaneidade* (São Paulo: FTL, 2016), p. 123.

and twentieth century discussions within the protestant mission movement. Similarly, both liberation theology and integral mission theology are influenced by contemporary theological trends in Europe and North America such as the theology of hope, political theology, secular theology, and the social gospel. Currently Latin American theological diversity has expanded to include Pentecostalism, Latin American public theology, and postcolonial theologies.

Beyond this shared social, historical, and cultural context, the concept of a hermeneutical circle provides Latin American theologies with a further unifying element. In Latin American theology the hermeneutical circle has three pillars: reality, Scripture, and praxis, known as seeing, judging, and acting in liberation theology. This allows theology to be both open and critical, to be renewed and remade without compromising one's identity, enabling theologians to respond to the demands of a dynamic and changing context. The doctrine of the incarnation justifies the risk of volatility which comes with such an approach. The incarnational demands of the gospel require a theology which itself is incarnational and able to adapt to a dynamic historical reality. Latin American theologies differ in how the hermeneutical circle is developed according to different Christian traditions and missiological objectives.

The integral mission movement, led by FTL, gave birth to integral mission theology, although the full influence of the movement extends beyond theological reflection. Integral mission theology is, therefore, a contemporary Latin American theology which always reaffirms its identification with the historical evangelical theological tradition.

Integral Mission Theology as Evangelical Theology

Evangelicalism began in the eighteenth-century as a movement seeking the renewal of European Protestantism. Its roots lie in pietism's focus on experience and the Great Awakening's call to evangelisation. Evangelicalism developed new theological and doctrinal understandings which energised protestant missions towards the Global South and evangelical churches were planted in Asia, Africa and Latin America.

Miguez Bonino describes the influence of evangelicalism on the emergence of "creole Protestantism" in Latin America. The first protestant churches were planted by immigrants and had little concern for evangelising the wider population. However, from the 1840s onwards many North American and British missionaries arrived in Latin America sharing a common theology despite denominational and geographical differences.[3] This theology was influenced by revivals, the holiness movement, social theologies, and fundamentalism.[4] These missionaries planted churches concerned with evangelisation, understood in

---

[3] J. Miguez Bonino, *Rostos do protestantismo latino-americano*, (São Leopoldo: EST/Sinodal, 2013), p. 29.

[4] Bonino, *Rostos do protestantismo latino-americano*, pp. 29-34.

conversionist terms. This is certainly one of the reasons for the rapid growth of the evangelical faith in our continent. Samuel Escobar compares evangelical fervour, characterised by evangelisation, with traditional Catholic practice in Latin America:

> Evangelicals have started with the assumption that the masses, although baptised, are not Christians and thus the first task is to evangelise. It is only through the deep conversion of the heart that a new people and new Christian praxis will emerge.[5]

Alongside evangelisation, Latin American evangelicalism has also affirmed other fundamental historical evangelical doctrinal and theological convictions:

1) The authority of the Bible and its primacy in theology.
2) The sinful state of all humans.
3) Salvation through the work of Jesus Christ.
4) The need for repentance and conversion.
5) The responsibility of every Christian with regards to evangelisation.[6]

Missionaries planted churches which were Latin American extensions of their European and North American denominations. We can, however, discern a form of autochthonous evangelicalism which deliberately takes Latin America as its context for living the Christian faith and engaging in theological reflection. Thus, traditional elements of evangelical theology merged with Latin American social, historical, and cultural experience creating a contextualised expression of evangelicalism. These evangelicals developed an understanding of sin shaped by Latin American problems and an integral vision of salvation. From this perspective, evangelisation should therefore include the fullness of human life in the world and seek to create a path towards liberation.[7]

An important role in the emergence of this autochthonous evangelicalism were the CLADEs (Latin American Evangelisation Congresses) organised by the FTL. These congresses were important in the development of FTL and integral mission theology. Their official documents are evidence that integral mission theologians affirmed both their evangelical faith and their commitment to Latin America and its social and cultural context. These theologians retained the missional emphasis in their theology but rethought the church's mission from their own context and in the light of the historical experience of protestant missions.

Although Latin Americans participate in the Lausanne movement, integral mission theology should be regarded as a distinct, autochthonous theology. Latin

---

[5] S. Escobar, *La fe evangélica y las teologías de la liberación* (El Paso: Casa Bautista de Publicaciones, 1987), p. 188.
[6] R. Sanches, *Introdução às Teologias Latino-americanas* (Campinas: Saber Criativo, 2019), p. 58.
[7] Sanches, *Introdução às Teologias Latino-americanas,* p. 58.

American integral mission theologians are in dialogue and overall agreement with the Lausanne movement, yet they display their theological autonomy in their concern for a wider understanding of the scope of mission and its theological foundations.

Integral Mission Theology as Missional Theology

Given its roots in the evangelical theological tradition, it is not surprising that Latin American integral mission theology has such a strong emphasis on mission. What is noteworthy are the differences with both classical theology and liberation theology. In classical theology, missional practice is the outcome of theological labour; in integral mission theology, missional practice is the starting point for it is the church's activity in the world that draws it to examine its social context in the light of Scripture. In liberation theology the starting point is the comprehension of social reality mediated through the social sciences; in integral mission theology, this role is played by the living presence and witness of the church in its context.

Nonetheless, uncritiqued missional practice risks degenerating into a project to control and dominate persons and groups. Thus, constant biblical reflection and investigation of the social context are required to subject missional practice to a discerning, critical analysis. Authentic mission is open to verification and reformulation; it is both transforming and transformable. In the case of integral mission theology, this is carried out with the aid of new hermeneutical methods. Padilla proposes a model of contextual hermeneutics based on the hermeneutical cycle:

> Missional/pastoral insertion in the Latin American social and historical context identified important questions which were not being adequately answered in evangelical churches. Efforts were made in congresses, conferences, consultations, and other discussions to verify what worldview would lead to better comprehension of the concrete situation. This led to the conclusion that the context of suffering in Latin America required a new approach to the Bible, less concerned with evangelisation as a form of Christian indoctrination and more interested in perceiving the liberatory work of God's word in a world where men and women are marked by the struggle for survival. This labour led to an understanding of mission which is not only liberatory, but also deals with the various aspects of reality.[8]

Scripture is read through a missional lens, set in a concrete reality, and understood with the help of different forms of knowledge. The kingdom of God, which is at work in the world and which the Church represents in mission,

---

[8] R. Sanches, *Como fazer teología da missão integral* (São Paulo: Garimpo, 2016), p. 97.

becomes the hermeneutical key in this process. This kingdom's justice becomes the justice mission seeks in Latin America.

This new understanding not only proposes a theology of mission, but a missional theology which announces and testifies to the knowledge of God revealed in the world for its transformation. This is the turnaround in Latin American evangelical theology: a widening of how theological labour is understood so that it is no longer reduced to the mere construction of theories or the systematisation of knowledge. Its starting point is an integral understanding of the context, as the theological *locus* where the theologian and theological community are located, engage in mission, and develop a holistic understanding of human reality and creation in all its multiple interactions. Nonetheless, this understanding preserves the authority of Scripture throughout the theological process and its primacy even for understanding one's own context. This hermeneutical exercise is possible as the Word is the living word of God incarnated in our world and history. The Scriptures must be read from an integral perspective, a contextual hermeneutic that adopts a holistic understanding of both the biblical world and that of the reading community. This theological effort leads to a new understanding of the mission of the church in the world and thus to a new missional praxis, that is both integral and incarnated in concrete reality.

Modern protestant missions were important in the expansion of Christianity in the West. In Latin America, they contributed to greater religious freedom in the face of a resistant, hegemonic Catholicism. Yet critical analysis perceives that mission has been historically associated with conquest and dominion, representing new forms of colonialism, imposing Western development policies, and rejecting local cultures. Mission from Latin America needs to be thought about and carried out differently, learning from the historical practice of mission. A liberating evangelical faith requires a new way of reading and interpreting the Bible. As Costas demands, mission should lead to a hope which results in concrete actions of redemption and liberation:

> To talk about hope for a new world without becoming involved in concrete ways of making it a better place to live in is to deny hope itself; it is undoubtedly to escape to a vague and otherworldly abstraction which paralyses the transformative power of the eschatological mission of the gospel and ends up sacralising the *status quo*. To hope that the world will be redeemed without executing any redemptive act in the world is blasphemy.[9]

It is in this way that Latin American evangelicalism has sought to construct another theology of the Church's mission, suitable for new times, to the rich and diverse cultures and societies of Latin America which struggle to solve serious socio-economic problems, a theology of mission which overcomes the model it

---

[9] O. Costas, 'A vida no Espírito', *Boletin Teológico* 18 (1986), p. 59.

has received. Thus, it is the mission of a church which although mainly poor, is numerically large, culturally diverse, and full of possibilities.

Integral in Mission and Theology

Protestant missions revealed their concern with the development of Latin American societies by setting up schools, hospitals and even universities. Nonetheless, these institutions generally served the upper classes rather than the impoverished masses. Even these days it is the wealthier who can access the institutions set up by missionary agencies.

Missionaries tended to teach a scholastic, dogmatic theology expressed in academic language, distant from Latin American reality. Church services proclaimed high-brow doctrines and theology in a foreign liturgy while church leadership was initially centralised around the missionary and his representatives. Christian faith focused more on a post-historical reality than on life in the present, and holiness was interpreted as separation from one's culture and one's body, alienating individuals from their own circumstances and personal relationships. Padilla associated this to an ideologically charged Western model of Christianity, linked to forms of imperialism:

> The end of the colonial era led the church to a stage where it is hard to clearly discern the real problems Christian mission faces. It is no longer possible to assume that persons in the Third World will accept Christianity due to its association with the West's political, economic, and cultural power. Rather, many will interpret this association as a hindrance. Consequently, Christian mission needs to be carried out from a position of weakness. There is a new opportunity to present the gospel as a message centred on Jesus Christ and not as a Western ideology.[10]

Protestant Christianity in Latin America followed the same path as Roman Catholicism, developing an official form acceptable to ecclesiastical leaders. Nonetheless, since Iberian colonisation, popular religiosity has developed forms of life-affirming resistance to external cultural, economic, and political forces. Among evangelicals this was expressed in homes and communities, taking on forms that were more adapted to local cultures. What was initially a silent resistance to established foreign models led to a popular model of evangelical faith which acquired an official form in the emergence of Pentecostalism.

The historical and cultural critique offered by the integral mission movement not only focused on the divorce between evangelical faith and Latin American culture, but also on the radical, sociological faith proposed by liberation theology. Integral mission theology declared that the mission of the church should avoid both extremes, as human reality involves both social aspects which

---

[10] C.R. Padilla, *Missão da Igreja– ensaios sobre o reino e a igreja* (São Paulo: FTL-B/Temática, 1992), p. 144.

are clearly exposed and deeper spiritual elements. The church's mission should cover all of reality affected by sin. The mission field was anywhere where life was in some way damaged.

This was not about a new evangelisation strategy, but a new way of looking at the world from the perspective of Christian faith, a holistic gaze. Writing in the 1990s, Padilla affirms the need to proclaim the full scope of the Christian hope with strength and conviction. Reflecting on the biblical understanding of the world, he affirms that "God's work in Christ Jesus is directly related to the world in its totality, not merely the individual. Therefore, a soteriology which does not take into account the relationship between the gospel and the world does no justice to Biblical teaching."[11] For Padilla, secular eschatologies such as Marxism also offered a hope, but the Christian hope, based on a wider understanding of the world, was incomparably superior.

Undoubtedly, these were the initial theological sketches required to develop an outline of integral mission. A serious historical critique was essential to give birth to a new missiological thinking which could overcome the individualistic theology and imperialistic practice of the older Western model. This task also demanded, without exception, that theologians avoid becoming enchanted by prevailing ideologies which reduced humans and their reality to class struggles. An understanding of mission which one can call "integral" was the net result of these reflections.

Thus, in this new way of doing theology:

> The integral, or integrating, gaze should guide the hermeneutical task of theological labour, both towards biblical texts and to human reality in general. A dynamic, integrating gaze constructs integral theology by understanding the past in a wide perspective, the present in its totality and the future as eschatological and historical hope.[12]

The idea of integrity had been employed in diverse social spheres, including Christian documents. The first part of Pope Paul VI's discussion of the development of peoples in his encyclic *Populorum Progressio* (1967) describes the "Integral development of Man", relating it to faith, the church and theological understanding itself.[13] Currently the expression is used in systemic and holistic approaches to reality as part of an understanding of the contemporary world.

When Latin American theologians first coined the idea of integral mission, they probably had little idea of the deeper implications of using this term for they were ahead of their days, yet these implications are clearer now. Currently, we

---

[11] Padilla, *Missão da Igreja*, ps. 16–17.
[12] Sanches, *Introdução as teologías latinoamericanas*, p. 100.
[13] Pope Paul VI, *Populorum Progressio: Encyclical of Paul VI on the development of peoples,* Vatican: Holy See, 1967. Available online at http://www.vatican.va/content/paul-vi/en/encyclicals/documents/hf_p-vi_enc_26031967_populorum.pdf. Accessed 28 April 2021.

know that it is impossible to talk about integral mission without considering the complex relationships involved and engaging in a genuinely multidisciplinary dialogue. It is also impossible to talk about the integral mission of the church without a theology which is also integral, which gives Scriptures and concrete reality the same hermeneutical treatment. This is the long-term task of Latin American evangelical theology.

Conclusion

Latin American understandings of mission and theology start from a deep comprehension of the apostolicity of the Church. This requires an integral approach, a complex interaction between observation of contextual problems and scriptural analyses. This leads to the emergence of liberatory activity in the life of the church, understanding social, historical contexts in the light of faith and Scripture. Although this new understanding was born within the Latin American evangelical missionary movement it is much more than a missiology, or a subset of theological knowledge and teaching. It has become a theology, which through the hermeneutical cycle, leads to a missional praxis.

Integral mission theology is undoubtedly a Latin American theology born in a cultural context where ancestral knowledges, such as those of African descent and indigenous peoples, intersect with contemporary scientific studies and new technological developments. Yet integral mission theology still retains the fundamental doctrinal elements of historical evangelicalism which establishes it as an evangelical theology. Nonetheless, as a Latin American theology, its great novelty lies in its methodology.

3. Integral Mission 'At the Car Wash': Facing the Challenges of Post-Odebrecht South America
Daniel Clark

Introduction[1]

As a Brazilian living in Lima, Peru, I am often asked about two subjects: football and political corruption. The corruption scandals associated with *Operação Lava Jato* (Car Wash Investigation) and the Brazilian construction company Odebrecht have become common topics of conversation for many South Americans. Nonetheless, there has been little theological reflection on the impact of these scandals, even by those who advocate an integral approach to mission, which has as one of its concerns the relationship between churches and society.

This article suggests that the current context in South America, post Odebrecht, presents significant challenges to those who wish to articulate an integral approach to mission, challenges which have yet to be faced successfully. However, to understand these challenges it is necessary to define integral mission in the South American context.

Integral Mission in the South American Context

Definitions of integral mission are arguably clearer on what they reject, rather than what they affirm. A common theme is the rejection both of attempts to reduce the mission of the church to verbal proclamation as well as eschew evangelism in favour of social transformation and humanisation. The Micah Network, which presents itself as 'a **global** community of Christians ... drawn together because of their passion for integral mission',[2] affirms:

> Integral mission or holistic transformation is the proclamation and demonstration of the gospel. It is not simply that evangelism and social involvement are to be done alongside each other. Rather, in integral mission our proclamation has social

---

[1] This chapter has been updated from an original version published in *Baptistic Theologies* 10.1 (2018). We thank the journal editors for permission to republish.
[2] Micah Network, 'Who we are', *Micah Network* available online at http://www.micahnetwork.org/who-we-are accessed 31 January 2018 (bold in the original).

consequences as we call people to love and repentance in all areas of life. And our social involvement has evangelistic consequences as we bear witness to the transforming grace of Jesus Christ.[3]

Despite these global aspirations, the definition is framed to solve a problem emerging from Western theological and missiological practice. In regarding evangelism and social action as distinct elements, it still allows the possibility of social action to be regarded as a secondary action, subordinate to verbal proclamation.[4] As it is focused on activities, there is little explanation concerning how integral mission is relevant in contexts where either open proclamation of the gospel or social involvement are not possible. Vinoth Ramachandra offers a useful corrective by shifting the focus away from what the church does to what it is. Integral mission is a 'way of calling the church to keep together, what the Triune God of the Biblical narrative always brings together',[5] thus refusing to draw artificial distinctions between proclamation and social action.

The use of the term 'integral' in South America draws on the image of wholemeal bread (*pan integral*) to affirm that the mission of the church cannot be broken down into separate components, such as proclamation and action.[6] In South America this affirmation of the integral nature of the church's mission has a strong Christological component. The incarnation points to God's willingness to step into the suffering and poverty of the world and becomes a model for the ministry of the church. Jesus' ministry was one in which verbal proclamation and works of compassion and mercy were inseparable, and his emphasis on the kingdom of God points to his Lordship over all aspects of creation and human life, denying the reduction of mission to a quest for converts.[7]

For much of the twentieth century evangelical Christians in South America retreated from social action to focus solely on the verbal proclamation of the gospel, in contrast to the late nineteenth-century missionary strategy of using social action, especially educational and medical projects, as a gateway to

---

[3] Micah Network, 'Integral Mission', *Micah Network* available online at http://www.micahnetwork.org/integral-mission accessed 05 November 2015.
[4] C.R. Padilla, 'The Future of the Lausanne Movement', *International Bulletin of Missionary Research* 35.2 (2011), p. 88.
[5] V. Ramachandra, 'What is Integral Mission?', *Micah Network* available online at http://www.micahnetwork.org/sites/default/files/doc/library/whatisintegralmission_imi-the-001.pdf accessed 02 February 2018, p. 1.
[6] D. Kirkpatrick, 'C. René Padilla: Integral Mission and the Reshaping of Global Evangelism' (PhD thesis, University of Edinburgh, 2015), p. 44. Other terms which are used include 'holistic' and 'transformative'. Kirkpatrick indicates that Padilla, who coined the expression *mission integral*, initially used different English concepts in translation.
[7] M. Clawson, '*Misión Integral* and Progressive Evangelicalism: The Latin American Influence on the North American Emerging Church', *Religions* 3 (2012), p.792. Escobar articulates a relevant Christology for the Latin American context in S. Escobar, *En Busca de Cristo en la América Latina,* Buenos Aires: Ediciones Kairos, 2012.

evangelism. This was partly a consequence of the reluctance of many mainstream protestant denominations to regard South America as a mission field, due to its Catholic heritage, so that missionaries came primarily from theologically conservative denominations and faith missions.[8] These missionaries adopted a dispensational eschatology in which the involvement of the church in social issues was considered a distraction from the urgent task of evangelising individuals. Fears regarding the global spread of communism accentuated this suspicion towards social action, as did developments within the World Council of Churches, in which the mission of the church was reduced to humanisation and the uniqueness of Christ was underplayed.[9]

Different factors coalesced in the second half of the twentieth century to encourage the emergence of the concept of integral mission. The slow transfer of power from missionaries to indigenous leaders in many denominations encouraged Latin American theologians to respond by gathering together. Missionary domination of the first Latin American Evangelism Congress (CLADE 1) in 1969 led to a meeting of indigenous theologians the subsequent year in Cochabamba, Bolivia, through which the Latin American Theological Fraternity (FTL) was born, which would become a major promoter of integral mission.[10] The endemic poverty in most Latin American countries and the spread of military dictatorships supported by the United States in the 1960s and 1970s encouraged a desire for a contextual reading of Scripture, which became accentuated with the growing concern of the Roman Catholic Church for the plight of the poor, expressed in the Base Ecclesial Communities and in liberation theology. During this period evangelical university students were exposed to Marxist ideas and turned to their Christian unions for help. Many of the leaders of the FTL, such as Padilla and Escobar, were heavily involved in campus ministry, through the International Fellowship of Evangelical Students (IFES), and the FTL became a hub to articulate a theological and missiological response to these changing circumstances, based on the centrality of the concept of the kingdom of God and a critical engagement with social sciences.[11]

---

[8] Clawson, '*Misión Integral* and Progressive Evangelicalism', p. 792.
[9] D. Bosch, *Transforming Mission: Paradigm Shifts in the Theology of Mission* (Maryknoll: Orbis, 1991), p. 383; Al Tizon, 'Precursors and Tensions in Holistic Mission: An Historical Overview', in B. Woolnough and W.Ma (eds), *Holistic Mission: God's Plan for God's People*, (Regnum Edinburgh 2010 series, Oxford: Regnum, 2010), p.63; T. Paredes, 'Holistic Mission in Latin America', in Woolnough and Ma, *Holistic Mission,* pp. 110–111 and E. Vílchez-Blancas, 'Signos y Condiciones de un Nuevo Contexto Misiológico', *Integralidad* 4 (2008), p. 29.
[10] Clawson, '*Misión Integral* and Progressive Evangelicalism', p. 791.
[11] The history of the FTLA is discussed in M. Ocaña Flores, 'Poder Político: Desafío para la Misión Integral en América Latina', *Integralidad* 3 (2008), pp. 19-22. The emergence of an integral approach to mission is described in M. Guerrero, 'El Pacto de Lausana (1974): Una Contextualización vista desde 2010', *Integralidad* 8 (2011), pp. 5–9; T. Paredes, 'Hipótesis de Trabajo para Comprender la Misiología de la Fraternidad

The Lausanne Congress for World Evangelisation held in 1974 in the eponymous Swiss city is widely regarded as a watershed in evangelical attitudes to social involvement. While many North American and European missiologists expected the Lausanne Congress to have a focus on proclamation, Escobar, Padilla, and others were instrumental in bringing the issue of social involvement to the heart of the Lausanne Covenant, which emerged from the congress.[12] While there are debates concerning the significance of integral mission for the Lausanne Committee for World Evangelisation (LCWE),[13] from a Latin American perspective the LCWE is of much less importance than the 1974 Covenant, which is the source of inspiration and legitimation for many ventures in integral mission.[14]

In the first decade of the twenty-first century the proliferation of projects in South America bringing social action and evangelism together seemed to confirm the statement by one missiologist that 'today the issue of social action or evangelism among evangelicals is largely a historical footnote'.[15] Many denominations had some form of social engagement so that, on the whole, preaching about integral mission was no longer an apologetic task but a matter of inspiring congregations and providing biblical and theological foundations. This positive environment for integral mission is evidenced in Brazil with the formation of a national evangelical social action network, *RENAS*, in 2006, which included many evangelical organisations and churches from diverse theological traditions such as Lutherans, Baptists, and the Assemblies of God. Nonetheless, many denominations, especially among newer Pentecostal churches, did not join *RENAS*.[16]

The apparent success of integral mission, and its contemporary challenges, is in many ways tied to the Brazilian social and political context and its impact on the whole continent. In Brazil, many advocates of integral mission were also

---

Teológica Latinoamericana', *Integralidad* 16 (2014), pp. 5–10 and U. Sallandt, 'Ética Social: Más Allá de la Misión Integral' *Integralidad* 3 (2007), p.15.

[12] Tizon, 'Precursors and Tensions in Holistic Mission', pp. 64–65; B. Woolnough, 'Good News for the Poor: Setting the Scene', in Woolnough and Ma, *Holistic Mission*, pp. 3–4; B. Myers, 'Holistic Mission: New Frontiers', in Woolnough and Ma, *Holistic Mission*, p. 119 and V. Samuel, 'Mission as Transformation and the Church' in Woolnough and Ma, *Holistic Mission*, p. 128.

[13] Critics suggest that under pressure from Northern American missiologists, the Committee regressed to a narrower understanding of mission, maintaining a dualistic opposition between social action and evangelism. Tizon, 'Precursors and Tensions in Holistic Mission', pp. 67–69.

[14] The support of John Stott for integral mission is a significant aspect in this legitimation. The importance of the friendship between Stott and Padilla is discussed in D. Kirkpatrick, 'C. René Padilla and the Origins of Integral Mission in Post-War Latin America', *Journal of Ecclesiastical History* 67.2 (2016), pp. 351–371.

[15] Myers, 'Holistic Mission', p. 120.

[16] RENAS, 'Histórico', *RENAS Rede Evangélica de Ação Social*, available online at http://renas.org.br/historico/ accessed 23 April 2018.

members of the *Movimento Evangélico Progressista* (Progressive Evangelical Movement-MEP) and celebrated the victory of the former metal worker and union leader Luis Inácio 'Lula' da Silva of the *Partido dos Trabalhadores* (Workers' Party-PT) in the 2002 presidential elections. While in previous elections the PT's roots in progressive Catholicism led to a neglect of evangelical voters, in 2002 the party proactively engaged with evangelicals and Lula's first cabinet included two women from the Assemblies of God, Benedita da Silva, a former governor of Rio de Janeiro and the internationally known environmentalist Marina da Silva.[17]

Lula enjoyed unprecedented levels of popularity during his two terms as President between 2003 and 2010. A commodities boom, fuelled by the Chinese economy, meant that while much of the world faced a serious recession, South American economies continued to grow. This in turn financed the expansion of welfare programmes in Brazil, especially the *Bolsa Familia* and the *Bolsa Escola*, which gave families cash payments while their children remained in school. As a result, millions exited absolute poverty, leading to claims that there were more middle-class Brazilians than those living in poverty.[18] The discovery of large oil reserves off the Southeast coast of Brazil, and the fact that the nation's Gross Domestic Product was fifth in the world, overtaking that of the United Kingdom, suggested that the nation was ready to exercise international leadership. In South America, Lula's administration was surrounded by sympathetic left-wing regimes in Venezuela, Bolivia, Ecuador, Chile, and Argentina. In many of these countries, Brazilian companies, such as Odebrecht, earned contracts for expensive public construction works. For many among the Latin American left, including advocates of integral mission, this economic growth amid a global recession was evidence of the superiority of state driven capitalism over liberal capitalism.[19]

The good times did not last long. As Chinese demand for South American commodities retracted, many economies entered recession. As Brazil faced its worst economic crisis in recent decades and corruption scandals afflicted the PT, Lula's hand-picked successor, Dilma Rousseff, faced controversial impeachment proceedings shortly into her second term of office. As the nation became increasingly polarised, advocates of integral mission, who overall had

---

[17] The PT's reluctance to engage with evangelical voters in previous elections is discussed in P. Freston, *Evangelicals and Politics in Asia, Africa and Latin America* (Cambridge: Cambridge University Press, 2001), pp. 30–34.

[18] See, for example, G. Duffy, 'Brazil sees Middle Class Emerging', *BBC News*, available online at http://news.bbc.co.uk/2/hi/business/6993546.stm accessed 12 December 2009 and The Economist, 'Half the Nation, a Hundred Million Citizens Strong', *The Economist,* available online at http://www.economist.com/world/americas/displaystory.cfm?story_id=12208726 accessed 12 December 2009.

[19] S. Fausto, 'The Lengthy Brazilian Crisis is not yet over', *Rice University's Baker Institute for Public Policy Issue Brief,* 17 February 2017, p. 2.

supported the PT administration, especially its income redistribution policies, found themselves subjected to strident criticism. A key watershed came when three Presbyterian scholars, Augusto Nicodemos Lopes, Fabio Costa, and Jonas Madureira engaged in a discussion and critique of integral mission on the Mackenzie University YouTube channel.[20] The fall-out from this controversy led Jorge Barro, founder of the Faculdade Teologica Sul Americana in Londrina to complain that it 'has become fashionable to attack integral mission in Brazil'.[21] This might have remained confined to the Brazilian context, especially considering the linguistic and cultural differences between Brazil and the rest of the continent, had it not been for the continent-wide aftermath of the Car Wash Investigation and the scandals involving the Brazilian construction company Odebrecht.

The Car Wash Earthquake and The Odebrecht Tsunami

The Car Wash Investigation initially sought to investigate financial transactions between companies doing business with Petrobras, the Brazilian state-owned oil company. What emerged was an unprecedented scheme of bribes and kickbacks, which involved payments to the PT and other members of the governing coalition. Executives at Petrobras and other companies negotiated plea bargains which reduced their prison sentences in exchange for information implicating politicians. Lula spent over eighteen months in jail,[22] and Eduardo Cunha, a former President of the Congress with ties to the Assemblies of God remains incarcerated. Some Brazilians regard the judge presiding the Car Wash Investigation, Sérgio Moro, as a national hero; others consider him part of a right-wing conspiracy to reverse the social gains of Lula's administration.[23]

---

[20] A. Nicodemos Lopes, J. Madureira, and F. Costa, 'Academia em Debate 37: Teologia da Missão Integral', available online at
https://www.youtube.com/watch?v=ng257P3XXOc accessed 05 November 2015.

[21] Quoted in S. Baggio, 'Teologia da Missão Integral em Debate', available online at https://archive.fo/5xTS3 accessed 02 February 2018.

[22] Lula faced five charges of corruption and was condemned to a twelve-year prison sentence for receiving a bribe in the form of an apartment from construction company OAS. He was released in November 2019 on appeal, before the Supreme Court in April 2021 quashed all the charges against him on procedural grounds. The Supreme Court affirmed that the court in Paraná where Lula was condemned did not have jurisdiction to try these charges.

[23] The details of the corruption scheme are described in M. de Almeida and B. Zagaris, 'Political Capture in the Petrobras Corruption Scandal: The Sad Tale of an Oil Giant', *The Fletcher Forum of World Affairs,* 39.2 (2015), p. 89. The operation itself was named after a car wash used to launder money. Dilma Rousseff's impeachment itself, however, was not linked to the corruption probe, but based on claims that she manipulated the federal budget in the run up to the 2010 election to hide the extent of the government deficit. Lula's condemnation meant that he was ineligible for the 2018

If the Car Wash investigation shook Brazilian politics, the practices of the construction company Odebrecht engulfed nearly all South America in a corruption scandal. Leveraging Brazil's influence, and the PT's contact with ideologically sympathetic governments, Odebrecht had a separate, clandestine department, the Division of Structured Operations, for arranging bribes and kickbacks for public officials in different countries and for laundering the money involved.

The fall-out has shaken various countries, not least due to Odebrecht's practice of paying bribes across the political spectrum. For example, in Peru, Pedro Pablo Kuzynscki was forced to resign as President, due to a scandal involving his ties to Odebrecht. His predecessor, Ollanta Humalla, has been arrested; there is a warrant for the arrest of former President, Alejandro Toledo, who resides in the United States; and there are investigations into connections between Odebrecht and the main leader of the opposition, Keiko Fujimori, and another former President, Alan García.[24]

The pendulum has swung away from the trend towards moderate left-wing regimes in South America, a context in which integral mission thrived in the first decade of the century. Dilma Rousseff was replaced by her Vice-President, Michel Temer, who sought to reverse many of the PT's policies. The subsequent 2018 presidential elections witnessed the surprise victory of a controversial far-right candidate, Jair Bolsonaro. Right-wing governments have returned to Ecuador, Chile, and Argentina, while the governments of Evo Morales in Bolivia and Nicolas Maduro in Venezuela have become increasingly authoritarian, in the latter case leading to an economic and humanitarian disaster.

Advocates of integral mission have not provided an effective response to these changing circumstances. There has been a tendency to downplay the scale of the corruption scandals and the economic challenges many countries are facing. For example, Padilla attributes these changes to media outlets promoting a 'conservative mentality and reactionary political thought' to achieve the impeachment of Dilma in Brazil, 'the return of neoliberalism with the election of the new national government in Argentina ... and attempts to destabilise other progressive democracies such as those in Venezuela, Ecuador and Bolivia.'[25] Similarly, in Brazil, Baptist minister Ariovaldo Ramos interprets recent events as a 'coup' and seeks to organise evangelicals campaigning for Lula's release.[26]

---

elections. Sérgio Moro subsequently became justice minister in Jair Bolsonaro's far-right government.

[24] The workings of the Odebrecht scheme and the countries involved are described in BBC News, 'Odebrecht Case: Politicians Worldwide Suspected in Bribery Scandal', *BBC News* available online at http://www.bbc.com/news/world-latin-america-41109132 accessed 01 February 2018.

[25] C.R. Padilla, 'Carta abierta a Harold Segura', *Fundación Kairos,* available online at http://www.kairos.org.ar/blog/?p=997 accessed 01 February 2018.

[26] A. Ramos, 'Os evangélicos descobriram o que Lula não conseguiu: para vencer é preciso mídia', *Brasil de Fato,* available online at

A better approach is to recognise that the social, political, and economic reality of post-Odebrecht South America means that advocates of integral mission need to respond to significant challenges, beginning with the role of integral mission in the life of churches

The Ecclesiological Challenge

In researching the legacy of the Catholic Base Ecclesial communities, Maria Domezi and David Lehmann independently arrived at the conclusion that they reflected the middle-class ethos of priests and scholars rather than the culture of the poor themselves.[27] A similar problem affects advocates of integral mission and local evangelical churches in South America. 'Integral mission arose from within the revolutionary Latin American university environment',[28] and the way in which its history is often told, in terms of successive theological conferences and consultations,[29] suggests that it is predominantly the perspective of a diffuse network of scholars, missiologists, seminaries, journals, and Wstern-funded NGOs. Consequently, despite the local church being considered the primary agent of integral mission, overall, only a small minority of churches have fully embraced integral mission in South America.

In part, this is because the fastest growing churches in South America are Pentecostal congregations. Although there are some Pentecostal advocates of integral mission, such as Dario López in Peru, most Pentecostal pastors and leaders do not participate in the same academic and missiological networks as advocates of integral mission. The fact that many more recent Pentecostal churches, referred to as Neo-Pentecostals, enthusiastically embrace prosperity theology and adopt aggressive models of spiritual warfare significantly reduces the possibilities of approximation with advocates of integral mission.

Consequently, even the aforementioned proliferation of social action projects may have exaggerated the apparent success of integral mission. For some

---

https://www.brasildefato.com.br/2017/01/03/os-evangelicos-descobriram-o-que-lula-naoconseguiu-para-vencer-e-preciso-midia/ accessed 23 April 2018.

[27] M. Domezi, 'A Devoção nas CEBs: Entre o Catolicismo Tradicional Popular e a Teologia da Libertação' (PhD thesis, São Paulo: Pontifícia Universidade Católica de São Paulo, 2006), p.15 and D. Lehmann, 'Dissidence and Conformism in Religious Movements: What Difference, if any, Separates the Catholic Charismatic Renewal and Pentecostal Churches' available online at http://www.davidlehmann.org/david-docs-pdf/Pubpap/DISSIDENCE%20AND%20CONFORMISM%20IN%20RELIGIOUS%20 MOVEMENTS.pdf accessed 12 November 2012, p. 2.

[28] Kirkpatrick, 'C. René Padilla and the Origins of Integral Mission in Post-War Latin America', p. 353

[29] For example, C.R. Padilla, 'Integral Mission and its Historical Development', in T. Chester (ed.), *Justice, Mercy and Humility* (Carlisle: Paternoster, 2003), pp. 42–58. Hence, David Kirkpatrick's PhD thesis on Padilla focuses predominantly on his role in universities, seminaries, and global missiological networks. Kirkpatrick, 'C. René Padilla', pp. 144–198.

churches, this did not emanate from a biblical theology of mission but was a form of patronage to increase the church's clientele base as part of a wider political project. An example of this is the *Projeto Nordeste* (Northeast Project), an irrigation project in the northeast of Brazil, of the Brazilian *Igreja Universal do Reino de Deus* (Universal Church of the Kingdom of God), which was used to raise the political profile of one of the church's main bishops, Marcelo Crivella, and propel him first to the Brazilian senate and then to the role of mayor of Rio de Janeiro.[30]

Hence, in Post-Odebrecht South America, the challenge to adequately engage with churches is as important as ever. Most Pentecostal churches are in deprived areas, led by poor pastors, and provide the poor – including women – with many opportunities for service.[31] They are, therefore, ideally situated for an integral approach to mission. Nonetheless, the track record of advocates of integral mission in engaging with these churches is not promising, especially as many identify primarily as members of seminaries, mission organisations, and NGOs rather than as members of local churches. Chris Sugden laments the way in which proponents are often very critical of churches and seek to impose their own development agenda, a process which David Bosch describes as making the church 'be constantly goaded into action, as though it has to prove itself, has to earn its credibility through its own imposing schemes and in this way secure salvation'.[32] As very little theological work has been done to develop the insights of Padilla, Escobar, and others in the 1970s and 1980s, consequently, especially at the level of grassroots NGOs, theology and mission have been replaced by a sociological pragmatism, which risks both underplaying the uniqueness of Christ and being taken over by a secular development agenda, further alienating local churches.[33]

---

[30] The significance of the *Projeto Nordeste* in launching Crivella's political career is discussed in A. Souza, *Igreja in Concert: Padres Cantores, Midia e Marketing* (São Paulo: Annablume, 2005), p. 89 and M. Machado, *Política e Religião: A Participação dos Evangélicos nas Eleições* (Rio de Janeiro: Fundação Getúlio Vargas, 2006), pp. 72–73.

[31] D. Clark, 'Outward Mission or Serving a Ghetto: An investigation of the Missiological Impact of Brazilian Churches in West London' (PhD thesis, University of Wales, 2013), pp. 44–49 and M. Machado, 'Representações e Relações de Gênero nos Grupos Pentecostais', *Estudos Feministas* 13.2 (2005), p. 391.

[32] Bosch, *Transforming Mission*, p. 387 and C. Sugden, 'Mission as Transformation: Its Journey among Evangelicals since Lausanne I', in Woolnough and Ma, *Holistic Mission*, p. 35.

[33] See Bosch, *Transforming Mission*, p. 398 and Sugden, 'Mission as Transformation', p. 35. The lack of theological work is lamented in Myers, 'Holistic Mission', p. 121.

The Teleological Challenge

The difficulty that advocates of integral mission face in engaging with churches is compounded by a lack of clarity on what precisely churches should be aiming for. Churches are criticised for focusing on local level assistance and are encouraged to engage with the structural causes of poverty and injustice, with little indication of what this engagement entails or the expected result that should be aimed for. Integral mission thus suffers from what Scot McKnight calls a lack of 'an explicit teleology'. By this term he asks 'What will happen if they "win" the influence?'[34] Arguably, in South America there was little expectation that any influence would be achieved, so that when left-wing administrations came into power, supported by many advocates of integral mission, the lack of a clear goal became evident.

Guilherme de Carvalho suggests that a focus on missiological praxis and a desire to keep those from different theological backgrounds together is responsible for this lack of clarity regarding the objectives of integral mission. Consequently, beyond an emphasis on greater involvement of lay members in the mission of the church, there is no 'ecclesiological model able to accurately explain the relationship between the local church, institutions and non-ecclesial Christian actions with society as a whole'.[35] This weak ecclesiology stems in part from the fact that, despite the kingdom of God being a central category in integral mission, there are different understandings of the kingdom and its relationship with contemporary society and politics.[36]

Critics claim that the lack of a theologically based teleology leaves integral mission vulnerable to being overly dominated by social scientific perspectives, especially Marxist ideology.[37] However, this critique often takes the form of guilt by citation, for quoting a Marxist, or guilt by vocabulary, for using a term developed by a Marxist. Although Orlando Costas accepted the role of Marxist analysis, this was rejected by Samuel Escobar and the prevailing position among advocates of integral mission such as Padilla, Tito Paredes, and Robinson Cavalcanti is to seek a critical use of the social sciences.[38] Nonetheless, integral

---

[34] S. McKnight, 'Evangelical Progressives: A Public Theology of Community' available online at http://www.patheos.com/blogs/jesuscreed/2015/11/04/evangelical-progressives-a-public-theology-ofcommunity> accessed 06 November 2015.
[35] G. Carvalho, 'A Missão Integral na Encruzilhada: Reconsiderando a Tensão no Pensamento Teológico de Lausanne', in L. Ramos, M. Camargo and R. Amorim (eds.), *Fé Crístã e Cultura Contemporanea*, (Viçosa: Ultimato, 2009), p. 34.
[36] Carvalho, 'A Missão Integral na Encruzilhada', p. 43. Carvalho himself singles out three competing models of the relationship between the kingdom and the world: Calvinist, Lutheran, and Anabaptist
[37] Lopes et al., 'Academia em Debate'
[38] Paredes, "Hipótesis de trabajo', p. 10. The debate between Costas and Escobar is described in Kirkpatrick, 'C. René Padilla and the Origins of Integral Mission in Post-War Latin America', p. 187. While Jose Miguéz Bonino embraced revolutionary socialism, it is arguably more accurate to consider him a representative of liberation

mission in South America has been characterised by a vague, narrow focus on statist solutions to structural problems, through the transfer of resources by taxation, and a lack of a positive role for markets in human development. This reflects an anti-market approach in many sections of South American social sciences, especially in the sociology of religion, where market metaphors abound which are pejorative in nature.[39] Hence, integral mission has tended to be the domain of those who are politically on the left, and thus becomes vulnerable to rejection at a time when left-wing administrations are experiencing record levels of unpopularity.

South American proponents of integral mission tend to be more comfortable playing the role of a Jeremiah, bravely denouncing the injustices of the system, than that of a Joseph, Obadiah, Nehemiah, or a Daniel who needed to work within existing structures. This outsider perspective results in a lack of clarity regarding what one should do if one has the means to bring about change. In post-Odebrecht South America, clear, competing visions are being articulated, based upon business-friendly policies, the scaling back of state welfare support, the repeal of environmental legislation and laws protecting indigenous land rights, and the violent repression of crime, often articulated as an expression of Christian principles.[40] While this may allow some to return to their preferred prophetic role, it raises questions regarding the potential of integral mission to shape the mission of South American churches.

The Challenge of Violence and Polarisation

Urban violence, in which young, poor males are both the main perpetrators and victims, is a major issue in South American cities and which appears regularly on lists of highest homicide rates.[41] The climate of fear and insecurity leads to the popularity of repressive measures against crime, including support for the return of the death penalty, the use of torture, police violence against suspects, and stricter prison sentences, despite the fact that most South American prisons

---

theology with close ties to advocates of integral mission. See Ocaña Flores, 'Poder político', pp. 21–22.

[39] See Clark, 'Outward Mission or Serving a Ghetto', pp. 44–49 and B. Martin, 'Pentecostal Conversion and the Limits of the Market Metaphor', *Exchange* 35.1 (2006), p. 67. For an example of such a pejorative use of market imagery see N. Pereira, 'Empire and Religion: Gospel, Ecumenism and Prophecy for the 21st Century', *The Ecumenical Review* 58.1 (2006), p. 94.

[40] See for example F. Ferreira, 'Uma Agenda para o Voto Conciente', *Teologia Brasileira* available online at http://www.teologiabrasileira.com.br/teologiadet.asp?codigo=402 accessed 01 February 2018.

[41] For example, T. Clavel, 'Latin America Dominates World's 50 Deadliest Cities Ranking', *Insight Crime* available online at https://www.insightcrime.org/news/brief/latin-america-dominates-world-50-deadliest-cities/ accessed 01 February 2018.

are over-crowded and dominated by criminal gangs. The fact that many advocates of integral mission emphasise the long-term structural causes of crime, the need to respect legal rights, and humane prison conditions leads to the unfair accusation that they are more interested in the human rights of the perpetrators of crime than of the victims.[42]

The difficulty in presenting a moderate perspective on crime is symptomatic of the wider polarisation in South American societies. A key issue is that of same-sex marriage and gender identity. For many on the South American left, the defence of same-sex marriage and fluid gender identities has become an axiomatic position. The educational system is thus perceived as a key medium to change social attitudes regarding gender. This has led to an alliance between evangelicals, Catholics, and right-wing politicians to counter what they perceive as a 'gender ideology' threatening family life and social stability. In Brazil, Assemblies of God pastors Silas Malafaia and Marcos Feliciano, a member of Congress, successfully led the campaign against same-sex marriage, while in Peru, the #conmishijosnosimetas (#don't mess with my children) movement successfully galvanised opposition to obstruct proposed government changes to the school curriculum, claiming the scalp of the Education minister in the process. As the hashtag indicates, the movement made extensive use of social media, distributing materials produced in Colombia and other countries against 'gender ideology'.

As political discourse becomes polarised, the possibility of being politically progressive on economic issues, but still defending a more historically Christian perspective on marriage, becomes curtailed. With many evangelicals equating concern for social justice with advocacy of 'gender ideology', the challenge of interacting with churches becomes even greater.

The Legacy Challenge

The challenges of post-Odebrecht South America come at a time when many of the pioneers in articulating the concept of integral mission are reaching the end of their careers. The polarisation of South American societies means that advocates of integral mission and their critics inhabit different academic, ecclesial, and missiological networks. This leads to an insularity among some advocates of integral mission who fail to deal with the substance of critiques and often resort to angry, *ad hominem* attacks. Thus, critics are often simply dismissed as being under North American influence, or, according to Ariovaldo

---

[42] The way in which security and crime issues are becoming the Achilles heel of integral mission mirrors what happened with Liberation theology as discussed in Clark, 'Outward Mission or Serving a Ghetto', p. 43 and P. Freston, 'Researching the Heartland of Pentecostalism: Latin Americans at Home and Abroad', *Fieldwork in Religion* 3.2 (2008), p. 131.

Ramos, being motivated by ignorance, self-interest, intellectual dishonesty, lack of academic rigour, and prejudice.[43]

This insularity and lack of engagement with critics raises the issue of the legacy of integral mission; that is, will there be a new generation of theologians, missiologists, and biblical scholars to carry on the work of Padilla, Escobar, and others? The answer is uncertain, as there are plenty of alternatives in South America for young Christian leaders, such as prosperity theology and various church growth strategies. Nonetheless, among seminary and university students, from where integral mission has traditionally recruited, what has become known as the 'New Calvinism' is the main alternative. Popularised by the Gospel Coalition and John Piper's Desiring God ministry, it presents complementarian gender roles, pro-market policies, and restrictions on the role of the state as the only biblically faithful and theologically sound approach. With articles and videos freely available on the internet in Spanish and Portuguese, university students are more likely to read materials by authors influenced by Abraham Kuyper than Padilla or Escobar. Although it is possible to reconcile Kuyper and integral mission,[44] his concept of sphere sovereignty is often presented to suggest that social justice is a concern which falls out of the domain of the church's mission. For example, for Brazilian theologian Franklin Ferreira there is no other role for the church beyond worshipping God, proclaiming the gospel, and administering the sacraments, the quest for social justice being the responsibility of Christians operating in other spheres.[45]

Tentative Steps Forward

It is hard to suggest more than a few tentative steps forward, given the complexity of the challenges faced by an integral approach to mission in post-Odebrecht South America. Rather the way ahead may be for a humbler and chastened form of integral mission to emerge. This involves recognising that, while definite gains were made in reducing poverty in the first decade of this century, this legacy has been tainted by corruption scandals and economic mismanagement. This humility involves, as Bosch indicates, rejecting the heresy that Christians can bring about salvation through their own works and remaining critical of 'all current human theories of human self-redemption'.[46] A chastened integral approach to mission abandons the shrill, self-righteous tone with which

---

[43] Baggio, 'Teologia da Missão Integral em Debate'.
[44] See P. Freston and R. Freston, 'A tão famigerada missão integral', *Ultimato,* 362 (2016), pp. 66–76.
[45] For example, see F. Ferreira, *Curso Vida Nova de teologia básica: Teologia sistemática* (São Paulo: Vida Nova, 2013), pp. 212–218 and F. Ferreira, 'Crentes no poder', *Revista Expressão Cidadania Cristã,* 1 (18 January 2002). More radical is the claim by another new Calvinist theologian Jonas Madureira that social action is little more than a 'decorative trinket' for the gospel, in Lopes et al., 'Academia em Debate'
[46] Bosch, *Transforming Mission,* p. 400

criticism has often been answered. It also rejects regarding critics of integral mission as enemies of the kingdom:

> When we claim the seriousness of the structures we build, they easily become oppressive ... we think we know who the enemies of the kingdom are, but too often we are the enemy.[47]

This humbler approach to integral mission should be more ideologically diverse. Traditionally, integral mission has been the preserve of the minority of evangelicals in South America who are politically progressive. Yet, the polarised context of many post-Odebrecht South American societies requires a broad coalition of churches, with individuals of different political persuasions committed to witnessing to the kingdom in word and deed. This ideological diversity needs to be reflected in a greater ability to contextualise the advocacy for integral approaches to mission in forms which are compatible with the vocabulary and liturgy of the Pentecostal churches attended by many of the poorer members of South American societies.

A humbler approach to integral mission should be market friendly, but not market driven. The minimalist state proposed by some neo-Calvinists, which focuses basically on law and order, is unlikely to redress the multiple historical injustices that prevail in South America. Likewise, the statist, redistributionist model, suspicious of the market, which is preferred by many progressive evangelicals, is unlikely to foster the creativity necessary to promote economic growth, whilst encouraging corruption and nepotism in an increasingly larger and indebted state, as has occurred in Brazil. A market friendly approach requires widening the inter-disciplinary dialogue partners of those theologians and missiologists who support integral mission. Until now, the main dialogue partners have been social scientists, yet the dialogue pool needs to be widened to include the expertise of economists and business leaders.

Conclusion

The immediate prognosis for integral mission in South America is not favourable. There is the unfair perception that it is the domain of left-wing academics, ecclesial outsiders who support the regimes responsible for the corruption scandals and economic difficulties in South America and are allies of those groups which would impose a 'gender ideology' upon South American societies. The popularity of the new Calvinism among many seminary and university students, which tends to exclude the concern for social action and social justice from the church's sphere, suggests the emergence of a new generation of leaders less congenial to the basic tenets of integral mission.

---

[47] J. Ingleby, 'Introduction', in M. Hoek, J. Ingleby, A. Kingston-Smith and C. Kingston-Smith *Carnival Kingdom*, y (Gloucester: Wide Margin, 2013), p. xv.

Liberation theology stands as a cautionary tale that it is possible for concepts born in South America to achieve popularity in global academic and missiological circles, while declining in the continent itself. Yet the following words of Tito Paredes serve as a timely reminder of the need to find contextual forms of expressing the mission of the church in ways which follow Christ's example of witnessing to the kingdom in both word and deed:

> What is the role of faith when a young person must leave university because they cannot afford to pay the fees despite working full time? How does one relate faith with the diversity of expressions of family that have emerged including single mothers (there are also a few single fathers) many abandoned by their husbands, and families separated as one of the partners has migrated to another city or country seeking employment? How does one relate faith with the demands of workers and indigenous peoples for more dignified work and treatment? What is the role of Christians when faced with protest marches caused by abuses by mining companies or harsh bosses?[48]

---

[48] T. Paredes, 'Reflexiones sobre los Desafíos y Oportunidades de Misión para las Iglesias Evangélicas Pentecostales Latinoamericanas', *Integralidad* 4 (2008), p. 9.

4. Christianity and Culture in Brazil: A Reformational Approach[1]
Josué Reichow

Introduction

The religious scenario in Brazil has changed significantly in the last thirty years. Since Portuguese colonisation there has been a considerable Catholic majority but now the country witnesses increasing numbers of evangelicals (*evangélicos*), propelled by exponential Pentecostal and Neo-Pentecostal growth. In the census in 2010, twenty-two percent of the population identified themselves as *evangélicos* – a figure of around forty million people. Some estimates suggest that figure had reached thirty percent in 2020. New challenges and theological questions emerge in this new scenario. This chapter attempts to address how *evangélicos* approach culture, discussing the major views present among Brazilian evangelicals and presenting a reformational perspective which is growing in influence in Brazil.[2]

In his classic work *Christ and Culture*, Richard Niebuhr presents five models of possible relationships between Christianity and culture.[3] This framework, adapted to the singularities of the Brazilian context, provides an interpretative apparatus to understand evangelical attitudes to culture, as long as it is recognised that no pure example of these types exists in isolation from the others. This chapter presents and discusses three different models of approaching culture in Brazil: 1) Christians against culture; 2) cultural Christians; and 3) Christians

---

[1] This chapter is adapted from J. Reichow, *Reformai a Vossa Mente: Uma introdução à filosofia cristã de Herman Dooyeweerd*, Brasília: Editora Monergismo, 2019.
[2] This reformational perspective refers to the legacy of the Dutch neo-Calvinist movement of the late 19th and early 20th centuries. The central figure of this movement is Abraham Kuyper (1837-1920), but other names worth mentioning are Herman Bavinck; (1854–1921) and Herman Dooyeweerd (1894–1977).
[3] H.R. Niebuhr, *Cristo e cultura*, Paz e Terra: Rio de Janeiro, 1967. This chapter does not seek to offer a full interpretation of Niebuhr's works but focuses on the types of relationship between Christianity and culture. The two models not quoted in this chapter are Christ above the culture and Christ and culture in paradox. A helpful guide to Niebuhr's ideas is J. McGregor, 'Christ and Culture Revisted', available online at http://labri-ideas library.org/do-download.asp?Lecture=1544.

as culture's reformers. The third is presented as a response and alternative to the first two.

Brazil is now both the most Roman Catholic and the most Pentecostal country in the world, leading emergent *evangélicos* to face a whole new set of challenges. Liberation theology has raised the theological theme of the poor,[4] yet financial prosperity and the growth of the middle-classes lead to new theological questions such as how *evangélicos* comprehend and approach culture.

One of the great dilemmas Brazilian Christians face is their relationship with the world and with its cultural systems. Does a Christian belong to this world? The apostle John commands "Do not love the world or anything in the world. If anyone loves the world, the love of the Father is not in him" (1 Jn. 1:15). Nevertheless, the same apostle writes "For God so loved the world that He gave His one and only son" (Jn 3:16). Do both texts refer to the same thing? What is the world from a Christian standpoint? In the Brazilian context it is possible to discern an enormous confusion between the world as a sinful system and the world as God's creation.

Christians against Culture

In this perspective, Christianity and culture are at odds, having no common ground whatsoever so that integration is impossible. Religious groups prone toward charismatic and evangelical expressions of faith are more inclined to this understanding. Much of the emphasis in their preaching is given to personal sanctification understood as separation from the world.[5]

This interpretation of the relationship between Christians and the world, including the cultural sphere, has its roots in the Platonic and neo-Platonic dualism of body and soul.[6] This dualism, rooted in the Greek ground motive of matter and form was transformed in the Middle Ages into a new ground motive: nature and grace.[7] The core belief of this dualism is that matter, the visible world, is evil as it contains the sinful passions that destroy and fight against the soul. The solution lies in the systematic denying of the body, valuing instead the soul and its activities.[8]

---

[4] See G. Gutiérrez, *A Theology of Liberation: History, Politics, and Salvation*, Revised Edition with a New Introduction, Maryknoll: Orbis, 1988.
[5] See the critical perspective of Rick Nañez regarding this position, as well as his study on the origin of this sort of dualism within Christianity. R. Nañez, *Pentecostal de coração e mente: um chamado ao dom divino do intelecto* (São Paulo: Editora Vida, 2007), p. 160.
[6] See F. Albano, 'Dualismo corpo/alma na teologia pentecostal' (Master's Dissertation, Escola Superior de Teología, 2010), p. 13.
[7] H. Dooyeweerd, *No Crepúsculo do Pensamento: estudos sobre a pretensa autonomia da razão,* São Paulo: Hagnos, 2010.
[8] M. Inwood, 'Platonism' in T. Honderich (ed), *The Oxford Companion to Philosophy* (Oxford: Oxford University Press, 2005), pp. 723–725.

Consequently, what is natural and visible is understood as a mere distortion of a superior, supernatural reality. This belief is developed from Plato's theory of forms. In his classical work *The Republic,* Plato presents his famous allegory of the cave as an illustration of his philosophical outlook.[9] In his Socratic dialogues, Plato understands the world we see and experience as a prison and the exercise of reason as a window opening to a superior and elevated reality, a way out of bodily imprisonment. This view has parallels in the way many Brazilian evangelicals regard the world and its structures as intrinsically evil so that ideal Christian spirituality involves exercising spiritual disciplines to abandon the world.[10]

This perspective is suspicious of all cultural production, demonising it as sinful. Nineteenth and twentieth century missions to Brazil, whose origins were mainly in North American revival movements, displayed a strong separatist attitude towards the relationship between Christians and culture.[11] Nañez claims that this results in an anti-intellectual fideism that reduces all interpretation of reality to faith categories, rather than acknowledging faith as part of a broader structure of meaning.[12]

In North America, the term fundamentalist was applied to anti-intellectual fideistic movements. In 1925, for example, there occurred the paradigmatic legal case known as the Monkey Trial, in which the state of Tennessee forbade the teaching of the Darwinist theory of evolution for supposedly contradicting the biblical teaching of creation. Many of the facets of the discussion between Christianity and science in Brazil are rooted in this North American dualism between creationism and evolutionism as if the theory of intelligent design were the only position Christians could adopt.

Evangelical fear of cultural and intellectual activities has a counterpart in the tremendous influence of Auguste de Comte's positivist movement in Brazilian academia. The legacy of this nineteenth century French movement is an extremely hostile environment towards the use of religious categories, be it at an academic level or in the public sphere. Thus, the Swiss-Brazilian theologian Rudolf von Sinner affirms that "public universities in Brazil have a tradition of

---

[9] Plato, 'A República', in D. Marcondes, *Textos Básicos de Filosofia: dos Pré-socráticos a Wittgenstein*, second edition, Rio de Janeiro: Jorge Zahar Editor, 2000.
[10] Platonic thought has undergone a significant historical process of transformation, being synthesised with other forms of thinking. Therefore I am not suggesting an immediate or direct Platonic influence on Brazilian evangelicalism.
[11] See J. Miguez Bonino, *Rostos do Protestantismo Latino-Americano* (São Leopoldo: Sinodal, 2002), p. 29. The character of evangelical mission to Brazil cannot be reduced to this separatism, involving complex religious and sociological aspects not discussed in this chapter.
[12] Nañez, *Pentecostal de coração e mente*, p. 187. See also H. Dooyeweerd, *Roots of Western Culture: Pagan, Secular and Christian Options*, Toronto: Wedge Publishing Foundation, 1979.

strong reservations against religion and theology".[13] According to a Dooyeweerdian understanding, this is evidence of the myth of the religious neutrality of reason at work.

Understanding Brazilian evangelical attitudes to culture requires paying attention to the media. There are numerous evangelical television programmes on mainstream networks and many channels offering exclusively Christian content. One example is *Nossa TV* (Our TV), an evangelical cable network associated with a well-known televangelist, R. R. Soares, seeking to provide alternative entertainment for the Brazilian evangelical audience.

Likewise, gospel music is one of the most profitable markets in Brazil.[14] However, there seems to be a constant tension with regards to the arts. According to Magali do Nascimento Cunha: "one of the marks of the gospel music praise and worship category is the fact that singers insist that they are not artists, but worshippers." This indicates that "the artistic career ... is incompatible with God's purpose".[15]

While there is significant evangelical cultural production in Brazil, it is aimed at an evangelical market segment, rather than seeking to influence the whole culture. An example of this segmentation and differentiation is *Espirítoval*, an evangelical celebration to celebrate the "feast of the Spirit" in deliberate opposition to the "feast of the flesh" (the Carnival). This distinction reveals a strong exclusivism as for evangelicals the cultural artefacts produced by specific groups are taken as holy, in opposition to the sinful worldly culture:

> The so-called language [of the] world, in the evangelical tradition, [is used to] refer to the space which is not of the church, of the saved ones, of those who are guarded from evil and sin [...]. The church-world dualism, constituted as a base for the theology and for the action of Brazilian evangelicals, is conserved even amid the transformations caused by the composition of pop melodies, sung by pop singers.[16]

This point conflicts with the idea of *common grace*, stressed by Abraham Kuyper: "whereas the special grace is that one through which God saves the sinner through Jesus Christ, common grace would be that one through which

---

[13] R. von Sinner, 'Teologia Pública no Brasil' in A.Soares and J. Passos (eds) *Teologia Pública: Reflexões sobre uma área de conhecimento e sua cidadania acadêmica* (São Paulo: Paulinas, 2011), pp. 265-276. Sinner also points to eclecticism, associated to Maine de Biran and Victor Cousin as a further significant influence.

[14] One of the most well-known magazines in Brazil dedicated a full report to this subject, see R. Levino, 'Música Gospel: trinados fé e dinheiro', *Veja* 25 November 2011, available online at https://veja.abril.com.br/cultura/musica-gospel-trinados-fe-e-dinheiro, accessed 14 Abril 2021.

[15] M. Cunha, *A explosão gospel: um olhar das ciências humanas sobre o cenário evangélico no Brasil*, Rio de Janeiro: Instituto Mysterium, 2007, pp. 107–108. Cunha is a Brazilian specialist in the interface of media and religion.

[16] Cunha, *A explosão gospel*, p. 131.

God restricts corruption in the world caused by sin, allowing the development of life and human culture."[17]

Kuyper clarified that God's common grace enabled every human being, whether Christian or not, to create good things including cultural artefacts that reflect God's glory. Therefore, cultural productions should not be analysed or rejected according to the religious confession of their authors but as an expression of the common grace shed over creation.

Cultural Christians

An attentive look at Brazil's evangelical boom in recent years reveals the growth of Neo-Pentecostal churches, such as the *Igreja Universal do Reino de Deus* (Universal Church of the Kingdom of God) and the *Igreja Internacional da Graça de Deus* (the International Church of the Grace of God). Other evangelical groups include charismatic, youth-oriented churches such as *Bola de Neve Gospel Church* (the Snowball Gospel Church), which originally ministered to surfers and has now spread to young urban middle-class groups. These new ecclesiastical models share a desire to make Christianity attractive to those unfamiliar with church environments. In this relationship the onus is on the church to adapt to contemporary changes, accept new forms of thinking and contemporary cultural artefacts.

Historically, according to Richard Niebuhr, some movements sought a harmonisation between Christ – or Christianity – and culture. Arguably, liberalism, which Niebuhr called cultural Protestantism, is the most well-known example.[18] For Niebuhr, "although their fundamental interest has to do with what relates to this world, they do not reject that which transcends this level (other worldliness) but seek to understand the transcendent kingdom as a continuum in time."[19] Liberalism is characterised by an acceptance of the neutrality of reason in modern epistemology. Similarly, Brazilian Neo-Pentecostal movements also accommodate contemporary cultural dynamics, although in their case these take the form of an acritical reception of modern consumerism. Critics of this model start from the assumption that a naïve accommodation between Christianity and culture distorts central biblical ideas and affects orthodox Christian faith and its fundamental beliefs. A coherent understanding of the main features of Western culture is required to understand the distortions such an accommodation would cause.

The period after the Second World War is often designated as postmodern and is characterised by a crisis of metanarratives.[20] Its main features are a

---

[17] R. Ramlow, *O Neocalvinismo holandês e o movimento de cosmovisão cristã*, São Leopoldo: EST/PPG, 2012, p. 25.
[18] Niebuhr, *Cristo e cultura*, p. 111.
[19] Niebuhr, *Cristo e cultura*, p. 110.
[20] See Z. Bauman, *Modernidade Líquida,* Rio de Janeiro: Jorge Zahar, 2001.

fragmentation of the idea of truth, an inability to find rational or religious meaning to life and disintegration at many levels, especially regarding personal identity.[21] As a result, universal interpretative categories have been weakened, opening space for individualistic and relativistic narratives. This results in an extremely dynamic scenario leading to constant change.

Many social theorists, philosophers, and theologians use a postmodern paradigm to analyse religions in Brazil, establishing parallels with the individualistic and market-oriented approach of our times, stating that "religions and theologies that arise from a postmodern worldview diverge greatly from a biblical orthodoxy [...] and from modernity as well".[22]

This chapter does not seek to deepen this reflection but instead to indicate a few examples of this *modus operandi* within some Brazilian evangelical movements. The most noticeable example is the prosperity gospel, which could be broadly defined as an "inter-confessional charismatic movement that emphasises physical health and financial prosperity as basic evidence of the divine blessings in the Christian life. [It] is, with no doubt, the highest expression of the accommodation of the Christian life to the capitalist ideal of physical and material prosperity."[23]

From a reformed perspective, prosperity theology shifts the focus from God's sovereignty, one of the pillars of the Christian faith, towards a profound concentration on the individual, who sees God as a means for his personal self-fulfilment. There is an inversion – the individual's will becomes sovereign, supposedly achieved through religious rituals such as campaigns of spiritual and financial victory, mediated by contemporary techniques of motivation and self-help.

In this model of interaction with culture, the *modus vivendi* of the church is characterised by a pragmatic agenda of attracting those who are outside, and requires the transformation of services and liturgy into something more palatable and acceptable for the world. This is illustrated by a flyer from a *Bola de Neve* church in Rio de Janeiro, inviting people to a *"balada gospel"* (gospel nightclub): "You can come and bring that friend of yours who enjoys electronic music, *forró*[24] and other rhythms, who loves a good football match and excitement. Let us show them that we know how to party and together worship God!"[25]

From a reformational standpoint, neither the total rejection nor an acritical accommodation to culture reflect the Christian ground motive of creation, fall

---

[21] See A. Giddens, *Modernidade e Identidade*. Rio de Janeiro. Jorge Zahar, 2002.
[22] R. Ramos, *Evangelização no mercado Pós-Moderno* Viçosa: Ultimato, 2003, p. 91.
[23] A. Timm, 'Teologia da Prosperidade', in F. Bortolleto Filho, *Dicionário Brasileiro de Teologia* (São Paulo: ASTE, 2008), pp. 966-968.
[24] A Brazilian rhythm emerging in the North Eastern region of Brazil.
[25] Available online at http://www.boladeneve.com/eventos/balada-da-zona-sul. Accessed 20 April 2021.

and redemption. The next section provides a panoramic perspective of an alternative: the reformed proposal of the interaction between Christianity and culture.

Christians as Culture's Reformers

Reformed thinkers stress the complete harmony between God the Creator and God the Redeemer and offer a broad worldview emphasising the sovereignty of Christ over all of life (Col. 1:15–20). Herman Dooyeweerd's cosmonomic philosophy has the subjacent theological principle of the cultural mandate, which occurred before the fall. In this sense, the theology of creation plays an important role in the understanding of the scope of redemption.

Hence, "[…] the comprehension of the cultural mandate is in the account of creation in Genesis. Human beings are created in the image and likeness of God, receiving the order to develop culture".[26] The mandate to work and care for the garden (Gen. 2:15) would imply a series of complex activities, such as the administration of different techniques of dealing with the land and the development of the necessary tools to work and cultivate it. Social norms would also need to be created to organise the process of work.[27]

This understanding of the cultural mandate is attached to the concept of vocation, so stressed by Martin Luther and John Calvin.[28] Vocation was not confined to ecclesiastical ministry, but every form of work would be a way of glorifying God. Consequently, a blacksmith gives glory to God while working in the same way that a pastor pleases the Lord when he delivers a sermon. Abraham Kuyper insisted upon a Christianity that would not divide reality between sacred and profane.[29] From a reformed Christian understanding of cultural activity, Guilherme de Carvalho observes:

> In contrast with isolationist and synthetic forms of evangelicalism, it is necessary to pursue a dialogic-antithetic form of evangelicalism: with a permanent and critical contact with culture, acknowledging its creational and intrinsically good character, but also being aware of the perverse and universal consequences of the fall.[30]

Given that creation is good, its different dimensions express God's will for his creatures. Nevertheless, along with this affirmation, the Reformed tradition

---

[26] Ramlow, *O Neocalvinismo Holandês e o Movimento de Cosmovisão Cristã*, p. 28.
[27] G. de Carvalho, 'A objeção reformada ao dogma da autonomia religiosa da razão', *Diálogo e Antítese*, 1.1 (2009) pp. 4–53.
[28] See M. Luther, *Pelo Evangelho de Cristo* (Porto Alegre/São Leopoldo: Ed. Concórdia/ Ed. Sinodal, 1984), p. 81.
[29] A. Kuyper, *Calvinismo*, São Paulo: Cultura Cristã, 2003.
[30] G. de Carvalho, 'O dualismo natureza/graça e a influência do humanismo secular no pensamento social cristão', in M. Cunha et al (eds), *Cosmovisão cristã e transformação: espiritualidade, razão e ordem social* (Viçosa, MG: Ultimato, 2006), p. 143.

gives importance to the view of the fall as total depravity, a total distortion of created order. As stated by Dooyeweerd, the human heart is inclined to a religious ground motive, seeking for its origin – *arché* – as a way of giving meaning to reality. Whenever the human heart is not oriented to God it expresses its fallen and apostate condition.[31] This is the only dualism existent in reality: the religious antithesis of the heart, introduced by sin in the fall. The antithetical, therefore, would be at work within the human heart – the religious centre – and not in the external structures of society. This erroneous orientation affects every aspect of life, from scientific and philosophical production to the cultural dimension.

As an answer to the consequences of the fall, the Dutch Neo-Calvinist tradition points to a comprehensive redemption in Jesus Christ. This includes the cultural sphere as well as every human enterprise that involves creativity. Besides, given that culture is understood as a good thing within creation, it is both a gift and a task to be attained. For de Carvalho:

> "[…] human culture as a whole is also part of God's creational order. Many of its aspects (state, family, economy, morality, etc.) already existed before the church and continue to be valid with the coming of the kingdom of God. New creation does not imply the destruction or the dissolution of the original creational order; it is not subversion, but the restoration and the glorification of creation's original architecture."[32]

Many Christian ministries have been developed, grounded in a Neo-Calvinist worldview. One example that has a *modus vivendi* applying principles derived from the Dutch tradition is the *L'Abri* Fellowship. Founded in 1955 in Switzerland by Francis and Edith Schaeffer, *L'Abri* was deeply influenced by the ideas of the Dooyweerdian art historian Hans Rookmaaker.[33] One of the features of this ministry is the integration of different aspects of life under the lordship of Christ. According to Steve Turner, a former L'Abri student in the 1970s in Switzerland:

> Life at L'Abri sharpened our perceptions. Many of us had come from backgrounds which encouraged us to categorise all culture as either Christian or non-Christian,

---

[31] Dooyeweerd, *No Crepúsculo do Pensamento*, p.83.
[32] de Carvalho, 'A objeção reformada ao dogma da autonomia religiosa da razão', p. 73.
[33] Hans Rookmaaker (1922–1977) was for many years Professor of Art History at the Free University of Amsterdam, where he applied neo-Calvinism to the arts. A few years later Rookmaaker founded the Dutch branch of L'Abri Fellowship, which exists to this day. See C. Duriez, *Francis Schaeffer: an authentic life*, Nottingham: InterVarsity Press, 2008. For an overview of the beginnings of L'Abri, see E. Schaeffer, *L'Abri*. Wheaton: Crossway, 1992. A lecture given by Edith Reitsema, 'The Intriguing Friendship Between Francis Schaeffer and Hans Rookmaaker' helps understand the influence of Dutch neo-Calvinism on Schaeffer. Available at: http://www.labri-ideas library.org/download.asp?fileID=711

spiritual or fleshy. Schaeffer, influenced by the Dutch art historian Hans Rookmaaker, instead proposed that we should look at works individually. Rather than asking, is this artist saved? Ask, Is this piece of work technically excellent? Is it a valid expression of the artist's view of the world? Are form and content well integrated? Is truth communicated?[34]

The reference to L'Abri and to Francis Schaeffer is important because his work has become well known among Brazilian evangelicals as new editions of some of his main books have been released.[35] This offers a partial explanation for the increased interest in the Reformed tradition in Brazil, especially with reference to Hans Rookmaaker and Herman Dooyeweerd. In 2010, Rookmaaker's book *Art Needs No Justification* was translated and published in Portuguese, and in 2012 the same publisher released a biography written by Laurel Gasque entitled *Rookmaaker: Arts and the Christian Mind*.[36] L'Abri workers Guilherme de Carvalho and Rodolfo Amorim have emphasised the connection between reformed thinking and L'Abri for Brazilian readers in various articles and book chapters and by translating Dooyeweerd's *In the Twilight of Western thought*. Dooyeweerd's book about the state was translated and published in Brazil in 2015 and *The Roots of Western Culture* in 2015.[37] *The Contours of a Christian Philosophy* by Kalsbeeck – an introduction to cosmonomic philosophy – was also translated and published in the same year.[38]

The influence of the Dutch neo-Calvinist tradition can also be seen in the establishment of the Kuyper Association for Transdisciplinary Studies (Associação Kuyper para Estudos Transdisciplinares, or AKET). AKET took the initiative, supported by the John Templeton Foundation, in setting up the Brazilian version of *Christians in Science*: *Associação Brasileira de Cristãos na Ciência*. AKET seeks to bridge a gap within Christian communities in Brazil by relating all areas of life to the Christian faith.

Thus, recent publications, the development of associations such as the one mentioned above, and communities of Christian thinkers and artists are evidence that an understanding of Christians as culture's reformers has started to gain strength in the Brazilian context. There are many challenges yet to be faced, though the first fruits of reformational thinking can already be seen in culture

---

[34] S. Turner, *Imagine*: *a vision for Christians in the arts* (Downers Grove: InterVarsity Press, 2001), p. 11.
[35] For example, F. Schaeffer, *A Arte e a Bíblia*. Viçosa: Ultimato, 2010 and F. Schaeffer, *A morte da Razão*. São Paulo: ABU Editora;2014.
[36] H. Rookmaaker, *A arte não precisa de justificativa*, Viçosa: Ultimato, 2010 and L. Gasque, *Rookmaaker*: *Arte e mente cristã*, Viçosa, MG: Ultimato, 2012.
[37] H. Dooyeweerd, *Estado e soberania: ensaios sobre cristianismo e política*, São Paulo: Vida Nova, 2014 and H. Dooyeweerd, *Raízes da cultura ocidental: as opções cristã, secular e pagã*, São Paulo: Cultura Cristã, 2015.
[38] L. Kalsbeeck, *Contornos da filosofia cristã: a melhor e mais sucinta à Filosofia Reformada de Herman Dooyeweerd*, São Paulo: Cultura Cristã, 2015.

and it stands as a powerful and meaningful response to the question raised at the start of this chapter concerning the relationship between Christians and the world.

5. Economics, Theology and the "Kingdom of God" in Latin America
Martín Ocaña

Can someone tell us how we are going to feed those who are hungry, if private hands control the means of production and destine their use to increase capital rather than satisfy the needs of the population?[1]

Approaching the Theme

The theological category of the "kingdom of God" has been a central theme in different Latin American theological projects across the last five decades. Thus, *Iglesia y Sociedad en América Latina* (Church and Society in Latin America – ISAL), different liberation theologies, the *Fraternidad Teológica Latinoamericana* (Latin American Theological Fraternity – FTL) and the New Apostolic Reformation (NAR), have all turned to the "kingdom of God" to explain their theological proposals.

This chapter explores how the kingdom of God has been related to the materiality of life, that is, satisfying bodily needs in these different theological projects. In the words of Norbert Lohfink, "what relationship does the vast and fundamental field of human activity that we call 'economy' have with the salvation God offers to humans and which the Bible describes through the concept of 'kingdom of God'?"[2] Latin America has produced much theological reflection on themes in which economic issues are implicit, such as "the social responsibility of the church", "integral mission" and "the political responsibility of Christians." Nonetheless, there is still an urgent need for direct, explicit reflection on the economy.

From "To Be or Not to Be" towards "To Eat or Not to Eat"

ISAL, liberation theology and the FTL share a common starting point: the close connection between theological reflection and the context it takes place in. In liberation theology this led to a radical rupture with how theology is done in

---

[1] J.P. Miranda, *Comunismo en la Biblia* (Mexico City: Siglo XXI, 1981), p. 20.
[2] N. Lohfink, 'Reino de Dios y economía en la Biblia', *Communio* 2.8 (1986), p. 112.

North Atlantic countries. For liberation theology, the North Atlantic context focused on issues of "to be or not to be" and led theologians into dialogue with different contemporary philosophical currents. In Latin America, the fundamental issue was the suffering of those who were non-persons, the economically poor, those who were deprived of the conditions which allowed them to have a dignified life.[3] Liberation theologians have therefore turned to the social sciences, especially certain sociological theories, as dialogue partners. From this perspective, one moves from concerns with "to be or not to be" to the flagrant reality of "to eat or not to eat", from philosophy to economics. The Latin American context provides many reasons to support Jung Mo Sung's claim that "the economic-theological theme should ... occupy a central place in theological reflection in Latin American and the Caribbean."[4]

This point of view leads to a series of theological affirmations: (1) the God in whom we believe is the God of life; (2) God is concerned with human life; (3) God desires to satisfy the vital needs of all, particularly the poor; and (4) God will judge how the means of production and reproduction are employed. God, therefore, has something to say about the economy and Latin American theology is not only in direct dialogue with the social sciences, but also the economic sciences. Manuel Gracio das Neves explains this as follows:

> The generic and abstract affirmation that God is the God of life itself is of no use without being related to the concrete, material elements of life, which are what allow real life to exist (...) a coherent preferential option for the poor requires a concrete option in the production and reproduction of the material elements of human life. The economy is the locus of production, distribution, and consumption of the material goods necessary for the perpetuation of human life. Thus, theology and economics find themselves intrinsically united. From the God of life and his preferential option for the poor, we come necessarily to a *critical judgement of the economy*.[5]

Disconnecting theology from the economy is dangerous. In the words of Jung Mo Sung:

> To announce the God of life and, likewise, defend the life of all, especially the poor, *without discussing theologically the problems of production and reproduction of material life,* means to accept, in practice, that the utopia of the kingdom of God will be carried out in a "magic" way, an "assault", with no need for any institutional

---

[3] G. Gutiérrez, *La fuerza histórica de los pobres,* Lima: CEP, 1979.
[4] J. M. Sung, *Economía, tema ausente en la teología de la liberación* (San José: DEI, 1994), p. 88.
[5] M. das Neves. *Dios resucita en la periferia: Hablar de Dios desde América Latina* (Salamanca: San Esteban, 1991), p. 81. My italics.

mediation – a position close to anarchism; or also to accept the thesis that theology should not "mix" with "profane" subjects.⁶

Certain ecclesial and theological circles do, indeed, hold to the unbiblical idea that the kingdom of God will be established, and all needs satisfied, without explaining through which historical mediators this will take place. This has a paralysing effect on social actors, impeding any changes to the dominant economic system. A rarely admitted assumption of this perspective is that faithful biblical interpretation must retain a certain ideological purity, uncontaminated by worldly ideologies. This would suggest that a Biblical contextual theology is one that is able to abstract itself from all aspects of a specific worldview, such as economics, language, and ideology. Is it possible to have a theology without ideology? What would be, in any case, the relationship between both? Is liberation theology more ideological than contemporary prosperity theology?

Emilio Núñez has correctly observed that it "is also possible to submit theology to a right-wing ideology."⁷ Sharon Heaney's evaluation of Latin American theologies, warns that "active biblical faith expressed through theology should not be used to cover up an ideology of the status quo".⁸ However, in Latin America certain ideologies have been subjected to more criticism than others. There is little controversy with regards to the critique of ideologies considered dangerous such as the different forms of Marxism. In comparison, the fall of the Berlin Wall in 1989 and the enthusiastic embrace of Francis Fukuyama's concept of the "end of history"⁹ mean that there is little debate on market friendly ideologies.

Economy: Presence and Absence

Since the end of the nineteenth century, theologians and churches have been commenting on economic themes. For example, the Roman Catholic Church has produced documents such as *Rerum Novarum* (1891), *Quadragesimo Anno* (1931), *Mater et Magistra* (1961), *Pacem in Terris* (1963), *Populorum Progressio* (1967), *Octogesima Adveniens* (1971), *Laborem Exercens* (1981), *Sollicitudo Rei Socialis* (1987), *Centessimus Annus* (1991), *Veritatis Splendor* (1993), *Evangelium Vitae* (1995), and *Caritas in Veritate* (2009). Alongside these we have documents from the *Pontificia Iustitita et Pax* Commission and the theoretical production of the neo-conservative theologian Michael Novak

---

⁶ Sung, *Economía*, pp. 200–201. My italics.
⁷ E. Núñez, *Teología de la liberación: Una perspectiva evangélica* (Miami: Caribe, 1986), p. 28.
⁸ S. Heaney, *Contextual Theology for Latin America* (Carlisle: Paternoster, 2008), p. 87.
⁹ Cf. F. Hinkelammert, *El asalto al poder mundial y la violencia sagrada del imperio*, San José: DEI, 2003.

and his followers.¹⁰ Protestant writers such as Walter Rauschenbusch, Reinhold Niebuhr, and the authors of *The Fundamentals* have clearly identified themselves with specific political and economic positions.¹¹

Political and economic themes are clearly articulated in all these examples. This makes the lack of clarity and specific details in certain Latin American evangelical theologies, or in Latin America as a whole, even more noteworthy, suggesting that they wanted to avoid engaging economics face on. Maybe economics has always been present, but through its absence?

The Kingdom of God and the Materiality of Life

Latin American theological movements understand the kingdom of God and its earthly concrete expression as follows:

ISAL and liberation theology: History belongs to all, so that Christians and non-Christians participate together in the process of constructing the kingdom of God. The poor, alongside their organic intellectuals are the privileged social subjects of this Christian imperative. Socialism (in one of its forms) provides social historical mediation, offering a viable structure for the kingdom to be expressed.¹²

FTL: It is impossible to construct the kingdom of God in history as we are living in the "now" and "not yet". The church is both the sign and agency of the kingdom and should reflect its values such as justice, equality and *shalom*. FTL writings were generally silent concerning the social and historical mediation of the kingdom of God. However, FTL's true position was possibly made implicit in its repeated condemnation of the option towards socialism in ISAL and liberation theology.¹³

Prosperity theology and the New Apostolic Reformation: There is also a Christian imperative to construct the kingdom of God in history, with

---

¹⁰ See, from different political perspectives, J. de Santa Ana, 'Economia e teología', in A. da Silva (ed.), *América Latina: 500 anos de evangelização* (São Paulo: Paulinas, 1990), pp. 140–141, M. Novak, *El pensamiento social católico y las instituciones liberales* (San José: Libro Libre, 1992), pp. 32–33 and J. Moltmann, *God for a Secular Society. The Public Relevance of Theology* (London: SCM Press, 1999), pp. 153–166.
¹¹ Russell Moore indicates that conservative theologians avoided the concept of the kingdom of God as in "the construction of an evangelical political theology, a situation that would paralyze any such effort since the problematic features of both fundamentalism and the Social Gospel in relation to the public square were directly related to kingdom concepts". R. Moore, *The kingdom of Christ: The New Evangelical Perspective* (Wheaton: Crossway Books, 2004), p. 22.
¹² This was made clear from early on in Liberation theology. A Protestant perspective is presented in J. Miguez Bonino 'El reino de Dios y la historia' in C.R Padilla (ed.), *El reino de Dios y América Latina* (El Paso: Casa Bautista de Publicaciones, 1975), pp. 75-95.
¹³ Cf. S. Escobar, *La fe evangélica y las teologías de la liberación,* Nashville: Casa Bautista de Publicaciones, 1987 and E. Núñez, *Teología de la liberación.*

businesspeople and other economic agents being the privileged subjects. Capitalism provides social and historical mediation as its institutions, such as unlimited free markets, and transnational companies provide a viable structure for the kingdom to be expressed.[14]

This summary raises the issue of FTL's lack of clarity and precision concerning critical issues such as social historical mediation, and the reluctance towards making implicit ideas explicit. The consequence was a timid discussion of economic themes in comparison to issues related to politics and integral mission.[15]

In my opinion, one of the most valuable contributions comes from the final document of the Jarabacoa Consultation in 1983. Considering its theological importance, I transcribe the section related to "The Economy":

> 5.1 We understand economic activity as the social relationship which guarantees the full satisfaction of a human being's temporal necessities. The economic goal is not exclusively directed to profit and the accumulation of capital, but mainly towards social investment and the production of essential goods and services.
>
> 5.2 We consider that the means of production (land, capital, labour, and organisations) have, above all else, a social function, and their use, benefits and exploitation should be conditioned to collective interests and the whole nation.
>
> 5.3 Economic self-determination is an essential element of a people's sovereignty. For this reason, in our countries, there is an urgent task to recover economic concessions granted to foreign groups and interests, and to privileged minorities, which go against our national heritage and autonomy.
>
> 5.4 We defend the democratisation of property, especially land, through a property regime that guarantees access to land ownership for those who work on it.
>
> 5.5 We support a new international economic order, which guarantees the defence of our natural resources and a more just participation in markets. We likewise insist on the emergence of equitable financial relationships and that scientific and technological resources can be within reach of our countries on favourable terms.
>
> 5.6 Considering similar circumstances in Latin American countries, we defend a greater cooperation and economic integration at a regional and continental level. Likewise, we are in favour of a more significant cooperation with other countries which have not yet reached their development potential.
>
> 5.7 We declare that God, having placed humans as stewards on the earth, did not renounce his lordship over creation. For this reason, we stand against the misuse of

---

[14] M. Ocaña Flores "The New Apostolic Reformation and the Theology of Prosperity in Peru" in D. Salinas (ed.), *Prosperity Theology and the Gospel* (Peabody: Hendrickson, 2017), pp. 123–135.

[15] See the documents referred to in the postscript.

the environment through irrational and indiscriminate exploitation which threatens to destroy the biological basis of our existence, degrading our quality of life.[16]

Why did FTL not continue this line of reflection started at Jarabacoa? The lack of academic expertise in economic sciences among FTL members helps understand the superficial initial treatment of economic themes but not their subsequent absence. Another hypothesis is that the International Fellowship of Evangelical Students left its mark, once again, by not allowing the discussion of alternative economic models to capitalism. This should be set in the context of dramatic global changes after the fall of the Berlin Wall in 1989 when the dominance of the neo-liberal economic model seemed incontestable so that detailed theological reflection on the economy no longer seemed necessary.

While this lack of economic reflection does not constitute a methodological crisis, an anomaly emerges in the incongruence between FTL's theological and theoretical reflection and its implicit or explicit acceptance of the prevailing economic model.

Theology, Praxis, and Feasibility

Life in its diverse expressions is a central theme in Christian theology. Unfortunately, some mistakenly emphasise eternal life at the expense of present, historical, and bodily life. Conservative theology has spoken about God as a "God of Life", but, on what terms? Juan Stam affirms that this theology:

> Speaks about eternal life, spiritual life, true life, abundant life, but manages to accommodate the biblical message so that it does not disturb the existing social and economic structures. This is carried out through a spiritualizing rereading of the Scriptures, systematically and thoroughly supressing the messianic thread with its concrete hope for this land and this history (utopia) translating it into the Platonic categories of the bodyless spirit and timeless heaven. Above all, this theology manifests a compulsive need to empty the biblical message of its promise of the "new earth" as the final goal of history.[17]

One of the greatest contributions of ISAL, liberation theology and the FTL has been to offer a counterpoint to this position, emphasising that human life comes from God, as our God is a God of life.[18] As John's Gospel reminds us, Jesus the Messiah declares "I have come so that they may have life and have it abundantly" (Jn. 10:10). One of the main contributions of Latin American

---

[16] FTL, 'Declaración de Jarabacoa: os cristãos e a ação política' *Boletim Teológico* 2, 1984.
[17] J. Stam, 'La teología dominante y el derecho a la vida' in A. Piedra (ed.), *Haciendo teología en América Latina: Juan Stam: un teólogo del camino, Volumen 2* (San José: Visión Mundial y otros, 2005), p. 168.
[18] Cf. G. Gutiérrez, *El Dios de la vida,* Lima: CEP – Instituto Bartolomé de las Casas, 1989.

theology has been to reflect on this theme, especially its relationship with the kingdom of God. What is the kingdom? A future kingdom? A present kingdom? Now but not yet? A kingdom which is a gift of the Father? A kingdom which needs to be built on earth? If so, by whom? What is its socio-economic mediation, and is such mediation sustainable? A liberation theologian, Raúl Vidales, who in my opinion is representative of the wider movement affirms:

> *The kingdom as a perfect society is impossible, nonetheless, those who do not try to conceive the impossible, will never discover what is possible, or most possible.* What is possible comes from submitting the impossible to the criterion of feasibility, and feasibility is what brings us close to the concrete anticipations of the ideal we pursue. It is evident that the kingdom of God becomes even more distant, rather than being anticipated, within the current international economic order. Thus, this economic order must be rejected in favour of building a new international economic order where life is truly guaranteed for all. And this can only be achieved in a socialist society.[19]

Leaving to one side Vidales' optimism towards a socialist state which guarantees life for all, the kingdom of God as a *perfect society* is impossible if one considers the biblical, anthropological element of personal and structural sin. Nonetheless, it should be indisputable that avoiding the fetishism or idolatry of the prevailing economic system requires maintaining an ideal, dream or utopia which goes beyond it. What is open to debate is whether this ideal should be a socialist state as liberation theologians affirm.

What do liberation theologians mean by a socialist state? Juan Luis Segundo affirms, "we describe as socialist the political regime in which *the property of the means of production is removed from individuals and handed over to superior institutions with regards to their concern for the common good*".[20] Socialism is considered a closer mediator to the kingdom of God in comparison to capitalism.[21] The challenge is to reflect on the difficult issue of what the Bible has to say about economic systems. There is always the temptation to declare that a certain economic system is defended by the Bible or at least most compatible with Scripture. The reality is that neither socialism, nor the welfare state, nor Keynesian economics, nor capitalism nor liberalism, nor the free market, or any of their many versions can claim that the Bible makes them "sacred."[22] It is arguably better to follow Lohfink who declares that *economic transformation is essential for salvation in history*. In the Old Testament the

---

[19] R. Vidales, *Teología e Imperio* (San José: DEI, 1991), p. 86, my italics.
[20] J. Segundo, "Capitalismo-socialismo, *crux theologica*", in R. Gibellini (ed.), *La nueva frontera de la teología en América Latina* (Salamanca: Sígueme, 1977), p. 231, my italics.
[21] Bonino, 'El reino de Dios y la historia'.
[22] G. Méndez, 'El sustrato teológico de la economía' *Kairós* 13 (1993), p. 35.

deliverance from Egypt and the year of Jubilee indicate that redemption, passing from death into bodily life, is associated with changes in the quality of life.[23]

Dealing with abundant and bodily life requires considering the contribution of two authors from opposing perspectives: Michael Novak, a philosopher from the United States and Franz Hinkelammert the German economist resident in Costa Rica. Novak proposes an explicit economic theology in which there is an overlap between Christianity and capitalism,[24] claiming that:

> Capitalism, alongside democracy, emerges from a specifically Christian soil. Its preconceptions are Judeo-Christian, its ethos is substantially, albeit not completely, Judeo-Christian. In a particularly significant way, its roots are evangelical.[25]
>
> What do I mean by "democratic capitalism"? With this expression I refer to three systems in one: a predominantly market economy; a political organisation which respects individual rights to life, liberty and the pursuit of happiness and a set of cultural institutions guided by ideals of liberty and justice for all.[26]

José Mardones aptly affirms that in North American neo-conservatism, as exemplified in Novak and his followers, "capitalism is the best economic system as it favours the best social structure, as it promotes the greater production of goods (efficiency and growth), the least unequal distribution and the least coercion by authorities over citizens and their ideas (liberty and pluralism)".[27] In simple terms, neo-conservatism declares that capitalism allows the poor to reach the prosperity needed for financial liberty. The fact that over a billion people on the planet still live in extreme poverty reveal that this is a myth and an illusion, but a myth proclaimed by prosperity theology and the New Apostolic Reformation.[28]

In comparison, Hinkelammert provides a liberationist economic theology. Hinkelammert develops a critical theory of fetishism, unmasking the anti-utopic utopia of the market which generates an ethics of sacrifice and leads to new processes of idolatry within Christianity. He proposes new alternatives for

---

[23] Lohfink, 'Reino de Dios y economía en la Biblia'.
[24] See the discussion in H. Assmann and F. Hinkelammert. *A idolatría do mercado: Ensaio sobre Economia e Teologia* (São Paulo: Vozes, 1989), p. 44.
[25] M. Novak, *Raíces evangélicas del capitalismo democrático* (San José: Libro Libre, 1989), p. 31.
[26] M. Novak, *El espíritu del capitalismo democrático* (Buenos Aires: Tres tiempos, 1983), pp. 11–12. See also G. Weigel. *Fieles y libres: Catolicismo, derechos humanos y democracia,* San José: Libro Libre, 1989 and A. Sherman. *Preferential Option: A Christian and Neoliberal Strategy for Latin America's poor,* Grand Rapids: Eerdmans, 1992.
[27] J. Mardones, *Capitalismo y religión: La religión política neoconservadora* (Santander: Sal Terrae, 1991), p. 83. Mardones offers an acute critique of neo-conservatism in J. Mardones, *Postmodernidad y neoconservadurismo: Reflexiones sobre la fe y la cultura* (Navarra: Verbo Divino, 1991), pp. 129–149.
[28] J. Schuldt. *Civilización del desperdicio,* Lima: Universidad del Pacífico, 2013.

reconstructing the economy to overcome the contemporary culture of hopelessness.²⁹ Jong Mo Sung laments how Hinkelammert's contribution has not been valued sufficiently.³⁰ Lately, his analysis has lost space to theological agendas which focus on the rights of new political actors who displace the poor as agents for the transformation of society in agreement with the kingdom of God. In an interview with philosopher Germán Gutiérrez, Hinkelammert himself points to the short-sighted nature of these new developments:

> One cannot substitute the approach of liberation theology with feminist theology. The human being to be liberated is man and woman, child and adult, black and white, native, *mestizo,* etc. From these specific characteristics one must take the whole into consideration. There are legitimate reasons for taking these specific characteristics into account, yet if one forgets that at the base of everything is the ability to eat, they melt into the air. To eat is clearly not everything, but it is the base of everything. And this is since Plato, not since Marx.³¹

Thus, it is necessary to consider whether these new theological concerns in Latin America really touch on the fundamental issues or, unwittingly, help to effectively disguise the very system they claim to change.

An Economy for Life: Prophetic or Utopic Imagination

Which economic system or model allows all to achieve an integral quality of life? Who defines the model? Who gets to determine what "quality of life" is? Is such a model achievable and sustainable? In the words of Walter Brueggemann, this leads us into the "prophetic imagination",³² dreaming about a socio-economic reality that places human beings and their needs at the centre. Rubem Alves accurately affirms, "society should not determine whether a form of life is crazy. On the contrary it is life which should say if a society is crazy or not".³³ This leads us to reflect anthropologically on contemporary technological society and its diverse messianisms.³⁴

---

²⁹ Cf. J. Bautista, *Crítica ética del pensamiento latinoamericano: Introducción al pensamiento crítico de Franz Hinkelammert,* La Paz: Filigrana, 2007. Although Hinkelammert's production is voluminous, one should emphasise F. Hinlelammert, *Las armas ideológicas de la muerte,* San José: DEI, 1981.
³⁰ Sung, *Economía,*
³¹ F. Hinkelammert, 'Teología en el acontecer de la vida', in J. Duque and G. Gutiérrez (ed.), *Itinerarios de la razón crítica: Homenaje a Franz Hinkelammert en sus 70 años* (San José: DEI, 2001), pp. 41–42.
³² W. Brueggemann, *La imaginación profética,* Santander: Sal y Terra, 1978.
³³ R. Alves, *Hijos del mañana* (Salamanca: Sígueme, 1976), pp. 151–152.
³⁴ Ruben Alves was a pioneer in this area. Cf. R. Alves, *¿Religión, opio o instrumento de liberación?* Montevideo: Tierra Nueva, 1970. See Ellul's valuable contribution in J. Ellul, *La edad de la técnica,* Barcelona: Octaedro, 2003.

On the other hand, it is well known that neo-conservatism's critique of liberation theology lies in the specific and often antagonistic reading that the latter makes of "economic and social realities."[35] Rather than critiquing specific perspectives, theologians need to reject any model which compromises human life, subjecting the economy and its impact on human beings to critical judgement. Although alternatives to the current system are being presented, such as "an economy of solidarity", they lack clear content. More than the economic system, it is human life and its survival which are at stake in these debates. As Pedro Morante aptly affirms:

> In a society in which we have a surplus of reports from economic and financial experts and of ideological schemes which claim to have the answers, what we lack is a cultural interpretation of our contemporary challenges which ... offer criteria for judgement based on the dignity of each person and their experience as a subject and the need to be treated as bearers of the truth. This is precisely the Church's fundamental contribution.[36]

The different theological movements referred to in this chapter (FTL, New Apostolic Reformation, prosperity theology, and others), theological institutions and the wider evangelical community have yet to engage in this important task.

Final Reflections

We are living through a period of considerable change as globalisation has become the new name for capitalist domination.[37] This involves other issues beyond the economy, such as multiculturalism, the environment, identities and religious symbols. Hence, to reduce everything to the economy is a dangerous simplification. However, to avoid the economy would be a methodological error with severe consequences. Human beings need their daily bread to survive, and this is not a mere accessory. However as, "the concern for social and economic justice has not been resolved",[38] I propose the following for contemporary theological reflection in Latin America:

1) That theology and economics be companions. A theology which reflects on the economy has an urgent sense of relevance as it reflects and places pressure upon the present and does not concern itself solely with an abstract future. In my opinion, both theology and economics share a common labour in unmasking the

---

[35] M. Novak. ¿En verdad liberará? Reflexiones sobre teología de la liberación (Mexico City: Diana, 1994), p. 27.
[36] P. Morante, Iglesia y cultura en América Latina (Lima: Vida y Espiritualidad, 1989), p. 175.
[37] N. Míguez, 'Hacer teología latinoamericana en el tiempo de globalización' in G. Hansen (ed.), El silbo ecuménico del Espíritu: Homenaje a José Míguez Bonino en sus 80 años (Buenos Aires: ISEDET, 2004), pp. 81–101.
[38] Míguez, 'Hacer teología latinoamericana en el tiempo de globalización', p. 99.

sacrificial elements of market economy, even though this is possible only by developing a theological critique of the economy, and not just of ideology, as has prevailed until now.[39]

2) Methodologically, we should incorporate the contributions from economics into our theological analysis. This requires widening the interdisciplinary nature of theological labour. It involves looking further and analysing how capitalism is manifest in our countries. There are idolatrous and fetishist tendencies in the predominant economic model. What is required is a theological critique of capitalism's ideological and cultural components.

3) There is urgent need for further work on the biblical concept of the kingdom of God. We still lack a solid kingdom theology related to history. In fact, it becomes necessary to work on the meaning of history, a theme always delayed in Latin American theologies. It is evident that there is a dependency on theologians from the 1970s and 1980s. Their contribution is valuable but not sufficient. The corporeal nature of human life demands a reflection. The kingdom of God integrates all aspects of human life in the here and now.[40]

Postscript: List of FTL Events and Publications Related to Economics[41]

Consultation "Los evangélicos y el poder político" (Jarabacoa, República Dominicana, 1983).

Pablo Deiros, *Los evangélicos y el poder político en América Latina.* Buenos Aires: Nueva Creación, 1986.

Consultation "Hacia una transformación integral" (Huampaní, Lima, 1987).

Washington Padilla, *Hacia una transformación integral.* Buenos Aires: Fraternidad Teológica Latinoamericana, 1989.

Renato Espoz. 'La economía: una pseudo-ciencia natural', *Boletín Teológico* 34 (1989), pp. 183–206.

Consultation "Los cristianos frente a la dependencia económica y la deuda externa de América Latina" (Santiago, 1990).

Consultation "El evangelio y la cuestión de la pobreza" (Sao Paulo, 1990).

Renato Espoz. 'El testimonio de la economía en la perspectiva del cristianismo en América Latina', *Boletín Teológico* 38 (1990), pp. 101-111.

---

[39] Cf. P. Sedgwick. *The Market Economy and Christian Ethics*, (Cambridge: Cambridge University Press), 2004.

[40] Cf. A. González: *Reinado de Dios e Imperio: Ensayo de teología social.*, (Santander: Sal Terrae), 2003 y A. González, *El evangelio de la paz y el reinado de Dios*, (Buenos Aires: Kairós), 2008. Also J. Solalinde, *El reino de Dios: Replanteamiento radical de la vida*, (Toluca: Universidad Autónoma del Estado de México), 2016.

[41] It is possible to find evangelical publications dealing with economic issues even before the formation of the FTL. Cf. S. Escobar. *Diálogo entre Cristo y Marx*, Lima: AGEUP, 1967 and P. Arana. *Progreso, técnica y hombre*, (Buenos Aires: Certeza), 1971 (The original text dates from February 1970).

Franz Hinkelammert. 'Economia e teología: as leis do mercade e a Fe', *Boletim Teologico* 11 (1990), pp. 43–64.

Renato Espoz. 'Os cristaos frente a dependencia económica e a divida externa', *Boletim Teologico* 13 (1990), pp. 41-50.

Robinson Cavalcanti. 'A situacao socio-economica e política da America Latina', *Boletim Teologico* 18 (1992), pp. 5-20.

Regional consultations concerning "Economía y fe cristiana" (Santiago, Lima, Guatemala, 1993).

Consultation: "Economía y fe cristiana" (Buenos Aires, 1993).

Marcos Kruse. 'Economo-Teología. Preliminares', *Boletim Teologico* 20, (1993), pp. 7-18.

Padilla, C. R. *Economía humana y economía del Reino de Dios* (Kairos: Buenos Aires, 2002)

6. The Ultimate Betrayal:
Christianity's Triumph and Shame in Power
Lucas Magnin

> If as Christians we descend to the market, where humanisms compete among each other, with our predetermined model, we should not complain if our product becomes tied to market eventualities.
>
> José González Ruiz[1]

Religions seemed destined to disappear during the nineteenth century as science, knowledge and reason apparently undermined the West's religious soul, which had dominated the medieval millennium. Auguste Comte forecasted the arrival of the definite era in which a mature humanity, come of age, would leave behind the dark theological and metaphysical ages and live in the age of absolute progress, marked by the positivistic and scientific ideal. "Some sociologists of religion announced that religions would not survive the twentieth century and would become a purely residual phenomenon".[2] Nonetheless, the new millennium has exposed the ridiculous nature of the antiquated forms of rationalism expressed in Comte's arrogant prophecy.

For decades, we have been witnessing what Giles Keppel has called "the revenge of God."[3] The World Wars, Auschwitz and the atomic bombs weakened the multifaceted Enlightenment attack on religion, revealing that "the Enlightenment is totalitarian",[4] for "instrumental reason, daughter of the enlightenment, in its intent to explain, give reason and understand all, eliminates from its sphere a far from negligible part of reality".[5] For this reason, when the modern dream fails the religious dimension, repressed by modern totalitarianism, re-emerges. In these times of diversity, multiculturalism, and

---

[1] J. González Ruiz, *Dios es gratuito pero no superfluo*, Madrid: Ediciones Marova, 1970.
[2] J. Tamayo Acosta, *Otra teología es posible: Pluralismo religioso, interculturalidad y feminismo* (Barcelona: Herder, 2011), p. 25.
[3] See G. Keppel, *The Revenge of God: The resurgence of Islam, Christianity and Judaism in the Modern World*, (University Park: Pennsylvania State University Press), 1994.
[4] Adorno and Horkheimer quoted in Tamayo Acosta, *Otra teología es posible*, p. 30.
[5] Tamayo Acosta, *Otra teología es posible*, p. 30.

globalisation, "to combat religions face-on in an indiscriminate way with a militant antireligious attitude is sterile and counterproductive. This attitude results as outdated as some of the manifestations it seeks to combat and leads directly to attitudes of self-defence which regularly result in fundamentalism, fanaticism and sectarianism".[6]

One cannot ignore the fact that religions are once more occupying a place of importance in social and cultural debates. The concern now is the role of religions in this new global context, that is, the form that they should take and how they should participate in public life.

Both in Europe and in America this question is addressed particularly to the Christian faith, which has for centuries adjusted to a post-Christian historical configuration. The debate concerning the relationship between church and state is especially relevant in this context. In the past, the Christian faith was the backbone of Medieval Europe and the American colony, with all the criticisms that these systems lead to. What type of institutional relationship will Christianity have with the public sphere, with politics and especially the state in the present? This question appears regularly in contemporary debates.[7]

Believers and non-believers who support the separation between church and state mainly desire to restrict religion to the private sphere. The anticlericalism and antireligious prejudice of the French Revolution led to a secular political configuration which has been maintained until now, despite enormous changes in socio-political circumstances.[8] To associate religion with the private sphere is an Enlightenment and republican legacy according to which "even the idea that there might be a public expression of religions is considered to risk the return of clericalist positions."[9]

In this chapter, I seek to offer a theological, biblical, and historical reflection on the issue of the relationship between believers and temporal powers. Rather

---

[6] Tamayo Acosta, *Otra teología es possible*, p. 29. Cristián Parker affirms something similar: "Regimes which repress religious feeling or attack faith values can generate intolerant responses from the faithful." C. Parker Gumucio, 'Pluralismo religioso y cambio de paradigma identitario en el campo político latinoamericano actual' in A. Almeigeiras (ed.), *Símbolos, rituales religiosos e identidades nacionales: los símbolos religiosos y los procesos de construcción política de identidades en Latinoamérica* (Buenos Aires: CLACSO, 2014), p. 62.

[7] In my country (Argentina), there is wide social support for a law being developed which would dictate the total separation between church and state and eliminate the privileges of the established Catholic church. Currently, article two of the Constitution guarantees the "support of Apostolic Roman Catholic services", which is translated into salaries, allowances, discounts, exemptions, etc.

[8] Hans Küng clarifies that this anticlericalism was mainly directed at the Papal Curia in contrast to the 130,000 French clergy at the time. He also recognises that "for social and religious reasons much of the lower clergy initially collaborated in the decisive rupture towards the revolution." H. Küng, *El cristianismo: Esencia e historia* (Madrid: Editorial Trotta, 1997), p. 722.

[9] Parker, 'Pluralismo religioso y cambio de paradigma identitario', p. 63.

than base my answers on contemporary political theories and old enlightenment prejudices, I will turn to the New Testament concepts of the kingdom of God and the lordship of Christ. Antonio González's social theology will help us reflect on these principles in the light of the historical danger of Constantinianism.

"Christianity" should not be treated as a term with a univocal meaning, as its history points to a diversity of meanings, possibilities, and contradictions. It covers what took place in the medieval period, the history of the American colony as well as the Anabaptists, John Wesley, William Wilberforce, Martin Luther King Jr., Enrique Angelelli and Desmond Tutu. How do we assess Christianity's contributions to contemporary society if history is full of so many good and bad examples?

The Kingdom of God and the Lordship of Christ

Hans Küng provides a clear answer to what gives the Christian faith cohesion: "it is the name of a Jew: Jesus of Nazareth who received from his followers the supreme honorific title that the Jews could grant to a human being".[10] Christ provides cohesion to Christian history, a "golden thread" which does not depend "on an impersonal idea, an abstract principle, a general norm, or a mental system. In contrast to many religions, Christianity depends on a concrete person who is guarantor of a cause, of a complete way of life. Jesus of Nazareth.".[11] The key to understanding, without distortion or confusion, the potential social projection that Christianity can have today lies in the person of Jesus Christ and the cause he dedicated his life to, the kingdom of God.

Liberal theology in previous centuries erred in disassociating the "historical Jesus", with his essential message concerning the kingdom of God, from the "Christ of Faith", constructed dogmatically by the institutional church. In this reading, the latter theology and history of Christianity was regarded as alienated from its founder´s ideas. Rather we follow Antonio González in affirming the continuity between the life of Jesus, centred on the proclamation of the kingdom of God, and the life of the early church, centred on the lordship of Christ.[12] There is no major rupture between the life of Jesus and the practice of the early church because "what comes after Easter is the reign of the same God, exercised by Jesus".[13] The kingdom of God (in Greek: *basileia tou theou*) proclaimed by Jesus becomes the lifestyle of the early church.

---

[10] Küng, *El cristianismo*, p. 42.
[11] Küng, *El cristianismo*, p. 42.
[12] The Book of Acts concludes presenting this continuity in a symbolic way: Paul arrives in Rome, the heart of the empire, from where he was "preaching the kingdom of God and teaching about the Lord Jesus Christ quite openly and unhindered" (Acts 28:31).
[13] A. González, *Reinado de Dios e imperio: Ensayo de teología social* (Santander: Sal Terrae, 2003), p. 197.

In the New Testament, the church becomes the people of the kingdom of God under the leadership of one Lord: Jesus, the Christ.[14] Early Christians appropriated and transformed expressions and ideas from their surrounding culture giving them deeply subversive new meanings. I am going to look briefly at three key examples. First, the term "kingdom" (*basileia*) was used to directly name the Roman Empire. Similarly, the expression "lord" (in Greek, *kyrios*) which the first Christians applied to Jesus was used to recognise Caesar's reign and dominion.[15] The title "son of God", especially in the form which appears three times in Matthew's Gospel (*theoû hyiós:* Matt. 14:33; 27:43, 54) was applied to Roman emperors especially Augustus, Tiberius, Nero and Dominican.[16] The kingdom of God, Jesus's divine sonship and the church's confession of Christ as Lord were not dogmatic abstractions but political and countercultural statements declaring the birth of a new people and a new loyalty, thereby challenging Roman hegemony.

The early church sought to express Jesus's message in renewed, reconciled, and healed relationships. It declared the lordship of Christ both as the key to eschatology and as a reality which becomes actualised in everyday life. The reign of Christ in the *basileia* of God is not an abstract sovereignty for it establishes the foundations for a new form of existence; the early church was, with all its limitations and defects, a concrete expression of this reality. Following Christ implies a loyalty, which has led to contradiction, rejection, and persecution throughout the centuries. The first Christians recognised that to identify oneself with Jesus was to reject the *status quo*:

> To announce Jesus as a dead and resurrected messiah includes the affirmation that Jesus himself is king. This is not something abstract but supposes a concrete challenge to the kings of this world. A new form of sovereignty has emerged in history: the Messiah's sovereignty over his people as the fulfilment of God's definitive reign in the last days of history.[17]

The kingdom of God preached by Jesus and the first Christians has little to do with an introspective escapism or prosperity theology's neo-liberal version, where the kingdom is translated into positions of economic and political power. The early church preached Jesus as Lord of an alternative kingdom; this new human community of justice and peace is materialised in the present in renewed relationships among believers.

---

[14] This is expressed in Jesus' sovereign exaltation to the right hand of the Father. See for example Acts 2:32ff: 5:31; 7:55ff; Romans 8:34; Ephesians 1:20ff; and Hebrews 1:3,13. Other key passages for understanding the lordship of Christ are Romans 10: 9, 1 Corinthians 8:6; 12:3; 2 Corinthians 4:5; Philippians 2:9–11; etc.
[15] See, for example, the implicit yet daring critique by Paul of the imperial cult in 1 Corinthians 8:5–6.
[16] González, *Reinado de Dios e imperio,* p. 196.
[17] González, *Reinado de Dios e imperio,* p. 199.

Contrary to Caesar's empire, Jesus' *basileia* is not imposed from above with arrogance and violence. Love and loyalty towards the Messiah cannot be coerced by the state, nor by any other institution or the ideal of a Christian society. In Galatians 5 Paul points to an opposition between "the works of the flesh" and the "fruit of the Spirit"; all positive values and virtues such as love, peace, and patience, are a fruit which the Spirit of Jesus causes to grow. Without the Spirit, there is no fruit; or, to recover Luther's concept, "we do not become just by doing what is just, but on the contrary, being just we do what is just."[18] The kingdom of God is not imposed through force or coercion but begins voluntarily, from below. A personal decision is required to enter this new reality.[19] For this reason:

> The Christian *ekklesia* is not possible without an exodus. Both terms have the same prefix, *ek*, which indicates a going out, a separation, the rupture which begins something new. Those summoned to the Christian assembly are people who have left the old society to initiate new social relationships within the basic structures of the old world.[20]

The word *alternative* describes early Christianity as an option for renewal within the reality of the Roman Empire:

> Any alternative requires two essential conditions. It must be visible and understandable in its own context as a truly advantageous and attractive social form. Yet it cannot be alternative without being distinguishable from the society which surrounds it.[21]

From its decentred location, the Christian church developed practices of justice within its communities. The kingdom principles followed by the first Christians did not require the state's legitimisation, help or approval; there was a new king governing among those who recognised his rule. The church was not an ally of the state, on the contrary, it was banned and persecuted, its prerogatives interpreted as seditious.

The First Constantinianism

The Constantinian turn changed the face of early Christianity. After the Edict of Milan (313 CE), Constantine removed the proscription upon Christianity. In time, this liberty was followed by favouritism towards the church. This change "from the recent past in which Christianity was persecuted and oppressed was

---

[18] Quoted in M. Hoffmann, 'La Reforma, como un nuevo paradigma de la teología' *Espiga* 16 (2017), p.32.
[19] This recalls the dialogue between Jesus and Nicodemus, "unless one is born anew, he cannot see the kingdom of God" for "unless one is born of water and the Spirit, he cannot enter the kingdom of God" (John 3:3,5).
[20] González, *Reinado de Dios e imperio*, p. 304.
[21] González, *Reinado de Dios e imperio*, pp. 255–256.

met with enormous relief and joy".[22] Only twelve years after the Edict of Milan, Constantine summoned the Council of Nicaea, which he presided over through an appointed Bishop. The emperor "suspended and closed sessions; through his confirmation council decisions became imperial laws".[23] Eventually, this situation led to a complete alliance between church and empire, which defined European society through the medieval period and beyond.

This carnal alliance between church and state is often denominated *Constantinianism:* religion acquires a national character; the nation's government becomes confessional. It proved to be an expensive alliance as the privileges and responsibilities of being the established religion led the Christian alternative to lose the creativity it displayed under persecution. This alliance with the empire led to three fundamental changes in Christianity.

The first change affected how an individual belonged to the church: "under Constantinianism being a Christian ceases to be an exceptional condition received by grace and accepted in freedom and becomes a common characteristic of all members of a specific society".[24] A state religion no longer requires a personal exodus nor the voluntary acceptance of the lordship of Christ as conditions to enter the kingdom.

The second change affected the church's communitarian dimension:

> The conversion of Christianity into the official imperial religion initiated the disappearance of many specific forms of Christian solidarity. When the entire world is Christian by birth or obligation, Christian communities ceased to make sense as an alternative society.[25]

A state religion does not demand new relationships, just and merciful practices nor countercultural structures and has a negative impact on the effectiveness of Christian communitarianism. A new society imposed from above is nothing other than the same society dressed up in new clothes.

The third change affected the church's social ethics. Jesus preached a practice of radical non-violence, synthetically expressed in the Sermon on the Mount; the first Christians, following this example, renounced violence, even when it cost them their lives. One of the state's prerogatives is the legitimate monopoly of violence in its different forms. An established church must legitimise state violence, either explicitly, as seen in the Crusades and the conquest of the Americas, or implicitly as happened in many dictatorships and can still be seen in some current democracies. This means a direct denial of the Sermon of the Mount and Jesus' ethical teaching.

In practical terms, the alliance of the church with the empire completely disfigured Christianity; this legacy is still felt today. Only over time were the

---

[22] Küng, *El cristianismo*, p. 192.
[23] Küng, *El cristianismo*, p. 194.
[24] González, *Reinado de Dios e imperio*, p. 309.
[25] González, *Reinado de Dios e imperio*, p. 245.

risks surrounding the promising and comforting alliance between the church and temporal power revealed. "The church sacralised social structures and legitimised political systems. God was defined as the supreme being who created this world with a hierarchical order, which was a descending ladder to avoid social chaos."[26] The alliance with the empire meant that the church renounced its fundamental quality of offering an alternative. Alternatives cannot be hegemonic; when the church lost what made it special, it became solely a means to legitimise the *status quo*.

Latter Constantinianism

It is easier to condemn events which happened 1700 years ago, than to reflect on their contemporary meanings. Critics condemn religion, especially Christianity, through superficial references to the Crusades, the conquest of the Americas and the Inquisition. The problem is not that they offer a false reading, but one that lacks in nuance and attention to details. Consequently, the arguments which dominate the public domain are full of stereotypes, generalisations, and exaggerations. This is not conducive towards constructing plural societies that nurture and respect diversity.

The Christian faith has found numerous ways of allying itself with existing powers. In the Americas, two forms are most easily recognised. The first is the unpleasant aftertaste of colonial Roman Catholicism in Latin America, which has played a fundamental role in twentieth century dictatorships and in many current democratic governments. The second lies in Protestant political engagement in the United States, which is associated to a conservative agenda and is usually expressed in the republican party. A similar case can be observed recently in the Latin American evangelical church, especially in Brazil. Constantinianism, is easily perceived in the alliance between Latin American governments and the Roman Catholic church and between the Protestant church and a wing of the North American government. This alliance leads critical sectors on the left, popular movements, liberals and progressives to criticise Christianity. In Argentina, the slogan "Trash church you are the dictatorship" is an ever-present phrase on marches and protests. The identification of some form of established religion is evident in these cases.

It is slightly harder to perceive this temptation in other scenarios. Is the danger of Constantinianism merely a danger of the right, of retrograde, conservative, old-fashioned sectors? Do these Constantinianisms belong to past societies, which are in a process of extinction, and which will only survive for a few more generations? Are left wing or progressive governments the solution for a more evolved society and a less contaminated church? Antonio González answers this in his critique of Christians who place their hopes in revolutionary and left-wing groups. He suggests that Constantinianism does not disappear, "when Christians

---

[26] Hoffmann, 'La Reforma, como un nuevo paradigma de la teología', p. 22

become "revolutionaries."[27] In what is arguably a critique of many sectors of liberation theology he affirms:

> In this case, loyalty to a current regime is replaced by loyalty to a future regime. Rather than identify themselves with the current power system, Christians start to identify themselves with a power system which does not yet exist, but which one expects in the future (…) The right political group obtaining political power becomes the hypothetical solution to all evils. Those who are sceptical that such a power grab may indeed lead to real change are accused of "not understanding the world." Constantinianism continues to stand.[28]

Progressive frames of reference systematically reject modern morality and present themselves as unalienable rights. They have caused a state of turmoil in ethics and politics in my country, in Latin America, and across the globe. Although few churches adopt these progressive frames of reference, there are many "unchurched" Christians,[29] or those critical of their own institutions who see in these demands the secular manifestation of the kingdom of God. This utopia is expressed in a universalist projection of the kingdom: as the state extends and projects individual and collective rights, society will be evermore healthier, pure, less selfish and will reach closer towards its utopic and eschatological horizon. According to this perspective, the approval of certain laws which universalise specific forms of education and transform government institutions and the market, will lead to full justice.

The theological problem with these utopias is that there is no need for Christ's reign for this liberating salvation to become reality. It simply requires the extension of rights under state tutelage. There is no longer any need for a spiritual and theological exodus, a new birth before God, only a collective and political exodus, a new birth before public opinion. God's people, through their renewed relationships, cease to be the agent of God's kingdom and become the declared enemy of the secular utopia. This utopia is not accepted through grace but constructed through politically correct actions and sustained by an increasingly fickle public opinion. This utopia often reaches the sophistication of pharisaic Victorian morality being reinforced by noisy protests and the rejection of those who fail one way or another to reach these ideals.

These mechanisms do nothing other than treat the state as the divine mediator connecting individuals and collective groups to reality. In the past, the idolatry of temporal powers took on the public face of the imperial cult, of the divine right of absolute monarchs, of the positivistic ideal of modernity; these days it takes on the public face of human rights. Many Christians are aligning with this

---

[27] González, *Reinado de Dios e imperio*, p. 314.
[28] González, *Reinado de Dios e imperio*, p. 314.
[29] A term proposed by Karel Dobbelaere. K. Dobbelaere, 'Towards an Integrated Perspective of the Processes Related to the Descriptive Concept of Secularization' *Sociology of Religion*, 60.3 (1999), pp. 229–247.,

secularised version of Constantinianism, and few voices are warning of the dangers. They regard this new society as the realised utopia and identify the enemy as the *status quo* of a previous era. All collective frustrations are directed against this past, intrinsically modern, society, which inhabits a world, which no longer exists and is ready to disappear.

Yet, this fails to challenge the current *status quo*; on the contrary, it reinforces the omnipotence of the spirit of this age by making current mechanisms, authorities, and strategies invisible. As happens with all the different forms of Constantinianism, believers no longer need to believe in God's mysterious sovereignty over history, nor in his authority in the face of temporal powers. In this new scenario, God is solely a diffuse materialised force, existing in an egalitarian society, disciplined by the state and under the surveillance of public opinion. We declare, emphatically, that this form of Christianity offers no alternative.

Should the Church "Use" the State to Carry Out Its Mission?

Historically, the institutional church and individual believers have been jealous of the legitimate violence the state can employ in pursuing its intentions and desires. After Constantine, Christianity has repeatedly regarded the state as an ally and struggled for the power to achieve not only its self-preservation but also to convert society from above into something which externally resembles the kingdom of God. Christians have made alliances which had little to do with Christ but sought positions of power and the ability to determine symbolic meanings. Except for some radical movements, Christianity since Constantine has sought to "introduce or guarantee a social order inspired by God through the power of the state. This is shared by both conservatives and progressives. It is, nonetheless, questionable from a biblical perspective".[30] The early testimony challenges and opposes this Christianity that remains captive to the state and dependent on what it has to offer:

> Christians do not think that social justice will primarily be the work of some of the powerful of this world, as if Caiaphas, Herod, or Caesar were the main agents of social transformation. Nor do they believe that social justice will begin the day that others occupy the palaces of Caiaphas, Herod, or Caesar. Such changes may have the advantage, *on some occasions,* of relieving injustice or oppression. Without doubt, many structures of domination can be substituted by others. However, the changes will not be *radical* if they do not touch the *root,* which always leads to new forms of oppression.[31]

The first Christians were not attracted to power disputes in the Roman Empire. There is much evidence that they perceived the state as a reality which

---

[30] González, *Reinado de Dios e imperio,* p. 284.
[31] González, *Reinado de Dios e imperio,* p. 224.

directly competed with God and which desired, under its own authority, to be considered divine. The New Testament indicates that temporal powers were directly responsible for Jesus' death (Acts 4:26–27; 1 Cor. 2:8); that the devil himself is the one who has power over the kingdoms of this world "because they are mine to give to who I want" and that the cost of this power is to worship him (Lk. 4:5–7). In apocalyptic symbolism, "the great dragon – that ancient serpent called the devil, or Satan, who leads the whole world astray" (Rev. 12:9) has given the beast, the Roman Empire, "his power and his throne and great authority" (Rev. 13:2). Revelation's eschatological call concerning the relationship between Christians and the symbolic Babylon is emphatic and recalls the exodus "'Come out of her, my people,' so that you will not share in her sins, so that you will not receive any of her plagues" (Rev. 18:4). Whereas in the Old Testament we can find figures such as Joseph, Daniel, and Esther, who carried out their spiritual mission from within the power of the state, nothing similar can be found in the New Testament books.

A third century work attributed to Hippolytus of Rome, confirms that the early church practiced what is implicit in the New Testament. This document states explicitly that "anyone who exercises the power of the sword, the city magistrate who wears purple, should resign or be expelled" from the Christian community and "those higher political offices (which exercise the power of the sword" and the magistrates who wear purple) are *always* incompatible with the faith".[32]

The Protestant Reformation sought to return to the practices and teachings of the early church, which had been disfigured by medieval imperial Christianity. The Reformation's contribution to Christian theology is undeniable but Luther failed in a crucial point and thus, the Anabaptists and other groups belonging to the Radical Reformation believed that he had not gone far enough. For these groups:

> The New Testament clearly contradicted the traditional practice, of both Catholics and Protestants, of confusing the church with civil society. In the New Testament, the Church is a community chosen out of the world, to be different from the world, and consists only of those who have made the personal decision to join the body of Christ.[33]

They considered the alliance with temporal powers a betrayal of the gospel even if it came with certain confessional benefits, as happened with Lutheranism in Germany. It is no surprise that both Protestants and Roman Catholics regarded the Anabaptist's radical critique subversive and persecuted and martyred them.

Becoming the established church requires commitments and alliances but this privilege comes with consequences, namely the disintegration of any alternative

---

[32] González, *Reinado de Dios e imperio,* p. 291.
[33] J. González, *Historia del pensamiento cristiano: Tomo 3* (Nashville: Editorial Caribe, 1992), p. 91.

the gospel has to offer. The church simply legitimises the *status quo* and can do little more than contribute to state idolatry:

> There is no state which does not demand loyalty oaths, which does not organise many ceremonies to worship its flag and symbols, which does not periodically demand the sacrifice of human lives, which does not build various 'altars to the nation', which does not raise statues of its violent founders.[34]

The alliance between church and state is doomed to pervert the identity of the movement established by Jesus.

The Master Calls Us to Keep Watch with Him

So far, our analysis has indicated the potential for renewed, countercultural relationships nurtured in a community under the rule of Christ, to influence the public sphere. It has also pointed to the dangers that come from an alliance with the powers of the age, knowing that Constantinianism has been a recurring temptation in the history of Christianity. The next theological, biblical, and historical challenge is to apply these lessons to contemporary conflicts Christians face. What are the possibilities and dangers of a dialogue between church and state in the present? Can we reconstruct a theological strategy? The final part of this chapter seeks to offer some preliminary, unfinished, tentative answers to these questions.

There are clear historical examples of the dangers of an institutional alignment of the church with specific political, economic, or cultural projects. This frequently results in the loss of any specifically Christian identity as the church is no longer able to offer a prophetic voice and becomes fully assimilated to a particular ideology. This awareness should not lead us to *fuga mundi*, desiring to escape history under a supposedly "apolitical" banner or to fear involvement in the "issues of this world". The truth is that living in society, living in the *polis*, is in itself a political act. Christians are called to make the *exodus* to the reign of Christ, but that is not the same as a self-imposed *exile* from all social, historical, or political involvement. The *exodus* of the *ekklesia* does not ignore the world but understands the renewing potential of the Gospel's power.

This leads us into difficult terrain and raises many questions. How do we understand the mission of individuals and the community on the public stage? Is there a specific vocation for public service? How should believers relate to social organisations, political parties, and the state? How should believers participate in ethical discussions in post-Christian societies like our own? How does the Christian responsibility to serve others translate into concrete decisions and commitments? How, as salt and light in the earth, can we promote justice and a commitment to those most in need, our environment, and human rights? These

---

[34] González, *Reinado de Dios e imperio*, p. 270.

questions must be answered with integrity and care by each person who embraces the Christian faith. Faithfulness to the gospel should be at the heart of our reflection on the relationship between the church and temporal powers; the hope of the gospel should be the foundation of our contribution towards the common good of society and creation.

The kingdom of God lives in permanent eschatological tension; it is, in the language of theologians, "already, but not yet". The gospel asks us to have one foot in our immediate reality and the other in the promise of hope. As the Catholic Bishop Enrique Angelelli, assassinated by the military dictatorship, affirmed, we must have "one ear with the people and another with the Gospel".[35] Those who follow Jesus live in a fragile balance between two paradoxical realities: *now* and *not yet*, or in the language of John 17, *being in this world* and *not belonging to it*.

When we only remember one of these truths, we lose our balance. A church that cannot be distinguished from the world, which does not offer any alternative, becomes so close to the world that it cannot speak to it and therefore loses its prophetic role. Similarly, a church with no involvement in the world also cannot speak to it, and has forgotten that its mission, like that of Jesus himself, begins with the Incarnation.

We affirm then that *we are in the world* and participate in the future of all of humanity. We are not extra-terrestials; we share the joys and miseries of the people who inhabit this planet. We cannot take refuge in the promise of heaven and forget about the world around us. At the same time, we affirm that we are not of this world and therefore, we must always ask ourselves where our loyalties lie. According to the Scriptures, we are pilgrims and strangers on their way to their true home. Although we can support or feel an individual identification with specific projects, candidates, and parties, it is a mistake to directly identify any of those utopias as the kingdom of God.

The problem that Christianity faces when it ceases to be an alternative is similar, in its sociological consequences, to what occurred with the historical vanguards of the early twentieth century. Shortly before dying, André Breton, the father of surrealism, declared to the filmmaker Luis Buñuel, "dear friend, nothing shocks anyone anymore".[36] The vanguards were born as a radical alternative to modernity's bourgeoisie art; their *modus operandi* was to scandalise, disturb, disrupt, and shock. However, when the *status quo* of Western art adopted the alternative spirit of the vanguards, canonising and domesticating it in museums, the scandal disappears. "A repertoire of similar resources can

---

[35] See CONFAR, 'Monseñor Enrique Angelelli: Un oído en el pueblo y otro en el evangelio', available online at http://www.confar.org.ar/descargas/textos/memoria_angelelli2015.pdf (accessed 20 April 2021).

[36] T. Pérez Turrent y J. de la Colina, *Buñuel por Buñuel* (Madrid: Plotediciones, 1993), p. 124.

cause a symmetrically opposing effect, by becoming incorporated into the cultural establishment as a legitimate way of doing art; what was previously a scandal now is applauded."[37] This is the paradox of success. The vanguards challenged the meanings of traditional art and sought to make their alternative visible; yet when this possibility becomes hegemonic, the vanguard disappeared. Christianity was born as an alternative to the prevailing options of its age and spread rapidly throughout the Roman Empire; nonetheless, when it became hegemonic, it became impotent. The victorious church is that of the cross, not of glory.

The natural desire to seek comfort and reputation is potentially the most dangerous enemy the Christian alternative faces. We do not wish to suffer or lose prestige; we instinctively resist pain and being treated as inferior. For this reason, when faced with testing and criticism the church has often chosen Peter's path: to deny Christ. The church in Constantine's days was the first to fall into this trap, but many have since followed in its footsteps.

Modernity's rationalistic theology is a paradigmatic case. For centuries, many of the most brilliant Christian theologians, especially among Protestants, joined the ranks of those who supported the ideology of progress, reason, science, technique, democracy, and capitalism. When the Enlightenment was in its zenith, it took considerable courage to criticise these values. No one desired to be judged by the Enlightenment nor to suffer the shame of rebelling against these modern gods. To distrust reason was absurd, retrograde, and almost inhuman. Thus, modern Protestant theology sought to defend bourgeoise ideology believing that it was impossible to affirm certain truths of the Christian faith in the face of issues that were so evident for the spirit of the age. Thus, Christianity seasoned and legitimised modernity. Yet this theology drowned in the shipwreck when the ship of modernity hit the rocks. Tamayo Acosta follows Johan Baptist Metz, in criticising theologies which follow the Enlightenment "mimetically and uncritically". This leads to two forms of reductionism, "a rationalistic reduction, which renounces the world of myths and symbols, and a privatising reduction, which converts religion into a private subject, located in the realm of the conscience and reclused in places of worship".[38]

Nonetheless we should be wary of criticising the errors of the past according to the values which the spirit of our age considers useful, avant-garde, or prestigious. If we do this, if we simply mimic what others are offering, then we are not offering any alternative. We will have lost the unique proposal made by Jesus and his followers which is at the core of the Christian faith.

Evidently, it is hard to support the alternative offered by the gospel when it is seen as useless, retrograde or in bad taste. Yet, to renounce the gospel's radical proposal in favour of prestige is to remove the creative and alternative value of

---

[37] A. Longoni and R. Santoni, *De los poetas malditos al videoclip: Arte y literatura de vanguardia* (Buenos Aires: Cántaro, 1998), p. 16.
[38] Tamayo Acosta, *Otra teología es posible*, p. 31.

faith in Christ. The Constantinian church felt the urgent need for a political alliance to avoid martyrdom and strengthen ecclesial structures. In the medieval period, it was preferable to live in a pseudo-Christian society than to live under Turk harassment. During the Reformation, a deal with the nobility appeared to be the only way to assure the survival of Protestantism during chaotic times. Faced with rationalism, modern theology preferred to jettison certain truths which risked sounding mediaeval.

In Latin America, the same dynamic is revealed in the way the Roman Catholic church fears the high economic, social, and symbolic cost of losing its alliance with national governments. Similarly, conservative Protestant groups in the United States fear that to cease lobbying Congress would mean losing visibility and impact on the nation's politics. Likewise, evangelical churches in Argentina and Brazil have become totally associated with far-right groups in their desire to oppose feminism, "gender ideology" and abortion, even though this means losing all their legitimacy in the eyes of much of society. Many progressive Christians, following in the footsteps of modern theology also succumb to this temptation. Fearing exclusion from the contemporary public sphere they adhere to all the slogans, banners, movements and causes that have become prestigious and undeniable; even if, in the process, they must ignore central Christian themes.

The faithfulness of the Christian community to Christ's life, work and message lies at the centre of the Christian alternative. The New Testament themes of the lordship of Christ and the kingdom of God are the foundation for Christian understandings of salvation, justice, and utopia. To hide this golden thread behind interests, internal struggles or external pressures is to deny Christian faith the essence of its paradoxical alternative. The tradition of the early Church teaches that individuals and collective relationships are changed when "Christians have a personal encounter with Jesus and take the message of the gospel seriously, without glosses."[39]

There will always be internal and external pressures seeking to disfigure Jesus' message and the loyalty of Christian communities. Therefore, it continues to be necessary to insist upon the gospel's alternative which meets our age's needs, offering something that no state can offer. Against all predictions of the expiration and uselessness of the gospel message, "this strategy of the early church has the capacity of being much more effective than all apparently "revolutionary" intentions of sitting in the palaces of Pharaoh or the Roman empire. For the Christian strategy transforms society, not at the top, but at the base."[40]

Matthew 26 narrates the heartrending scene of Jesus' prayer, hours before the Passion. At this time of anguish and anxiety, he asked his closest friends, Peter, John, and James, to keep watch all night alongside him. The Lord prayed for

---

[39] González, *Reinado de Dios e imperio*, p. 316.
[40] González, *Reinado de Dios e imperio*, p. 233.

heavenly intervention, to be rescued from the cross, but accepted his Father's will. Amid his clamour, he searched for his disciples, who were sleeping and said: "So, could you not watch with me one hour? Watch and pray that you may not enter into temptation. The spirit indeed is willing, but the flesh is weak" (26:40–41). A second time he prayed and returned to find them sleeping. He went to pray yet again; when he returned to the disciples it was no longer important whether they were keeping watch or not: "Sleep and take your rest later on. See, the hour is at hand, and the Son of Man is betrayed into the hands of sinners. Rise, let us be going; see, my betrayer is at hand" (26:45-46). This symbolic account, full of sarcasm, reads as a parody of Christian history. Time after time, the disciples have failed to keep watch with their master in his hours of greatest anguish. The flesh is weak and cannot bear the weight of the night. Yet, sooner or later, the moment comes when denial has become a habit, and it no longer matters if we keep watch or sleep: The Son of Man has been betrayed yet again.

There are no easy solutions to rescue Christianity from its universal shame. In a post-Christian era, it seems an absurd utopia to seek to change the world through faith in Christ. Yet, nonetheless, "to try and take the way of Christ seriously may be the most important way that Christians can contribute to change the world today".[41]

Yet are we able to watch all night alongside our teacher?

> People have fallen into a foolish habit of speaking of orthodoxy as something heavy, humdrum, and safe. There never was anything so perilous or so exciting as orthodoxy. *G. K. Chesterton.*[42]

---

[41] González, *Reinado de Dios e imperio,* p. 321.
[42] G. Chesterton, *Orthodoxy* (London: John Lane, 1908), p. 13.

7. The Absence of Dialogue in a Technologically Faceless Age: An Augustinian Response of Embrace and Confession
Davi C. Ribeiro Lin

> Men become accustomed to listening to machines and talking to machines, as, for example, with telephones and dictaphones. No more face-to-face encounters, no more dialogue. In a perpetual monologue by means of which he escapes the anguish of silence and the inconvenience of neighbours, man finds refuge in the lap of technique, which envelops him in solitude and at the same time reassures him with all its hoaxes.[1]
>
> Yet allow me to speak, though I am but dust and ashes, allow me to speak in your merciful presence, for it is to your mercy that I address myself.[2]

While researching in Belgium in 2017, I had the opportunity to participate in events related to the celebration of the 500th anniversary of the Protestant Reformation. One remarkable experience was the *Luther and the Reformation: Saint Augustine and the Augustinian Order* conference held at the *Institutum Patristicum Augustinianum* in Rome. There is no doubt that the father of the Protestant Reformation, the German Augustinian monk Martin Luther (1483–1546) read and memorised part of the works of Augustine of Hippo (354–430). The African Bishop of Hippo, who lived amid the decay of the ancient Roman Empire, provided the reformers with a pastoral and theological reference with which to confront the sixteenth century Roman Catholic Church. As one can imagine, the conference was immersed in irony, as Catholic Augustinian friars were gathered to assess Luther's legacy. On one hand, as one of their own, Luther resembles an old great uncle of their monastic order. On the other hand, Luther is considered to have disrupted church unity and spoke against monasteries. At

---

[1] J. Ellul, *The Technological Society* (New York: Knopf, 1964), pp. 379–380.
[2] Augustine of Hippo, *Confessions* 1.6.7. English quotations of *Confessions* are from M. Boulding *The Works of St. Augustine: A Translation for the 21st Century* (Hyde Park: New City Press, 1997).

the time of the Reformation, Augustinian friars were considered a source of misfortune to the Catholic Church.[3]

After thought-provoking discussions, one of the participants (whom I will call Father Bill) stood up and vehemently criticised Luther's appropriation of Augustine's thought, calling it partial and insufficient. Father Bill accused Luther of selectively adapting the doctrine of grace while neglecting Augustine's teaching on church unity. This has, over the centuries, been a Roman Catholic criticism against the Protestant reception of Augustine and his legacy.

A presentation on the last morning of the conference by a Protestant nun, Sister Anna Maria Aus der Wiesche, led Father Bill to change his attitude. She lectured movingly on the rebirth of consecrated life in the churches of the Reformation. With simplicity and humility, she testified how Lutherans in Germany recovered monastic life after the Second World War. This touched the hearts of Father Bill and all the audience. Deeply moved, he publicly asked for forgiveness for the many times he had spoken badly about Luther. I marvelled watching from afar their personal exchange after the lecture. Mercy and truth met together, and their hearts attuned in an embrace. I perceived in Father Bill a true Augustinian: while willing to disagree, he humbly initiated a public confession which allowed the audience to witness an encounter of reconciliation.

But would that transformative encounter have happened over the internet, through an online conference? Would this be possible if they were not seeing each other in flesh and bone? As Miroslav Volf points out, a physical embrace is a living metaphor of reconciliation, a dynamic relationship between the self and the other that is both symbolised and enacted.[4] Open arms signal that I am opening up space in myself for another, an invitation for a reciprocal openness of self-giving. The fact that an embrace carries a visible movement towards the recognition of otherness should not lead us to disregard the relevance of online meetings and Zoom conferences for the development of relationality. If one establishes an attentive posture towards the other, a person is impelled to hear a voice and a call. Nevertheless, a visible presence seemed to have taken Bill and Anna Maria a step further, as their embrace became a visible reconciliation (or at least a ceasefire) of a historical and inner conflict. This experience exemplifies how an incarnate presence carries the possibility of taking someone out of enclosed prejudices, mobilizing our common humanity. An incarnate presence establishes an *I-Thou* encounter that facilitates the unity of hearts (*cor unum*).

In the contemporary context of lowered relational responsiveness and loss of dialogical posture, I would like to suggest that Augustine of Hippo can be recovered as an inspiration for a fuller dialogical posture which involves a recognition of being embraced by another and responding humbly through the

---

[3] The Protestant Reformation was born within the Augustinian Order and its first martyrs were two Flemish Augustinian friars from Antwerp, Hendrik Voes and Johann Esch, condemned in Brussels in 1523.
[4] M. Volf, *Exclusion and Embrace* (Nashville: Abingdon Press, 1996), p. 141.

language of confession, of sin, and praise. Augustine's narrative in *Confessions* is a highly interpersonal account expressed through a metaphor of embrace, a narrative framed under the prodigal son motif, a lost heart led by grace towards the open arms of a father. His response to God's embrace is a double cry, weeping not only due to his vulnerability and sins but weeping even more in the recognition that he has been accepted and comforted. As a response to God's embrace, his narrative is framed within the structure of a continual double movement of confession of sin (*peccati*) and confession of praise (*laudis*), both opening the wounds and praising the divine doctor. *Confessions,* both in its content and form, establishes a dialogical dynamism that vulnerably and relationally expresses his responsiveness to the gift of love:

> Let them turn back, and seek you, for you do not forsake your creation as they have forsaken their Creator. Let them turn back, see! There you are in their hearts, in the hearts of those who confess you, who fling themselves into your arms and weep against your breast after their difficult journey, while you so easily will wipe away their tears. At this they weep the more, yet even their laments are matter for joy, because you, Lord, are not some human being of flesh and blood, but the Lord who made them, and now make them anew and comfort them (*Conf.* 5.2.2.).

Little Dialogical Aptitude: Technology and Relationality

The twenty-first century has disconnected human beings from the heart, the centre of human vitality and hyper-connected them to information. The consequence is cultures that are incapable of comprehending or reflecting on antagonistic positions, but which enclose themselves in polarised bubbles with little dialogical aptitude. The current information society, fuelled by the internet's implicit Gnosticism, denying that life is made in material encounters, is the newest heterodox disincarnate posture that distorts contemporary life. The disincarnate immaterial form of the medium we use for communication reduces its content. Facebook is no face-to-face encounter and social media has amplified polarisation. Consequently, people who believe in the same foundations of Christian faith are no longer able to hear or encounter each other, fragmenting the church through the loss of a dialogical posture.

Doctrines are important as they establish the content that shapes our lives, nonetheless, Christianity is not primarily an intellectual arrangement, a package of dogmas, or a moralism; it is an encounter, a love story revealed through an exceptional presence, God becoming human, the Word made flesh. In God's communication, the revelatory event is an encounter, a relational experience. From Genesis Yahweh has demonstrated himself as a personal God, pursuing the face of Abraham, Isaac, and Jacob. The apex of God's historical self-revelation is the incarnation, death, and resurrection of Christ. Historically, living in community and discipleship, daily remembering Christ's human life by breaking bread together was a means of transforming hearts. How can this be replicated in a digital age, especially with regards to those one disagrees with in internet or social media discussions? One possibility might be to invite them over for a generous conversation over a cup of coffee. If time, location, or social restrictions such as those caused by a global pandemic make this impossible, then a second-best option might be to have a one-to-one online meeting. In other words, a Trinitarian faith which creates space for the other is intrinsically apt to offer a call for a fuller relational life, a counter-cultural incarnational and dialogical posture in bubble-oriented societies.

In a technologically driven era, one must be reminded that life is not primarily a technical process, but always has a relational dynamic. As Martin Buber pointed out, the fundamental fact of existence is that human beings construct meaning in a space of reciprocity and mutuality, an *I-Thou* encounter of another's responsive face.[5] According to Mauro Amatuzzi, often the only thing capable of promoting paradigm changes in a person is a qualitative movement towards another person. In this process the interpersonal relationship acts as a catalyst which triggers an internal transformation.[6] Our process of humanisation is a continuous experience of encountering and being attentive to otherness and alterity, a process that demands the giving of oneself in love and does not follow the fast-paced rhythm of technology. Mechanisms of digital communication abound in a technologically controlled society, but the capacity for intersubjective encounters has not kept pace with the speed of technical progress.

By diminishing distances, technology has surely brought novel possibilities for dialogue between persons and opened new horizons for human communication. Nevertheless, as Jacques Ellul had already pointed out over fifty years ago, encounters cannot rely exclusively on technological means.[7] Although technology decreases geographical distances, a relationally fulfilled life can remain miles away. When embodied face-to-face encounters are replaced by confessions over social media, intimate expression is both changed and reduced. As the body itself is a means of one's gift and presence to the other, the virtual medium of social media fosters impersonal exchange, even when the content remains the same. The present age has lost the ability to confess personally and has exchanged embodied relationality for digital Instagram posts.

I write from Brazil as an Asian-Latin American pastor-theologian and psychotherapist, a mestizo like Augustine.[8] I have been theologically trained in South America, North America and Europe, and come to realize that individuals from all over the world have the resources for non-superficial relations but experience the privation of true encounters. The loss of a dialogical posture has

---

[5] M. Buber, *I and Thou*, Edinburgh: Clark, 1984.
[6] M. Amatuzzi, *Por uma psicologia humana* (Campinas: Editora Alinea, 2001), p. 124.
[7] Ellul, *The Technological.* Jacques Ellul has aptly discussed how technology prompted the emergence of impersonal societies.
[8] See J. González, *The Mestizo Augustine: A Theologian between Two Cultures*, Downers Grove: InterVarsity Press, 2016)

created a context that has lowered relational responsiveness and contributed to mental distress. All over the world, there is an increased tendency to give technical solutions to relational problems; consequently, an automatised technical age has disconnected the present generation from the slow process of being attentive to one's inner life and the centre, described in the Christian tradition as the "heart". As anxiety and depression rise worldwide, they act as signposts indicating that the fundamental questions about meaning and interpersonal fulfilment cannot be extinguished.

Augustine of Hippo lived in late antiquity during the decline of the Roman Empire, a time of loss, anxiety, confusion, and the end of narratives which provided security, but found a theological vision of hope in the midst of chaos. The North African Bishop of Hippo exemplifies how the history of Christianity carries the potential to fertilize present times, opening novel possibilities to think and live in wise and hopeful ways. As we seek to faithfully reconstruct mindsets which are qualitatively different from ours, we realise that the present is not normative for all times. Augustine's world and ours share plentiful similarities, as both are times of transition and confusion; they exemplify a heterogeneous global arena of conflicting worldviews, in which elements of Christian faith are intermingled with other ideologies in an intellectual stew pot.[9]

The Dialogical Character of Augustine's *Confessions*

Augustine's *Confessions* is particularly relevant for our contemporary, non-dialogical, yet plural context. It describes crossing from a self-centred existence to an essentially dialogical posture, telling the story of his relational responsiveness to grace, of his *affectus*, the growth of his heart.[10] His narrative also critiques his rhetorical career in the late Roman Empire which promoted a self-centred mode of communicating. At the peak of his career in Milan, Augustine realized the putrid state of his heart and how his relationships had been bound to the selfishness of prideful individual achievement. Augustine's description of his own journey is a story of loss and inner fragmentation, either by death or for upward mobility; but this *aversio* which distanced him from God gave way to the movement of conversion, a return towards humility and love, in a fuller and responsive relationality to God and neighbour.

Augustine's *Confessions* selectively interweaves biographical content with the biblical doctrine of grace, describing the story of a dependent man before another who is greater than himself. *Confessions* is Augustine's first elaborated and integrated exposition on grace in which a middle-aged Augustine, after gaining a deeper understanding of Scripture and particularly of Saint Paul's

---

[9] J. Rist, *On Ethics, Politics and Psychology in the Twenty-first Century*, Reading Augustine (London: Bloomsbury Academic, 2018), p. 2.
[10] P. Brown, *Augustine of Hippo* (Berkeley: University of California Press, 2000), p. 163.

epistles, realised how God's grace and providence had guided his steps to conversion. Its narrative sustains a theological anthropology, humanity's position in relation to the Creator; Augustine testifies about God's action to transform and direct the itinerary of restless human hearts. Relevant stories are selected to highlight the redemptive activity of the divine being that sustains the uncertain journeys of those that move away from their own hearts but are called to return to their destiny in God. *Confessions* describes the inner journey of a middle-aged man who witnesses the action of divine grace in his past (books 1–9), recognises his dependent state in the present (book 10) and comments on the biblical account of creation in Genesis, highlighting God's activity in recreating him with hope for his future (books 11-13).

Confessions is not an autobiography, but a narrative of a relational response to grace, so that Augustine becomes, paradoxically, the non-central subject of his own narrative. The very beginning of *Confessions*, "You are great oh Lord", announces the narrative's main character and the displacement of Augustine's very self. One could question the integrity of a subject who forgoes narrating himself as an autonomous subject. Augustine is narratively proposing a biblical paradox, losing himself for God's sake to find himself anew (Matthew 16.25). Marion insists that the movement to decentralise himself is essential to *Confessions*. Nevertheless, this does not lead to the loss of the subject, but to a displacement that allows himself to be found anew in God, the proper place of his very self, *au lieu de soi*.[11] It is the place of the most authentic self, rediscovered and recovered after it ceases to be a self-sufficient autonomous being. By giving himself to another, Augustine regains his personal centre and the dynamism of his heart, forged to return, and rest in his Creator, his highest good.

In *Confessions*, Augustine depicts himself as a prodigal son in his homecoming, arriving in his father's arms where his tears are wiped away, because the Creator of human beings also encourages and consoles them (*Conf.* 5.2.2). Augustine narrates the wanderings of his heart through the motif of the parable of the prodigal son as described in the Gospel of Luke: "I took care that this excellent part of my substance should be under my own control, and I did not guard my strength by approaching you, but left you and set out for a distant land to squander it there on the quest for meretricious gratifications" (*Conf.* 4.16.30). Augustine had loved his own selfish ways and not God's, *amans vias meas et non tuas* (*Conf.* 3.3.5). The image places his story as an example of human constant distancing, *aversio*, to God – "where were you at the time? How far from me? I was certainly roving far away from you and debarred even from the pods I was feeding to pigs" (*Conf.* 3.6.10). As he returns home – *conversio* – the prodigal son cries twice, both in a lamentation of his woundedness and for the joy of being forgiven in spite of his vulnerability, "at this they weep the more,

---

[11] J. Marion, *In the Self's Place: The Approach of Saint Augustine* (Stanford: Stanford University Press, 2012)

yet even their laments are matter for joy, because you, Lord, are not some human being of flesh and blood, but the Lord who made them, and now make them anew and comfort them (*Conf.* 5.2.2.). The double weeping, lament, and joy, corresponding to sin and praise, is evidence that Augustine does not deserve his rehabilitated place, but the grace that upholds life in weakness must be answered by surrendering his life to love.

Since Augustine had been a former professor of rhetoric who questioned his previously self-centred use of words, after his conversion he pursues a rehabilitated language to respond to God's mercy. As a professor of rhetoric, he knew how cunning and misleading language could become, and therefore after conversion "withdraws the service of tongue from the market of speechifying" (*Conf.* 9.2.2). As a Catholic Christian Augustine continues to handle words powerfully, but his strive towards humility would lead him to dialogical communication. The mode of expressing himself as a convert becomes *confessio*, a prayerful and poetic heart-language, in a dialogical I-thou relationship. *Confessio* is no extravagant rhetorical discourse that expresses Augustine's achievements with the goal of self-affirmation. It is a "weak" speech which directs itself in vulnerability to a Thou, even to the point he begs for grace to pray: "Allow me to speak in your merciful presence" (*Conf.* 1.6.7). In Scripture, Augustine discovers the possibility of speaking in psalms, words given to him by God, an alternative to the presumption of his former speech: "Circumcise all that is within me from presumption and my lips without from falsehood. Let your scriptures be my chaste delight, let me not be deceived in them nor through them deceive others" (*Conf.* 11.2.3). Augustine's life would be permanently marked by speaking as a response to grace, in prayer, bursting with God's words in him. In *confessio* through the psalms, the public communication of an orator becomes the language of intimate relationality.

Confessions is neither monologue nor superficial conversation, but the reply of Augustine's heart attuned to the mouth of God. Far from chatter or gossip, the heart listens to what God's grace has spoken, and responds in a language of surrender, requesting nearness: "bring the ear of my heart close to your mouth" (*Conf.* 4.5.10). In such a conversation, God is apparently mute; but not every person is humble or attentive enough to hear. Many are non-dialogical partners, listening only to their own voices, projecting God to their wills. As Augustine points out, "your best servant is the one who is less intent on hearing from you what accords with his own will, and more on embracing with his will what he has heard from you" (*Conf.* 10.26.37).

The dialogical character of Augustine's *Confessions* is highlighted through a linguistic analysis of the main verb "to confess", *confiteri/confiteor* and its related words. Melchior Verheijen has concluded that the constant use of *confiteor/confiteri* linked with the pronominal second personal singular expression *tibi* institutes an incessant pattern of communicating to God as a personal thou. Out of the eighty-three contexts in which *confiteri* is used, in sixty-three of them *tibi* is present, emphasizing the importance of addressing God as his interlocutor. Verheijen indicates that in those twenty contexts where *tibi* is not used, it is substituted by a comparable expression, such as *nomini tuo* or *altitudini tuae*.[12] Furthermore, numerous references to *thou* at the start of *Confessions* established a dialogical posture of personal confession in the form of prayer.

Augustine's *Confessions* is a relational spiritual dialogue, oriented towards God but also towards fostering a confessing community of believers. As such, the work is not to be regarded as a kind of fenced interchange between Augustine and God, but as an open, vulnerable engagement with God with repercussions for his hearers: "that recital arouses the hearer's heart, forbidding it to slump into despair" (*Conf.* 10.3.4). Consequently, the three characters in *Confessions*, are namely, God, Augustine, and his audience.

Augustine's first writings show a communitarian sense right from the outset. Truth could not be discovered in isolation or seclusion, but in the company of friends, as the *Cassiciacum* dialogues attest. Augustine had a high regard for friendship and became increasingly convinced that Christ was the most significant factor in uniting friends. Augustine sought life in community and aspired to journey in the presence of others. Even in his first works, such as in *Soliloquia*, truth is materialised in interpersonal relationships in a community and not in an isolated individual. This is further developed after his ordination as Bishop in 391, as Augustine understood his ministry relationally, avid to serve the congregation entrusted to him by God, "a longing on fire not for myself alone but to serve the brethren I dearly love" (*Conf.* 11.2.3). As Augustine matured, he insightfully grasped how sin is associated to a self that denies living in community:

> Augustine's thought in his fifties began to be dominated by the notion that the roots of sin lie in the self's retreat into a privacy which is deprivation: the self is deprived of community. All community – with God, with one's fellows, and even with one's own self – is fatally ruptured by sin. The radical flaw in human nature is now transcribed in terms of a retreat into a closed-off self.[13]

Augustine realised that the *cor unum* of the first Christians described in the book of Acts was an important ideal for community life. After Pentecost, a restored community, empowered by the Holy Spirit is at the centre of faith rather than the individual. This community becomes the restored humanity that represents Christ to the world; consequently, the voluntary giving of possessions was a manifestation of being-for-the-other. Its communitarian character announced to the world the beauty of being of one heart and mind (Acts 4:32). The breaking of barriers was inspiring and world changing. Stories such as Peter,

---

[12] M. Verheijen, *Eloquentia Pedisequa: observations sur le style des confessions de saint Augustin* (Nijmegen: Dekker & Van de Vegt, 1949), pp. 23–24.

[13] R. Markus, *Conversion and Disenchantment in Augustine's Spiritual Career* (Villanova: Villanova University Press, 1989), pp. 31–32.

a Jewish fisherman, sitting at the same table in communion with Cornelius, a Roman centurion, signalled a reconciled and reconciling Spirit-filled community. Inspired by the book of Acts, Augustine's sermons developed the implications of oneness of heart experience, *anima una et cor unum*, both for monastic life and for his congregation; solidarity of heart attuned to the other, playing the symphony of the song of love for God and neighbour.[14]

Book 12 of *Confessions* poignantly describes this solidarity of the heart which allows a plurality of views to flourish as a concrete embodiment of the command to love the neighbour and pursue church unity:

> Of this I am certain, and I am not afraid to declare it from my heart, that if I had to write something to which the highest authority would be attributed, I would rather write it in such a way that my words would reinforce for each reader whatever truth he was able to grasp about these matters, than express a single idea so unambiguously as to exclude others, provided these did not offend me by their falsehood (Conf. 12.31.42).

Now we see as in a mirror, but then, one shall see face to face: direct knowledge of divine truth is opposed to indirect communication by finite beings.[15] This openness to a plurality of interpretations is based on the distinction between a sphere of eternal truths and the scope of our limited changing reality. Augustine's commitment to allow a multitude of voices within the church integrates the humble posture of recognizing the limitations of human language and the challenge to cultivate relational responsiveness in which truth is spoken in love.

Augustine's Dialogical Posture and Implications for the 21st Century

Augustine displays a sense of the uniqueness and unity of the human person so that *Confessions* is the first existential encounter in an I-Thou dialogue with a personal God in the history of Western literature.[16] By confessing, Augustine discovers a responsive language towards the healer of his pride. This dialogical communication, as a vulnerable, wounded patient before his doctor, desperate for God's intervention, transforms Augustine and places him even more under God's love and mercy, sustaining his continuous conversion.

God's gracious embrace leads Augustine, the returning prodigal son, to an experience of weeping. These tears of confession are not to be regarded as a loss of the self, the disappearance of the "I" into the "we", but a movement towards a place of surrender and love. The dynamics of embrace maintain the boundaries between two bodies. Nonetheless, as arms open again, each body is marked by

---

[14] A. Dupont and P. Walraet, 'Augustine on the Heart as the Centre of Human Happiness', *Studies in Spirituality* 25 (2015) p. 73.

[15] J. Brachtendorf, *Confissões de Agostinho* (São Paulo: Loyola, 2008), p. 279.

[16] J. Hugo, *St. Augustine on Nature, Sex and Marriage* (Chicago: Scepter, 1969), p. 19.

the vestiges of another, the self is reconfigured by the embrace. Consequently, after the embrace of grace Augustine no longer exists outside of his relationships, and his life finds meaning and order in loving God and others: "My God, I would not exist, I would not be at all, were you not in me. Or should I say, rather, that I should not exist if I were not in you, from whom are all things, through whom are all things, in whom are all things?" (*Conf.* 1.2.2).

Augustine's dialogical posture includes God and love towards neighbours without denying the possibility of frictions or contrasting perspectives. In complex situations divergences may rise and lead to disagreements. Augustine himself frequently positioned his theology in polemics, in anti-Manichean, anti-Arian, anti-Donatist and anti-Pelagian controversies. Augustine firmly positioned himself against those who denied fundamental beliefs such as the divinity and humanity of Christ or the saving work of Christ's grace. Nonetheless, such disagreement should entail respectful dialogue and attentive listening, for Christ himself united truth and grace, confrontationally looked people in the eyes and loved them. Stories such as "the rich young man" in Mark 10:21, or Zacchaeus' transformation model, a merciful paradigm for Christian confrontational engagement in its call to repentance.

Polarised positions have decreased the possibility of fraternal dialogue. In pluralistic societies, fragile identities decrease attentiveness to others as people become enclosed in like-minded digital bubbles and identity ghettos. This process leads to the accusation that Christians are intolerant close-minded moralists who cannot regard different lifestyles as valuable. If we are to raise a relevant and faithful generation of Christians, we are called to cultivate a dialogical posture and a renewed relational attitude. As the 2010 Lausanne Movement Cape Town Commitment suggests, dialogue is a legitimate part of Christian mission, combining confidence in the uniqueness of Christ with respectful listening, refusing to promote caricatures and resisting prejudice.[17]

As secularism rises in the twenty-first century, self-enclosed, non-dialogical fundamentalist postures may become unnecessary stumbling blocks for Christian mission. In such a context, Christians are called to cultivate patience, dialogue, and holy tolerance without losing their identity or beliefs. In the Augustinian tradition, a high dose of humility is the best antidote against fundamentalisms, secular or religious. Christians should have the humility to recognise that outsiders may help us recover an emphasis that we ourselves have forgotten. Biblically, a Spirit filled life is expressed in patience without meaning total agreement with diverse ideas. Christianity is more than an intellectual system, it is a transformative encounter, so that being in Christ means acknowledging something more essential in another, beyond the ideas I disagree with.

---

[17] Lausanne Movement, 'Cape Town Commitment', *Lausanne Movement Homepage* available online at https://lausanne.org/content/ctcommitment#capetown accessed 2 June 2020.

Responding to Father Bill's Provocative Call

To conclude, I would like to propose an exercise of Evangelical/Protestant humility by hearing what Father Bill would like Protestants to recover about Augustine, namely, finding in Augustine an inspiration for Christian unity. Considering that Catholic-Protestant relations have been historically confrontational in Latin-America, and being a Brazilian Evangelical myself, accepting Father's Bill call is an intentional embracing of a posture of listening and humility. Augustine is the theologian who most influenced Luther and Calvin, but their reception is more focused on Augustine's later works, particularly on the doctrine of grace and the anti-Pelagian controversy. A missing piece for Protestant reception of Augustine may be his anti-Donatist works. Donatism is the name of the schismatic movement within North African Christianity deep-rooted in the disputed election of the Bishop of Carthage, giving rise to a division within the African ecclesiological tradition. Augustine regarded the Donatists as purists, rigorists who valued morality above charity and were incapable of accepting that Christianity is constituted by an imperfect mixed body of sinners. The Bishop of Hippo's ideas about the unity of the church, particularly as proposed in his anti-Donatist sermons, may truly be a missing treasure for heirs of the Protestant tradition and Christians in general. Furthermore, in a non-dialogical age, these works are to be recovered as an inspiration for Christian mission: "So that the world may believe that you have sent me" – will the 21st century Christian church become the reconciled community of faith Jesus desired? I would like to suggest five central ecclesiological ideas in the form of five theses based on Augustine's anti-Donatist sermons. Hopefully, they will provide a provocative inspiration for a humbler, dialogical posture:

Five Theses on Ecclesial Unity

1. Since God is patient and merciful, the Church is patient and tolerant towards imperfect pilgrims on the way.

2. Since only God is righteous judge, no one can be an accuser of someone else's heart except the One who sees it. Judging ahead of time is pride: a congregation is a *corpus permixtum*, a mixed body, which includes chaff and wheat, goats, and sheep. Let the righteous judge separate them, let us not take His place.

3. Since the church is the body of Christ, let us not make Him two separate parts: Christ, the bridegroom, has joined his wife, the church in wholeness. Dividing the Church is to participate in a divorce that crucifies Christ himself.

4. The mystery of Christ and his body is rightly understood if we love humility. Those who separate the body usurp power and demonstrate pride: stay away from vanity, confess yourself humbly to the *Christus Medicus*.

5. Remain in unity where happiness is found, and do not go after multiplicity: keep yourself where you were planted and seek the preservation of the garden. For the love of Christ and in witness to the world (Jn 17), preserve the unity of his beloved Church.

8. Strangers or Friends? A Mexican Perspective on Cross-border Relations in Times of Immigration Crisis

Alejandra Ortiz

There is something autobiographical every time we write or speak about topics where life and theology intersect. There is something personal in the reasons that lead us to investigate a particular theme. My story is intertwined with the history, politics, and cross-cultural mission work on the border between the United States and Mexico, particularly between Tijuana and San Diego. I am a resident of this border neighbourhood. My dad has been a green card holder for almost 50 years, which means he can live and work in the United States. I was born thirteen kilometres to the north of *la linea*, the border wall, and brought back to Mexico three days later. Both my husband's family and my own migrated to Tijuana as job opportunities opened on both sides of the wall. Borders and migration intersect our lives, and my own blood bears testimony of the colonised and the coloniser, for I am a *mestiza*, someone with both European and native roots.

The border wall crosses over lands that were once part of the same region. The Californias were once the homeland of the Kumaii people, and even after the colonial period these lands were still part of Mexico. It was only after the end of the war between the United States and Mexico in 1848 that the United States took half of Mexico's territory. As of today, almost twenty-five percent of people in San Diego are native Spanish speakers,[1] and thousands of illegal immigrants from the United States live in Tijuana. The migrants from the United States call themselves "expats", but they are also economic migrants, seeking lower rent or cheaper properties and beach houses. This binational neighbourhood is divided by an infamous wall that fails to stop people, trade, mission, or drugs crossing the border.

My theological perspectives are framed in this context, as well as God's story in my life. This is no secret – we all speak or write from where we stand. In my case, I stand at a border in the farthest corner of Latin America which has been

---

[1] Data USA, 'San Diego County, CA: Race and Ethnicity', *Data USA*, available online at https://datausa.io/profile/geo/san-diego-county-ca/#demographics accessed 15 November 2020.

the focus of recent conversations and news about migration and politics. This is a pertinent and fascinating starting point for theological reflection. This endeavour intersects with history and politics as it involves understanding the relationship between the United States and Mexico, and particularly the engagement of the Church on both sides of the border. It allows one to observe the consequences of different cross-cultural activities and relationships which have been labelled mission.

This chapter explores historical and contemporary Christian cross-cultural engagement in the region. It investigates the understanding of mission which underwrites these activities and leads to missional practices that perpetuate imperial motivations and agendas. Our missiological reflection will focus on short term missions, mission relationships between the United States and Mexico and immigration. The arrival of caravans of migrants, asylum seekers and others in the Tijuana/San Diego region provides the context to understand the recent interactions between Christians from the United States and Mexico. Such interactions have produced personal and communal pain leading to lament, but also allow us to imagine a better future where citizens of God's kingdom work towards peace, justice, and solidarity on both sides of the border.

Crossing Borders as Strangers: Historical – and Present – Cross-Cultural Engagement of the Church in the Border

There has never been an easy relationship between the United States and Mexico especially after the United States took almost half of Mexico's territory. This relationship has been marked by Mexican subordination and the religious legitimation of the United States' dominion, through ideas such as Manifest Destiny. The Bible was interpreted to buttress the idea that God had destined the United States for dominion, legitimising expansionism as a means to spread democracy and capitalism.

Missionary efforts from the United States extended to Latin America in the nineteenth century. These efforts were tainted with the notions of whites being racially superior and chosen by God. Merk indicates that in the south of the United States, attitudes to Mexicans and freed slaves were fused with "the ethics of the enslavement of race into one conglomerate of emotion."[2] As Protestantism came south of the border, this racialised understanding also spread, with Mexicans being treated as a lower race.

The first female single missionary in Mexico was Melinda Rankin, although she did not minister in the northwest of Mexico. Rankin became a foreign missionary in Texas in 1847 and arrived in Mexico in 1862.[3] Although Rankin's missionary work took place within structures dominated by an imperialistic

---

[2] F. Merk, *Manifest Destiny and Mission in American History* (Cambridge: Harvard University Press, 1963), p. 161.
[3] Most church boards considered Texas a foreign mission field.

mindset, she was ahead of her time in several aspects, going beyond the roles usually assigned or taken by women. Rankin did traditional tasks such as establishing schools and fundraising, but she also sent missionaries into the foreign field, trained indigenous missionaries, and acted as a Bible sales representative. Rankin also confronted racist assumptions and challenged beliefs in white superiority.[4]

Protestant cross-cultural missional engagement from North to South has been marked both by godly people like Rankin and by the influence of imperialism and religion. Historically, evangelistic zeal has been mixed with national pride; a combination often seen at the border. Tijuana could claim to be the most evangelised city in the world, as the city has received short-term mission trips for decades. Thousands of youth teams and groups of adults travel each year from the United States to build houses for the poor, to help at orphanages or to participate in vacation Bible schools. However, prejudice, racism, and the lack of local knowledge prevail. Melinda Rankin herself complained about this in her memoir:

> The prejudices existing against the Mexicans, engendered during the late war, often proved great barriers to my success. The sentiment was expressed by many, that "the Mexicans were a people just fit to be exterminated from the earth." Even ministers of the gospel said to me, "We had better send bullets and gunpowder to Mexico than Bibles."[5]

While many have left behind such harsh declarations, a recent United States President was still capable of racially profiling Mexicans, referring to some as rapists and criminals.[6] Missionary engagements at the border mostly reflect a racialised vision based on the assumption that Mexicans and people of colour are inferior, and whites are chosen and blessed by God. These power dynamics are reinforced by the fact that historically Mexicans have struggled with an inferiority complex. Consequently, although Mexico is no longer at war with the United States it is still considered less favoured, so that mission can only move in one direction, from North to South. Mission groups arrive in Tijuana and Baja unable to engage in any critique of their country's wealth and power. In response, those they minister to are led to regard God's blessing in terms of wealth, power, and resources.

The three main options for short term mission activities in Tijuana and Baja California, are house building, vacation Bible schools, and orphanage visits.

---

[4] D. Robert *American Women in Mission* (Macon: Mercer University Press, 1998), p. 136.
[5] M. Rankin, *Twenty Years Among the Mexicans* (Cincinnati: Chase & Hall, 1875), p. 51.
[6] M. Mark, 'Trump just referred to one of his most infamous campaign comments', *Business Insider*, 5 April 2018 https://www.businessinsider.com/trump-mexicans-rapists-remark-reference-2018-4?r=MX&IR=T

These activities are carried out without any language training or efforts to understand the local context and culture. Translators are provided and people usually sleep in closed compounds that are safe, clean, and secure for United States citizens. Most encounters with Mexican Christians happen in controlled scenarios that do not allow deep personal encounters and real relationships to develop. The Gospel is brought and dropped into poor neighbourhoods, through evangelistic tracts and translators, or through the medium of candy and other junk food in orphanages. There is, of course, an element of over-simplification in this highly critical picture of short-term missions. In this chapter my intention is not to completely disparage short term missions, but to observe how the missiological context of the border has urgent implications for how we reflect on cross-cultural interactions and the way people understand missions.

Crossing Borders with Humility: Critiquing Colonial Models of Mission

Chris Wright reminds us that the mission of the church is derived from God's work, it is "our committed participation as God's people, as an invitation and God's mandate, to the mission of God in the history of the world, for the redemption of God's creation."[7] Mission is thus at the heart of Christianity, but missional practice will never be perfect so it is necessary to critique expressions of mission tainted by colonialism. This critique needs to extend to the motives and practice of those who engage in mission.

Al Tizon offers a comprehensive description of the gospel as "the good news from God, announced, demonstrated, and embodied most definitely in Jesus Christ, that salvation has come and is still coming in its fullness."[8] The Gospel is translatable into every culture, and no culture can claim exclusive ownership of the Gospel.[9] Confusing the gospel with the American way of life means that the whole gospel is not proclaimed and damages relationships between the United States and Mexico. Consequently, the fusion between evangelicalism and colonialism is one of the main problems in the border region and has created great damage to the advancement of the gospel, which no longer becomes good news for all. Theology produced in the United States is presented as biblically neutral, ignoring that all theology is contextual.

The idea that is perpetuated is that the American church has all it needs, while the Mexican church lacks money, power, and influence. This affirms the church's marriage with worldly power and does not live up to the kingdom's countercultural values. There is a long history of Christian desire for power, force, and influence; this is not exclusive to the United States, and the Latin

---

[7] C. Wright, *La misión de Dios: Descubriendo el gran mensaje de la Biblia* (Buenos Aires, Certeza Unida, 2009), p. 25.
[8] A. Tizon, *Whole and Reconciled* (Grand Rapids: Baker Academic, 2018), p. 57.
[9] L. Sanneh, *Whose religion is Christianity? The Gospel beyond the west* (Grand Rapids: Eerdmans, 2003), pp. 105–106.

American church is not exempt from these same habits and tendencies. Missionaries and short-term teams have imported an understanding of mission to Mexico that does not require incarnating the gospel fully, being restricted to urgently saving souls. The gospel is restricted to a ticket to heaven distributed by those who have the wealth to finance their activities such as distributing evangelistic tracts. God's blessing is equated with money and resources but no access to those resources is given.

A minority of organisations have changed their view and understanding of short-tern missions to emphasise learning and come in a posture of humility and realistic expectations. For a positive transformational relationship to develop, there needs to be a release of control. Some positive relationships have developed as Mexican pastors have been able to speak up and articulate their needs in the partnership. This usually happens when there is a long-term relationship with a local Mexican church, in which there is space to question practices and redefine needs, and when new generations are invited to the table.

When Christians are not willing to reflect biblically and theologically about the place where they will carry out their missionary activity and the type of work they are invited to do, then this mission will be carried out in an imaginary place devoid of context. Significantly, neither purveyors nor recipients will critique the cultures that they inhabit. If mission implies our participation in what God is doing in Christ to restore creation, then missionaries are not protagonists, but collaborators who come to join in what the Spirit of God is doing. Missionaries need to develop self-understanding, an awareness of their own culture and that of wherever they are going. The implications of the gospel need to be acknowledged first in the life of the missionary, and then in the missional context. This requires humility, laying down the resources provided by power and money and the capacity to partner and befriend others, allowing real encounters that bring the Gospel to life, as others encounter Jesus.

Most short-term teams that come to Tijuana are completely unaware of history, theological heritage, and past interactions. These teams function as a type of religious tourism allowing individuals to consume a missionary experience and purchase a specific product. These experiences vary according to their level of commitment, time, and money but usually involve building a house, painting a church, visiting an orphanage, or doing a vacation Bible school. For many people, these teams provide a positive experience because they get to value their own comfort and material blessings, and some are also able to meet and work with fellow Christians south of the border. However, these experiences often reinforce the restriction of God's blessing to material resources and an attitude of prejudice towards Mexicans. The capacity to develop an accurate understanding of Mexican people, their churches and their city is hindered by the limited scope of these trips, as well as the lack of information regarding the places they visit and their culture. Short-term teams often reveal a lack of curiosity, displaying a lack of love and desire to care in their cross-cultural engagement. Short term trips can and must be done under better frameworks, which will not create dependency. The emphasis cannot be placed on satisfying the demands of American Christians and doing what they desire, but on the creation of true partnerships that may lead to genuine relationships. Awareness, humility, confession, and a shift of power dynamics are essential for all of this to happen.

Crossings Borders to Become Friends: Immigration Crisis and Dealings at the Tijuana/San Diego Border

There are several ways to deal with immigrants at the border. The following example illustrates how many attitudes are determined by visions of masses of people arriving, seeking asylum. In early 2019, my husband and I were with friends at the beach in Tijuana, near where the border fence meets the ocean. We were sharing with them how a few weeks earlier, hundreds of men, women, and children from Central American caravans walked into Playas de Tijuana. As we were explaining what had happened, we suddenly heard and spotted three men preaching across the border wall while holding a huge banner that read "Fear the Lord". These men were on the beach, a hundred meters from the border fence, announcing through a megaphone, in English, that Central American migrants should trust in the Lord. The message was that crossing into the United States would not solve their problems and that they should trust and fear God with all their needs. Ironically, the Central American migrants were no longer there, so that this becomes a splendid and sad case of non-engagement, evidence of how ignorance, fear, and privilege may blind people. There is a need to connect faith, love for others and historical awareness to counteract the toxicity of American nationalism.

In the summer of 2014, a humanitarian crisis was declared as thousands of unaccompanied minors were crossing into the United States. That same year, the Mexican government created the *Plan Integral de Frontera Sur* (Integral Southern Border Plan-PFS) to control the influx of Central Americans into the United States of America.[10] In the first year, PFS detained ninety-three thousand people. Vigilance in the Mexican southern border made migrants choose perilous routes, exposing them to organised crime. In 2016, there was a transformation in the way people migrated; it became massive and international. That same year, thousands of Haitians arrived in Tijuana seeking asylum in the United States. After them, people from Honduras, El Salvador and Guatemala followed in 2018. Massive migrations in caravans are a way for people to protect themselves against violence, crime, and Mexican immigration laws.[11] In many ways, a

---

[10] A. Castañeda, '¿Qué es el Programa de la Frontera Sur?', *Boletín del Observatorio de Legislación y Política Migratoria*, COLEF-CNDH 1 (February 2016).

[11] A. Varela Huerta, 'La rebelión de las víctimas del Plan Frontera Sur', *Animal Político*, 13 noviembre 2018 available online at https://www.animalpolitico.com/blogueros-blog-invitado/2018/11/13/la-rebelion-de-las-

caravan is an indirect result of American foreign affairs and their constant intervention in the politics of Central American countries in the twentieth century. There are many complex reasons as to why people migrate, and some are strongly linked to the ways that rich countries continue to exploit more vulnerable nations.

Theological reflection requires further de-colonisation, that is, the need to grapple with the history of our nations and understand the power dynamics at work, as well as the notions we have inherited of God, of power, and of "the other". Theological frameworks for understanding complex issues like immigration or colonisation are not easily constructed or deconstructed as they challenge us to deepen our faith. They require learning history, increased biblical literacy and exposure to current realities and people directly affected by them. This requires crossing physical and symbolic borders, grappling with the hard questions that arise and developing a posture of lament. Theological perspectives or frameworks are about our position primarily as followers of Christ who should show our allegiance first and foremost to Christ, and not to a nation. In this sense, theology is not only something we read and write about in relation to God, but how we participate in God's actions in the world.

Evangelical churches responded admirably to the societal challenges generated by the arrival of Haitians in Tijuana. For decades, the Catholic Church had responded best to serving migrant communities with well-established shelters. But when the Haitians arrived, small and medium sized evangelical churches responded, developing sixteen temporary shelters. COLEF, the most important research centre and graduate school in Northern Mexico, explained that without the involvement of the evangelical churches in Tijuana, the arrival of the Haitians and their later adaptation to the city would have been even more difficult. In 2018, when Central Americans arrived, only one third of those churches re-opened to serve as shelters. There are many reasons. Some were still faced with huge water and electricity bills; others had lost membership and others did not find the Central Americans worthy enough. Sadly, the majority in Tijuana made many xenophobic statements, mirroring what we were used to hearing from the United States, and this led to corresponding reactions among many people in churches.

The practice of serving migrants has changed the self-understanding of our own church: *Iglesia Bautista Camino de Salvación* in El Pípila.[12] While many in Tijuana were worried and xenophobic as Central Americans approached our city, Pastor José Antonio Altamirano preached about hospitality. He reminded fellow congregants about love for neighbours, and the privilege and responsibility of

---

victimas-del-plan-frontera-sur/?fbclid=IwAR0O5mtx6QzNYmYi3zKSShbGpE4mI2KncVypXEN1ZNFChQ9KDq3JrpVYs1s, accessed 15 November 2020.

[12] This church has been present for twenty-six years in one of the most violent neighbourhoods in East Tijuana.

the church to host people on the move. The shelter came as a local initiative. The sustainability of the shelter for the past four years has come from local support as well as from American partners. One of the main differences of the United States based organisations that support the shelter, compared to those who come on short term trips, is their desire to support and learn from our church. The visits from American partners have focused on learning about the work of the shelter, hearing people's stories, and sometimes helping with specific needs pitched by Mexican Christians. Those partners who invest money trust that the church can administer the resources and bring only what is asked of them. Through the immigration crisis, strangers have become friends. To visit the shelter is a humbling experience, reminding people that the good news of the Gospel is not about having resources, but the simplicity of following Jesus. The relationships that develop from these interactions happen on a more level ground, in which the American partners come in a posture of humility, curiosity and wanting to participate in sustainable ways.

The reality has been that while many local and American partners supported the work of the shelter since its inception, few have persevered throughout the years. The challenge has been that as the months have gone by, the excitement of those willing to help has diminished. Initially, when Haitian and Central American caravans arrived, there was an overwhelming outpouring of resources. At this point, there were very few Mexican activists or ministers among those leading the support for migrants. Most advocates for those in the caravans were leaders of American aid organisations. The subsequent challenge has been to provide long term support, develop job opportunities, dignified shelters, temporary homes, and education. Investing in such projects requires time and solid relationships. In this context, there is evidence of new ways God's Spirit is working. The partnerships that have flourished are those involving people, churches and organisations who listen to different cultures and voices and trust locals to achieve results. These partnerships are able to support immigrants and enable their flourishing on both sides of the border.

An honest look at the past and the present, in the light of Scripture, leads us into lament. Yet Scripture also provides us with avenues for a prophetic imagination of the future. Acts 6, which describes the situation of a growing church, in numbers and diversity, is an example which offers a model for better cross-cultural relations at the border. Specific needs provide new opportunities and new horizons for God's mission. In the opening chapters of Acts, Luke describes believers in Jesus as generous and sharing what they had with each other, so no one was in need. God's Spirit moved his people to share their resources with one another and with the world that opened to them. In chapter 6 a problem arises, because the Hellenistic widows feel neglected, and claim that the Hebraic Jewish widows are receiving better treatment. The apostles are not willing to be drawn into cultural tension and ask the group of disciples to choose seven people from among themselves who would take on the important responsibility of feeding the widows.

The seven ministers chosen are holistic ministers, of good reputation, full of the Holy Spirit and wisdom who will distribute the resources, and they are all Greek. This allows the transfer of power and decision making to the community that understands its own needs. This is a new reality in God's mission that widens the scope of people reached by the gospel. This is God's Spirit at work, in which we see the transfer of power from the centre to the fringes, from Jewish apostles to Greek Jews so the word of God spreads as a result. These men have access to places the apostles did not. God uses them in unique ways. Philip goes to the Samaritans, and Saul listens as Stephen witnesses to Christ, and is stoned to death.[13] The history of the church is full of these stories, of God using those on the margins as key players in his story. The history of Christianity shows us that the centre of gravity of Christianity is changing and has made its home in different cultures.[14]

The reality at the border shows the clash been Western Christianity and the Global South, which has been deeply impacted by, but is also distinct from, the West. Service at the border requires a partnership between North and South, the United States of America and Mexico. Such partnerships need to honour history and culture, recognising the role of place and history. There is a need to live out God's mission in post-colonial contexts, resisting the temptation of using power and resources to impose faith or aid. The church is growing and is alive among refugees, asylum seekers, immigrants, and Mexicans, but it is not dead in the West. Cross-cultural relationships between Christians should take place as equals, recognising that both those in the centres of power and influence and those in the Global South need the experience and mentoring of other Christians to resist the seductions of power. As Western wealth has come from the exploitation of colonised nations, the transfer of resources from the Western church should be seen as a sign of repentance, not a sign of the weakness of the receiving churches.

---

[13] D. López, 'Hechos' in C.R. Padilla, M. Acosta Benítez and R. Velloso da Silva (eds.), *Comentario Bíblico Contemporáneo* (Buenos Aíres: Kairós, 2019) p. 1393.
[14] A. Walls, *The Missionary Movement in Christian History* (Maryknoll: Orbis, 1996), p. 22.

9. "Where Do You Come from and Where Are You Going?": Refugees in the Pentateuch[1]
Délnia Bastos

The treatment of foreigners is an important theme in the Pentateuch and there are significant examples of refugees. This chapter presents some of the most important cases, and then analyses the Pentateuch's teaching on refugees.

Adam and His Family

The first chapters of Genesis reveal "God's redemptive grace for humanity".[2] In the garden, humans lived in harmony with God, one another, and with nature; they had an abundance of food, dignified work, and welfare (Gen. 2:8-25). However, they were expelled from their homeland, the Garden of Eden, due to the Fall (Gen. 3:22–24). In exile, their harmonious relationships were broken, food depended on hard work and welfare gave way to tiredness (Genesis 3:16-19).[3] Nonetheless, God did not abandon them to despair and graciously provided for their continued existence after the loss of their original state of innocence.[4]

Moreover, ultimate hope is born, even in exile from the presence of God. The woman's descendant will strike the head of the serpent (Gen. 3:15). This protoevangelium announces the final victory of the Messiah. In Revelation we can see the fruit of his work, a new Heaven and new Earth in which refugees return to their good origins (Rev. 21:1ff). However much still needs to happen in the period in between.[5]

The narrative then focuses on Cain and Abel, sons of the first couple. One day, Cain turns against his brother and kills him in anger. Lane observes that

---

[1] This material has been adapted from chapters 3 and 4 of D. Bastos, *Donde vens e para onde vais?: Ensino bíblico sobre o tema do refugiado no pentateuco,* (Master's thesis, Escola de Missões Transculturais do Centro Evangélico de Missões, 2018).
[2] T. Carriker, *Missão Integral: Uma teologia bíblica* (São Paulo: SEPAL, 1992), p. 13.
[3] D. Kidner, *Gênesis: Introdução e comentário* (São Paulo: Mundo Cristão, 1979), p. 68.
[4] H. Braumer, *Gênesis 1: Comentário Esperança* (Curitiba: Editora Esperança, 2016), p. 82.
[5] J. Stam, *Profecia bíblica e Missão da Igreja* (São Leopoldo: Sinodal e CLAI, 2003), p. 97.

Cain's narrative follows the same sequence as that of Adam: sin (Gen. 4:7), an attempt to hide (4:8), God's question, (4:9), curse (4:11) and expulsion from God's presence (4:16).[6] Cain's punishment is worse than that of his parents, he becomes a nomad, a fugitive refugee, castaway from God's presence (Gen. 4:10–14).[7]

Cain, in Hebrew, resembles "used to have", and Nod, where Cain now lives (Gen. 4:16) echoes the sound for "wanderer" (*nûd*). This reminds us that the person alienated from God has no permanent place.[8] Sad is the life of the one who no longer has the presence of God, who no longer has land to work and live on but walks errantly through the world.

Nonetheless, amid sin and punishment, God pours out his grace protecting murderous Cain from vengeance with a mark "lest any who found him should attack him" (Gen. 4:15). This mark is not a curse but a form of protection, an act of mercy which "is almost a covenant, making him Cain's virtual *go'el* or protector".[9]

Schwantes affirms that although Cain deserved the death penalty for murdering Abel, his initial punishment is to cease to be a farmer and be forced to wander without protection. When Cain appeals to God, the first part of the punishment remains but "the second becomes reduced, as Cain is protected by a sign …. Cain joins the same category as Abel … a seminomadic migrant under Yahweh's protection".[10]

While it is the line of Seth, Adam's other son, which calls upon the name of the Lord (Gen. 4:25–26), God does not forget Cain the refugee. Genesis presents his descendants as the source of various cultural advances which God would later use to benefit his own people, including urbanism, cattle farming, music, and metallurgy (Gen. 4:17–22).[11] Although the Bible provides no closure to Cain's story, it is unlikely that he became like Abel. Nonetheless, the story reminds us of God's mercy and justice towards refugees, even those with criminal records. The sign that God places on Cain anticipates the cities of refuge established in the law.

---

[6] W. Lane, *Uma análise do propósito bíblico da missão* (Viçosa: CEM, 2013), p. 28.
[7] T. Carriker and J. Oliveira, *Bíblia Missionaria de Estudo*, (Barueri, Sociedade Bíblica do Brasil, 2014), p. 9.
[8] B. Waltke, *Comentário do Antigo Testamento: Gênesis* (São Paulo: Cultura Crista: Geográfica 2010), p. 119.
[9] Kidner, *Gênesis,* p. 71. See also W. Wiersbe, *Comentário Bíblico Expositivo: Antigo Testamento: volume 1: Pentateuco* (Santo André: Geográfica 2010), p. 45.
[10] M. Schwantes, *Projetos de Esperança – meditações sobre Gênesis 1-11* (Petrópolis: Vozes; 1989), pp. 60-61.
[11] Carriker y Oliveira, *Bíblia Missionaria de Estudo*, p. 10 and Kidner, *Gênesis,* pp. 72–73.

Noah and His Family: Literally Landless

The exponential increase of human evil leads God to make a covenant with Noah and his family. God gives Noah the task of building an enormous ark to host his family and a pair of each animal during the flood (Gen. 6:5-22).[12] Noah and his family become refugees and once the ark rests on the Ararat mountain range (Gen. 8:4) they settle in a land distant from where God first met Noah (Gen. 6:1 – 9:. 28). This leads to the first biblical record of the nations of the world, which significantly comes before any mention of the nation of Israel.

The word 'covenant' is mentioned eight times both before and after the flood (6:.18; 9:.9, 11, 12, 13, 15, 16 and 17). The story focuses on the universal covenant God establishes with all of creation through Noah and his family, signalled by the bow of grace. God could have destroyed all of creation because evil continues to prevail even after Noah. In this sense, we were all in the ark as refugees and our life on earth is possible because God maintains and renews his promise of life every day. This covenant includes all living creatures and all generations "being both unconditional and unmerited".[13]

Noah prefigures how Christ would one day inaugurate the greatest and most definite of covenants between God and creation. Just as God saved all life on earth including animal life through the "ark of salvation", he also saves us through faith in Christ. Just as God gave new land to Noah's refugee family, we who are sojourners will also inherit new heavens and a new earth. Finally, we can also offer an allegorical comparison of Noah and his family migrating to an unknown land in the ark with contemporary refugees, taking to the seas in the search for new beginnings.

Babel: All Are Refugees

Human sinfulness continues as the narrative progresses. The inhabitants of the earth seek power and fame by gathering to build a city and a tower. They wish "to invade the heavens, while resisting God's will for them on earth".[14] However, God frustrated their plans scattering "them over the face of the whole earth" (Gen. 11:9). Jehu Hanciles indicates that migration is a central theme of this narrative as "the Babel project is in opposition to the diasporic scattering of nations and peoples" and is thus "a metaphor for cultural absolutism".[15] God is faithful to his covenant with Noah and does not destroy humanity but intervenes to restrain human sinfulness, and all become refugees and are forced to leave

---

[12] This would also include seven pairs of "clean" animals to be used in sacrifices (Genesis 7:1–2, 8:20).

[13] Kidner, *Gênesis*, p. 95.

[14] C. Wright, *A missão do povo de Deus: uma teologia bíblica da missão da igreja* (São Paulo: Vida Nova, 2012), p. 78.

[15] J. Hanciles, *Beyond Christendom: Globalization, African Migration, and the Transformation of the West* (Maryknoll: Orbis, 2008), pp. 141–142.

their homeland. The nations are not abandoned at Babel as God sovereignly governs over their pilgrimages. They are included within God's mission which is the key to understanding the Biblical narrative between Genesis 11 and Revelation 22.[16]

Abraham: "A Nation the Other Side of the River"

Abraham begins a new chapter in the story of redemption. He lived with his family in "Ur of the Chaldeans", one of the most ancient South Mesopotamian cities, near the Euphrates estuary in the Persian Gulf, where, as Joshua indicates, the moon god Nanar was worshipped (Josh.24:2–3).[17]

Abraham was originally a foreigner, possibly a refugee rather than a Hebrew. We are not told why his family migrated but the destruction of the city by the Elamites in 1950 BC suggests that exile or prudence are possible reasons.[18] Abraham's father, Terah, died in Haram, on the way to Canaan. There, God called Abraham, in what is one of the most important missiological passages in Scripture:

> Go from your country and your kindred and your father's house to the land that I will show you. And I will make of you a great nation, and I will bless you and make your name great, so that you will be a blessing. I will bless those who bless you, and him who dishonours you I will curse, and in you all the families of the earth shall be blessed. Genesis 12:1–3

Abraham travels to Canaan, mainly out of obedience to and faith in Yahweh, probably experiencing many of the feelings of a refugee. In ancient cultures, identity was tied up with land and family and thus God's call to Abraham touches crucial elements.[19] Abraham is called to provide evidence of what "God can do in the life of the one who believes and obeys."[20] God's promise to Abraham is God's gracious answer to the problem of the nations.[21]

Genesis 14:13 refers to Abraham as a Hebrew for the first time. This expression means "the people from the other side of the river" referring to the location of Canaan relative to the Euphrates. It denotes nomads who preserve their culture in the face of migration and captivity. The promise of land can only be made to a landless people and points to a close association between Hebrew

---

[16] C. Wright, *A missão de Deus: desvendando a grande narrativa da Bíblia* (São Paulo: Vida Nova, 2014), p. 476, p. 487.
[17] G Livingston *Comentário Bíblico Beacon. v. 1 Gênesis a Deuteronômio* (Rio de Janeiro: CPAD, 2005), p. 57.
[18] Braumer, *Gênesis 1*, p. 191 and Kidner, *Gênesis* p. 104.
[19] Carriker y Oliveira, *Bíblia Missionaria de Estudo*, p. 17.
[20] E. César, *Cuide das raízes, espere pelos frutos: meditações diárias* (Viçosa: Ultimato, 2017), p. 51.
[21] Wright, *A missão do povo de Deus*, p. 85.

history and refugee contexts. This marvellous promise comes with a solemn warning "your descendants will be strangers in a country not their own" (Gen. 15:13), which emphasises that Abraham and his descendants were pilgrims.

Hagar: Where Are You Coming from and Where Are You Going?

After ten years in Canaan, Abraham needs to intervene in a serious family conflict. As Sarah still had no son, she suggested, according to a common custom, that Abraham have relations with her Egyptian slave, Hagar, who conceived and ended up despising her mistress. After being humiliated and persecuted, Hagar becomes a refugee (Gen. 16:1–6).

There is beauty in this tragic scene as God comes to the aid of this poor refugee promising that she would be the mother of many descendants (Gen. 16:7-13). These verses refer on four occasions to the "Angel of the Lord", interpreted either as a reference to God himself,[22] or as an angel authorised to speak on God's behalf. It is God who takes the initiative, finds Hagar, and intervenes. God's grace is not restricted to Isaac's line, as God is present to bless Hagar and reveals that the Ishmaelites, another branch of Abraham's descendants, are important for him. Waltke claims that this narrative is the only example in Ancient Near Eastern literature where a deity calls a woman by the name, and Hagar is the only woman in the Old Testament to give God a name.[23] The two questions that the Angel of the Lord asks, continue to echo in the mind of present-day refugees: "Where have you come from, and where are you going?" (Gen. 16:8). Since Adam, God is always asking the right questions.

Yet some refugees do not know the answer. An estimated twelve million persons are born at borders and have no country or documentation.[24] Some families live for generations in a particular country, but still do not officially exist anywhere, having no nationality. They do not have any sense of belonging and carry with them identity problems.

Hagar's encounter with God transforms her completely. She now has more certainties than doubts, she knows that the Lord has ordered her to return to her mistress, that God has promised that she will have many descendants and that he will always be with her (Gen. 16:3). God's inclusive blessing extends to the people of the desert, the despised refugees of this world.

Nonetheless, Hagar is destined to suffer once more as a refugee. The Lord fulfils his promise to Abraham and Sarah who now have Isaac. Ishmael, now a teenager, mocks his three-year-old half-brother Isaac on the day of his weaning.[25] Jealous and fearful of having to divide her son's inheritance with the "son of the

---

[22] So Kidner, *Gênesis*, p. 32 and p. 118.
[23] Waltke, *Gênesis*, p. 309, pp. 312–313, p. 363.
[24] UNHCR, *Manual de Proteção aos Apátridas* (Geneva: ANCUR, 2014), p. 9.
[25] Waltke indicates that the Hebrew suggests a malicious form of laughter. Waltke, *Gênesis*, p. 361. See also Kidner, *Gênesis* pp. 130–131,

slave", Sarah asks Abraham to send Hagar and Ishmael away. Despite his sorrow, Abraham wakes up early and gives Hagar food and a water canister and orders her and Ishmael to depart (Gen. 21:8-14).

Hagar wanders without direction through the Beersheba desert, once again not knowing where she is going. The water runs out and Hagar leaves Ismael in the shade of a bush and goes about a hundred metres away, as she cannot bear to watch her son die. God hears her cry and from the heavens the Angel of the Lord declares that Hagar should not fear as Ishmael will become a great nation (Gen. 21:17–18).

Once more God meets Hagar, despised by her mistress, but never by her Lord. If on the first occasion God sees Hagar's situation, the text now tells us that God hears the child's voice. According to Kidner, "Ishmael's name is almost the exact spelling of the Hebrew 'God heard'."[26] God reminds Hagar that he has promised that she will have numerous descendants. Although Ishmael and his descendants are despised, the Bible affirms that God fulfils his promise to Abraham (Gen. 17:20) and is with Ishmael making him into a great nation. Carriker affirms that both descriptions of Ishmaelite origins in Genesis (16:1–14 and 21:1–20) emphasise God's love and care for them and they should remain "a particular focus of the love and care of God's people in their missionary vocation."[27]

In both stories Hagar appears as a heroic character who receives grace and mercy from God during great adversity.[28] This story reminds us of the alarming circumstances of children involved in the current refugee crisis. Like Ishmael, they cry, and their parents suffer as Hagar did. Yet, just as God saw Hagar and heard the cry of Ishmael, so God sees contemporary refugees and hears the cry of their children. He is aware of their struggles and ready to help them in their affliction. This challenges us to reflect on how we can be God's answer to their prayers, conveying to them the message of God's love.

Jacob, the Paradigmatic Pilgrim

Isaac's descendants also become pilgrims and Abraham's grandson Jacob faced a life of persecution and pilgrimage. Having fooled his brother Esau to receive his father's blessing, he is advised by his mother Rebecca to escape from Canaan to the home of his uncle Laban in Pada-Hara (Genesis 27:42–45). According to Waltke this journey, in which Jacob follows the opposite path of Abraham and Tera, establishes Jacob "as a patriarch in his own right."[29]

Jacob's time as a refugee extends from the few days advised by Rebecca and lasts twenty years (Genesis 31:38). During this time Jacob works hard for Laban marrying both his daughters Leah and Rachel. Even after two decades he still

---

[26] Kidner, *Gênesis* p. 131.
[27] Carriker and Oliveira, *Bíblia Missionaria de Estudo*, p. 26.
[28] Waltke, *Gênesis*, pp. 304–305.
[29] Waltke, *Gênesis*, p. 479

sees himself as a foreigner (Gen. 32:3–5) a feeling shared by his wives (Genesis 31:15). The Hebrew word used, *nokriy*, denotes acertain contempt, such as "strange" or "alien".

A pattern emerges in Jacob's life. He leaves Canaan as a refugee to escape the wrath of his brother and the threat of death. He returns to Canaan as a refugee escaping from his father-in-law, seeking autonomy in his work. Yet again in his old age, Jacob leaves Canaan as a refugee to escape from a famine and reunite with his son in Egypt. Likewise, people continue to seek refuge for diverse reasons including war, conflicts, famine, and family reunion.

Migration is so important in Jacob's life that he describes his life to Pharaoh as the "years of my pilgrimage" (Gen. 47:9). For Waltke, Jacob never doubts the promise of land being "on a pilgrimage towards the celestial city".[30] Throughout this journey he names places with profound spiritual meaning such as where he meets angels: Bethel, Maanaim, and Peniel.[31] Peniel is by the Jabbok River where Jacob struggles with God and prevails. God blesses him, changes his name to Israel, and injures his hip. This radical encounter with God transforms Jacob (Gen. 32:30).

Jacob's story is a reminder that God is not restricted to specific locations or countries. God accompanies pilgrims and refugees in their travels, being able to provide profound life transforming experiences wherever they are.

Joseph: A Victim of Trafficking

Jacob's most beloved son becomes the most hated brother. His brothers tried to kill him but ended up selling their seventeen-year-old brother to Ishmaelites travelling from Gilead to Egypt (Gen. 37:18–28). Believing that his son has died, Jacob mourns him for many days (Gen. 37:29–36). This reminds us of those who have been abducted, sold, and even killed. Most are sold for sexual trafficking, others for slave work or the illegal drugs trade. Their families can never be sure that they have died, and grieving cannot take place properly, leading to much bitterness.

According to the United Nations, over two million persons every year are victims of human trafficking. Globalisation, has increased the opportunities for transnational organised crime, making human trafficking much easier.[32] Like Joseph, some are even trafficked by their own families.

Family conflict, especially among siblings, is present in all these Genesis narratives: Cain and Abel, Isaac and Ishmael, Esau and Jacob, Leah and Rachel, Joseph and his brothers. Many contemporary conflicts between nations and

---

[30] Waltke, *Gênesis*, p. 732.
[31] Waltke, *Gênesis*, p. 545.
[32] UNODOC, 'UN.GIFT – Iniciativa Global da ONU contra o Tráfico de Pessoas', UNDOC Homepage available at https://www.unodc.org/lpo-brazil/pt/trafico-de-pessoas/ungift.html.

churches also happen between brothers, those who have their roots in the same people. In a wider sense, all human beings are brothers as we share a common origin, something which pacifists have long referred to. Thus, it is useful to remember that Jews and Palestinians, for example, are brothers in their origins.

Joseph's life in exile is one of challenges and changes. He was a victim of injustice, but always behaved exemplarily, and God blessed him even more. Thus, Joseph reveals to his brothers that God had a plan for Joseph from the beginning, for him to be governor of Egypt during a terrible famine (Gen. 45:1–8). As a model of Christ, Joseph would not only save his people, but others as well. In this Joseph is different from contemporary refugees. The limitations of life in exile mean that, with a few noteworthy exceptions, most refugees do not reach their full potential. They face discrimination and difficulty in regularising documents and validating diplomas. In Brazil, Arab immigrants face disrespect and issues concerning the spelling of their names, leading to frustration in the present and difficulties in the future. God's intervention allowed Joseph to be an exceptional example of achieving success and fulfilment overseas.

Despite living all his adult life in Egypt, marrying an Egyptian and having Egyptian children. Joseph never ceased to regard himself as a pilgrim, even after becoming a high-ranking public official. Like Jacob, he never forgot God's promise and his homeland. Thus, the book of Genesis ends with the mummifying of the great governor of Egypt, waiting for his bones to be taken to the promised land. Likewise, many contemporary immigrants even after settling down in their new country still regard themselves as pilgrims until the end of their lives.

Moses: From Refugee to Liberator

Four generations later, the one who would deliver his people from Egypt is born. After Joseph died, a new pharaoh who did not know him came to power. This pharaoh feared that the Israelites, who had grown considerably while in Egypt, might become stronger than the Egyptians and rebel. Therefore, he enslaved the Israelites forcing them to work on major construction works and in the fields.

Israelite suffering was considerable, "bitter" (Ex. 1:14). They had gone from being refugees to abused slaves as "economic shelter transformed itself into house arrest within a policy of hatred, unfounded fear, exploitation and discrimination".[33] Nonetheless, God is faithful to his covenant and having fulfilled his promise of numerous descendants to the patriarchs, he would also provide them with land to live in and bless all the nations of the earth.[34]

However, God chooses a refugee in the land of Midian, Moses, to lead the Hebrews to liberation. Moses's life is a series of pilgrimages. He is born in a foreign land to a slave family. Pharaoh's daughter finds him in a basket on the Nile and Moses is raised in the Egyptian court as Pharaoh's adopted son. He

---

[33] Wright, *A missão do povo de Deus,* p. 118.
[34] Carriker and Oliveira, *Bíblia Missionaria de Estudo,* pp. 55–56.

escapes to Midian as a murderer and though he settles there and marries, his experience as a refugee is reflected in the name of his first son Gershom which means, "I have become an alien in a foreign land" (Ex. 2:22; 18:3). At eighty, Moses starts a mass pilgrimage, freeing his people from slavery in Egypt and taking them towards the promised land.

Moses is an authentic refugee, from the land of Goshen to the palace, from the palace to Midian, from Midian to the desert where he remains. He never enters the promised land, which he can only see from afar due to a single sin. In Moses' life we can see examples of the different reasons people seek refuge. Hunger led his ancestors to Goshen, oppression leads him to the palace, crime to Midian and God's call to the desert. The final pilgrimage is the most important. Despite resisting at first, he obeys God and frees the people from four hundred years of slavery and takes them to the promised land.

Moses is also a type of Christ, who would free his people from the slavery of sin, who also was a persecuted new-born baby, living in Egypt, travelling through the land, preaching, teaching, performing miracles and interceding for his people's sins.

The Israelites: Forty Years in the Desert

Exodus narrates Israel's pilgrimage under Moses' leadership, continuing the story of God's missionary covenant with Abraham and his descendants. It provides the main biblical model of redemption and is crucial for understanding the cross of Christ. In Jewish memory, Exodus provides the rationale for protecting and caring for the weak, especially the poor and strangers.[35]

Exodus reveals God justice and compassion in freeing an enslaved people. The initial chapters emphasise both Israel's suffering and God's sovereignty and initiative. God sees the affliction of the people, hears their cry, knows their suffering, is attentive to their condition, visits his people, remembers the covenant, and comes down to free them from the Egyptians and take them towards worship and conquering the land. As G. Wright, affirms God is "the God who acts… only he can direct and is directing the course of history".[36]

Croatto correctly emphasises the political nature of this oppression which sought the genocide of the Hebrew people, although other aspects of his hermeneutics are questionable.[37] As Wright indicates, the exodus is not merely towards freedom, but towards God's grace, to love and serve him exclusively.[38]

---

[35] Carriker and Oliveira, *Bíblia Missionaria de Estudo*, p. 55 and Wright, *A missão de Deus*, p. 275.

[36] G. Wright, *O Deus que age* (São Paulo: Aste, 1967), p. 55.

[37] J. Croatto, *Êxodo: uma hermenêutica da liberdade* (São Paulo: Paulinas, 1981), pp. 47–48.

[38] Wright, *A missão do povo de Deus,* p. 120, p. 187.

Israel's freedom to exclusively worship God should attract foreigners to participate, both those who live among the people and those outside.

Just as God saw his people's suffering, he also sees the suffering of contemporary refugees and persecuted people. Exodus presents God as judging injustice in a dramatic way. The Israelite refugees are protected from the ten plagues that God sends, with the text explicitly registering a distinction being made between the Israelites and the Egyptians in the fourth, fifth, seventh, ninth and especially the final plague, the death of the firstborn.

These plagues reveal God's judgment over Pharaoh and the Egyptians, his sovereignty, and the truth that "the earth is the Lord's" (Exodus 9:29). God's power extends over all of nature, and he is able to miraculously spare the victims of injustice, as in the case of Israelite homes being spared the three days of darkness that fell over all of Egypt.

The final plague provides the origins of the Passover and prefigures the salvation of those marked by the blood of the lamb (Ex. 12; Rev. 7:.14; 12:11; 22:.14). The Passover was established during refuge as God's people were preparing for pilgrimage; Jesus was slaughtered at Easter for the sins of all the people of the world, represented by the foreign pilgrims present in Jerusalem.

As they travel, God protects and guides his refugee people. He provides food and shade during the day and light and warmth at night. He gives the people Moses' leadership and the law to live by; yet they still rebel against God. Welcoming the stranger risks those we welcome turning their backs on us in ingratitude, rudeness, and sin. Even so, like God, we should continue to offer grace without prejudging the actions of those we welcome.

A Mixture of Peoples

Non-Israelites also left Egypt with the Israelites; therefore, God mentions foreigners four times in the instructions given to Moses and Aaron concerning the Passover (Ex. 12:37–51). Circumcised foreigners could participate in the Passover. These foreigners probably included other slaves, including those belonging to Israelites, those who were married to Israelites and those who feared the God of Israel. After settlement in Canaan, these foreigners would be from different ethnic groups, living and working among the Israelites, possibly including descendants of the Canaanites.[39] The deliverance of other slaves together with the Israelites, is a partial fulfilment of God's promise to bless all peoples of the earth, pointing to the eschatological fulfilment when both Jews and Gentiles are saved.[40]

Christopher Wright denies that Israel saw itself as a racially pure people. The tribes of Manasseh and Ephraim were descended from Joseph's Egyptian wife, and there were other mixed elements among the Israelites, so that the Old

---

[39] Wright, *A missão de Deus,* pp. 304–305.
[40] Carriker and Oliveira, *Bíblia Missionaria de Estudo*, p. 67.

Testament should not be used to justify theories of chosen, pure races.[41] Separation was understood in religious rather than ethic terms as there were many ways a foreigner could belong to the Israelite community.[42] Thus, the Passover lamb was shared among Israelites and foreigners, bosses and workers, a principle of equality overcoming cultural, social, and economic differences. This points to the welcome that God expects the church to show, sharing the gift of food with the sojourner among us without distinctions of class or anything else.

Moses' brother-in-law Hobab is an example of a stranger joining Israel in the Exodus. Moses insists that Hobab guide the people in the desert, promising to grant him the blessings that God gives the people. These foreigners had rights and duties while living among the Israelites. God's people should treat them, especially the most vulnerable, with justice and compassion.

The Pentateuch's Teaching on Refugees

Many refugees would have been covered by the commandments given concerning foreigners in the Mosaic law. Roland de Vaux emphasises that for desert nomads, hospitality is both a necessity and a virtue.[43] As isolated individual life is inconceivable, someone who is forced to leave their own tribe needs to find another tribe for it to provide "protection, defend him from his enemies and practice blood vengeance in his favour ... In the Old Testament we find echoes of these customs in the institution of the *ger* ... and in the cities of refuge".[44]

Sadly, as was common in that historical context, there would be many slaves, especially prisoners of war, among the foreigners in Israel.[45] This was not part of God's ideal, and the law sought to protect as far as possible those who faced this harsh reality. God's ideal can be discerned by exploring the ethical paradigm established in the law towards foreigners.

The Divine Paradigm

Israel was required to act towards others, including foreigners, as God has acted towards them, with compassion, justice, and generosity. Christopher Wright concludes that the uniqueness of Israel's election serves the universal nature of God's mission in this world. Commenting on Deuteronomy 28:9–10, he affirms that God's reputation is intertwined with that of Israel's, a risk that God is willing

---

[41] C. Wright, *Povo, terra e Deus: a relevância da ética do Antigo Testamento para a sociedade de hoje* (São Paulo: ABU Editora, 1991), pp.118–119.
[42] Wright, *A missão de Deus*, p. 268.
[43] R. de Vaux, *Instituições de Israel no Antigo Testamento* (São Paulo: Editora Teológica, 2003) p. 29.
[44] de Vaux, *Instituições de Israel no Antigo Testamento*. p. 29.
[45] H. Wolff, *Antropologia do Antigo Testamento* (São Paulo: Hagnos, 2008 p. 302), de Vaux, *Instituições de Israel no Antigo Testamento*, p. 106.

to take as part of his mission towards humanity.[46] God's people should act as God does so that other peoples would come to him. This ethical principle is expressed in the Old Testament through the metaphor "to walk in the ways of the Lord", which means to act towards others as God would act towards them, in the light of what one has received from him.[47]

The Triangle of Compassion

René Padilla describes foreigners, orphans and widows as forming a "triangle of God's special concern" as they appear together in many Old Testament passages, especially in Deuteronomy. Foreigners, alongside orphans and widows, were the most vulnerable persons in Israelite society so that responsibility towards them becomes an ethical and theological issue, being related to Israel's origin as God's people.[48] Widows and orphans faced the lack of a husband or father to provide and protect. Foreigners faced the complex challenge of life away from their own culture, tribe, clan, and family. There might be difficulty with language and customs, which would restrict access to dignified work. If they were not slaves, strangers were often restricted to the worst jobs, and always vulnerable to oppression.[49]

These groups faced socioeconomic poverty, so the law provided them with protection for important rights, establishing God "as their protector."[50] Nonetheless, the needs of foreigners, especially refugees, go beyond material needs including widespread emotional needs such as uncertainty, anxiety, boredom, depression, anger, despair, fear of the unknown, abandonment, impotency, confusion, and difficulties in adapting to new circumstances. Therefore, reports of mental illness among refugee children are increasing.[51]

The Rights and Duties of Foreigners

The Pentateuch determines the rights that foreigners were entitled to, and their duties.[52] This text will focus on six: following the law of Moses, Sabbath rest, freedom in the year of remission, to be loved and treated with justice, entitlement to the gleanings and a share in the triannual tithe.

---

[46] Wright, *A missão de Deus,* pp. 267–269.
[47] Wright, *A missão do povo de Deus,* p. 106.
[48] C.R. Padilla, 'Deus ama o estrangeiro' *Revista Ultimato* 367 (2017), p. 54. See Deuteronomy 10.18; 14.29; 16.11–14, 24.17; 26.12, 27.19. In these passages the Hebrew word used is *ger,* referring to a foreigner who has been assimilated, often a proselyte.
[49] de Vaux, *Instituições de Israel no Antigo Testamento,* p. 106–107; Wolff, *Antropologia do Antigo Testamento,* pp. 302–309 and J. Thompson, *Deuteronômio: introdução e comentário* (São Paulo: Mundo Cristão, 1982)
[50] de Vaux, *Instituições de Israel no Antigo Testamento,* p.63.
[51] J. Ferreira in J. Oliveira (org.), *Refugiados, peregrinos e forasteiros: a igreja respondendo ao desafio mundial da migração* (Londrina: Descoberta, 2017), p. 74–75.
[52] For a comprehensive list see D. Bastos, *Donde vens e para onde vais,* pp. 49–51.

Following the Law of Moses

Three passages in the Pentateuch, Exodus 12:49, Numbers 9:14 and Numbers 15:15, establish a clear principle, that there should be equality and justice under the law and thus each commandment would apply equally to Israelites and foreigners living among the people. Therefore, the law recognised the rights of the resident stranger *"ger"* but determined that he should also fulfil its duties. Numbers 15 emphasises that "you and the foreigners will be equal before the Lord". Thus the foreigner was under both the protection and the yoke of the law, receiving the blessings of the covenant, observing its statutes, and celebrating the religious festivals.[53]

Have Sabbath Rest

Foreigners are included in the sabbath rest in Exodus 20:10, 23:12 and Deuteronomy 5:14–15. Deuteronomy resorts to Israel's memory, that it once was a foreigner (*ger*) and a servant in Egypt and needed its rest as its servants now do. Keeping the sabbath was a means for foreigners to identify themselves with the Israelites, avoiding discrimination and promoting inclusion.

The sabbath was not simply about free time and worship, but also a means of just treatment for those who worked hard. Thus, Deuteronomy emphasises that slaves should be allowed to rest and Exodus 23:12 extends this to those who were most vulnerable to exploitation, the "son of the slave or foreigners." This emphasises God's lordship over time and creation and his concern for those who "are especially exhausted or dependent".[54]

Freedom in the Sabbath Year

In the ancient world prisoners of war were often reduced to slavery and traded. In this context the Sinai Covenant sought to humanise this practice and had laws concerning the treatment of slaves, be they foreigners or Israelites.[55] Thus, three passages, Exodus 21:1–11, Leviticus 25:39–46 and Deuteronomy 15:12–18, establish that Hebrew slaves should be released in the Sabbath year. Christopher Wright argues that these slaves were unlikely to be ethnic Israelites, but vulnerable, landless people from the surrounding areas who survived by selling their labour.[56] If this interpretation is correct, then foreign slaves were also released during the year of remission, after having worked for six years.

---

[53] Thompson, *Deuteronômio*, p. 144.
[54] Wolff, *Antropologia do Antigo Testamento*, p. 216. See also p. 305 and Wiersbe, *Pentateuco,* p. 290.
[55] de Vaux, *Instituições de Israel no Antigo Testamento*, p. 106–107.
[56] Wright, *A missão do povo de Deus,* p. 125–126.

To Be Loved and Treated with Justice

Many passages emphasise that Israelites should not oppress nor treat resident foreigners with injustice. Moreover, they should love the foreigner, remembering that they were once strangers in Egypt. According to Christopher Wright, Leviticus 19 teaches that holiness involves, among other things, "rejecting cruel treatment of ethnic minorities and displaying racial equality before the law and practical love towards the foreigner as to oneself".[57]

The fifth curse of Deuteronomy 27:14–26 refers to treating those in distress with kindness and justice, especially widows, orphans, and strangers. God would judge Israel if it did not display the same kindness God had displayed delivering the nation from slavery.[58] For René Padilla:

> God taught the people through this experience of living under oppression in a foreign land so that the responsibility for exercising justice to the stranger would be branded on Israel's moral consciousness. For Israel, the memory of slavery would link ethics to history to encourage obedience.[59]

Thus, not only is there a law to love and not oppress the "triangle of compassion", there is an explicit curse for those who do not obey this law. God is the defender of the exploited. Magistrates and judges should be careful to ensure that no party was denied justice because of their weakness.

Entitlement to Gleanings

Leviticus 19:10; 23:22 and Deuteronomy 24:19–22 established that Israelites should not be greedy but leave some of their harvest for orphans, widows, and foreigners. Significantly, this law not only refers to cereals, such as wheat, barley, and corn, as if the poor were only entitled to the basics, but also includes delicacies such as grapes and olives.

This entitlement allowed foreigners, orphans, and widows to gather food without the indignity of begging.[60] Gleaning appears twelve times in the second chapter of Ruth revealing that begging can be avoided through obedience to the law.[61] This law is one of various which emphasise justice, generosity, and special care towards vulnerable people.[62] One should not be tight-fisted towards the weakest, such as foreign residents and refugees. Sadly, we frequently see the opposite, as migrants are used as cheap labour, denied rights and legal protection due to their lack of cultural knowledge and urgent needs. Some work long hours

---

[57] Wright, *A missão do povo de Deus,* p. 150, de Vaux, *Instituições de Israel no Antigo Testamento,* p. 99.
[58] Wiersbe, *Pentateuco* p. 579.
[59] Padilla, 'Deus ama o estrangeiro', p.54.
[60] Wiersbe, *Pentateuco* p. 575.
[61] J. Every-Clayton in Carriker and Oliveira, *Bíblia Missionaria de Estudo,* p. 234
[62] Wright, *Povo, terra e Deus,* pp. 170–171.,

for a mere plate of food, as greed, which is condemned in God's law, takes over from generosity. The commands in Leviticus 19 regarding care for foreigners are particularly relevant nowadays when thousands of immigrants become a mission field.[63]

Receive a Portion from the Triannual Tithe

Deuteronomy 14:28–29 and 26:12–13 establish another tithe beyond that of Deuteronomy 12 which was to be given to the Levites. This triannual tithe should remain in a person's hometown and be used to feed the poor, the needy and the Levites.[64]

Recipients of this tithes were those who did not have land and access to harvests, such as the Levites, who were spread all over Israel and the resident foreigners (*ger*), orphans and widows, the triangle of compassion. The provision should be generous, as they should be able to eat until satisfied.[65] This tithe is given to God but is also relational in nature as it required the giver to encounter the needy.[66]

The giver is also commanded to declare to God, while giving the gift "my father was a wandering Aramean, and he went down into Egypt with a few people and lived there and became a great nation, powerful and numerous" (Deut. 26:5b). Obedience was encouraged through memory of the nation's experience as strangers in Egypt. The word "foreigner" appears four times in Deuteronomy 26 (verses 5, 11, 12 and 13) possibly to counteract the human tendency to ignore or discriminate against those who are different.

Conclusion

It is possible to discern four ethical and theological principals in the Pentateuch's teaching on refugees and foreigners: inclusion, participation in worship, being treated with justice and equity and protection of the vulnerable.

Inclusion

Foreigners were included in the community of God's people. All Israelites were of foreign stock as their forefather Abraham had been called out of a foreign nation. The first foreigners included in the Mosaic law were those who participated in the Exodus. While Israel was called to be God's exclusive people, separate from the nations as an example for them, there is no scriptural warrant for the concept of a racially or ethnically pure Israelite people. Future generations were obliged to remember the importance of including foreigners.

---

[63] So Wiersbe, *Pentateuco*, p. 369.
[64] Wiersbe, *Pentateuco*, p. 543 and Thompson, *Deuteronômio*, p. 177.
[65] Thompson, *Deuteronômio*, p. 246.
[66] Carriker and Oliveira, *Bíblia Missionaria de Estudo*, p. 171, Sanchez 2002, p. 357.

Participation in Worship

Foreigners were welcome to worship God and, if circumcised, had the right to participate integrally in religious festivals, such as the Passover, the Feast of Expiation, Pentecost, and Tabernacles. They could participate in expiation and purification rituals, listen to the public reading of the Law, and make offerings. The Law's demands regarding appropriate worship also applied to foreigners, such as not offering human sacrifices, not sacrificing outside the temple, not eating blood, and not blaspheming the name of the Lord.

This is a consequence of universal worship being "the ultimate goal of missions."[67] Habakkuk hopes for the time when "the earth will be filled with the knowledge of the glory of the Lord, as the waters cover the sea" (2:14). Hence Solomon, when dedicating the temple, prays that God will listen to prayers by foreigners in the temple (1 Kgs. 8:4–43) and Is. 56:1–7 announces that foreigners will have complete access to the temple as "my house shall be called a house of prayer for all peoples." As in both cases the Hebrew expression used *nokriy* is usually used for foreign pagans, one can only imagine the scandal these texts would have caused for Israelite readers.[68]

Being Treated with Justice and Equity

Justice and equity mean that the law established the same rights and duties for Israelites and foreigners. God´s concern for foreigners is revealed in their right to sabbath rest, gleanings, resort to a city of refuge in the case of involuntary manslaughter, receive a fair trial, have a portion in the triannual tithe, and receive their daily wage without delay. God's action in the exodus, redeeming Israel, signifies that the nation should love foreigners, displaying the characteristics of a redeemer, "sacrificial compassion, commitment to justice, charitable generosity and efficacious redemptive action".[69]

Protecting the Vulnerable

There is a particular emphasis in the law on the "triangle of compassion", the foreigner, the widow, and the orphan. Foreigners are referenced in at least thirty-two laws, so that their rights would not be forgotten. God is aware of the human tendency to forget, alienate, discriminate, and oppress those who are different, hence this repeated emphasis. Exodus 21–23 indicates that God's missionary people should be concerned with the protection of the most vulnerable.[70]

---

[67] Carriker and Oliveira, *Bíblia Missionaria de Estudo*, p. 79.
[68] Carriker and Oliveira, *Bíblia Missionaria de Estudo*, p. 871–872 and Wright, *A missão de Deus,* pp. 362–363, 509-510, 516-517.
[69] Wright, *A missão do povo de Deus*, p. 125.
[70] Carriker and Oliveira, *Biblia Missionaria de Estudo*, p. 76.

10. "Privileged Is The One Who Reads Aloud": An Open Letter from a Visually Impaired Peruvian Theologian
Julio Gonzáles Ulloa

Callao, Peru, November 2020,

Dear Colleague,
I write to you as someone who has been involved for a couple of decades in pastoral ministry and theological education in Peru. I also write as someone who due to a visual impairment is often excluded from access to good theological materials, and from effective participation in many theological conferences and networks. As such, my voice and those of many visually impaired Peruvians are often excluded from theological conversations.

I am aware that there is discussion in the English language on issues to do with disability. However, this is far removed from my context, where we still face issues of accessibility and inclusion. In this letter I wish to convey what a privilege it is to be able to read the words of Scripture and other literature with one's own eyes, and how you can use this privilege to bless those who are not able to do so and include us in theological dialogues:

> Blessed is the one who reads aloud the words of this prophesy, and blessed are those who hear, and who keep what is written in it, for the time is near. Revelation 1:3

This is the first of seven blessings that appear in the Book of Revelation and speaks powerfully to me as it relates to one of my favourite tasks, the act of reading. According to this verse, both those who read aloud, and those who hear are blessed. In the case of the Bible, the reader is especially privileged as in reading Scripture we can communicate with God. As I like to tell my students, the Bible is the only book where the author is present when we are reading.

The Greek word employed here, *makarios* refers in many texts to the freedom that the rich have from cares and worries. Thus, while the term is usually translated as "blessed", "happy" or even "joyful" in our Spanish Bibles, its semantic range is wider also conveying the idea of being "fortunate" or "privileged." It is important to remember that John was writing at a time when illiteracy rates were high, even in classical Athens. Hence, my preference is to translate *makarios* as "privileged" as it aptly describes those who were able to read at a time when many could not.

The one who reads is privileged, because they have received the educational opportunities which allows them to read. Reading is a reflexive, comprehensive and, in the case of the Bible, spiritual activity. Reading is not just the ability to translate phonemes and letters and decode signs and sounds. A child quickly learns how to do this, but this does not mean that she has the capacity to understand. Reading requires the ability to reflect and therefore understand what is written. It thus demands devoting time to learning, which traditionally Christians have sought to do through discipleship programmes and biblical studies.

The Greek term for reading, *avaginosko*, refers to the ability to recognise, know something. The one who reads can be certain of the content of the text that they are seeing. For this reason, the one who develops the capacity to read should regard him or herself as privileged, yet it saddens me to see that many pastors and leaders are unaware of this privilege. I believe that if many of my seminary students were truly aware of the blessing that they have received in their educational opportunities, they would devote more of their time to reading.

The one who reads is privileged as they have access to different texts. In the first century it was hard to have access to the different scrolls, papyruses, and parchments on which Biblical texts were written. I date Revelation in the last decade of the first century, a period in which Christians faced hostility and possibly persecution under the Emperor Domitian. This was a particularly challenging time to obtain and read copies of Scripture.

We can extend this understanding to the present and affirm that it is a privilege to have access to the Bible in one's own language. As a Spanish-speaking Peruvian I am blessed that the Scriptures have been translated from Hebrew and Greek into Spanish, and we have different versions which we can compare. However, linguists estimate that in Peru there are between forty to one hundred and twenty different languages. Nonetheless, beyond Spanish, we only have versions of the Bible in Quechua and Aymara. Yet the basic Bible study aids and other tools, which we take for granted in Spanish, have yet to be translated into either Quechua or Aymara. The lack of such resources affects the quality of Biblical teaching available, and thus helps facilitate the presence of syncretistic practices in different Christian communities.

Even Spanish speaking pastors and theologians in Latin America face difficulties in accessing more up to date information which is often only published in English and which very few church leaders in Peru can read. As a seminary teacher I often find it difficult to access Biblical commentaries or even theological articles translated into Spanish to assist me in preparing my classes. There is a need for a continued translation of resources into Spanish to improve the material we have available. There is also the need to translate works from

Spanish into English, so that Latin American theologians are better able to participate in global theological debates.

Finally, there is a physiological reason why the one who reads is privileged. Those who have good eyesight and are able to read the Bible with their own eyes are blessed. Although obvious this is often ignored, yet many in the world suffer from different forms of visual impairment. It is often only when one loses one's eyesight that one realises what a privilege it is to be able to physically read Scripture.

I suffer from retinitis pigmentosa which has led me to progressively lose my eyesight. Retinitis pigmentosa is a genetic disorder commonly known as night-blindness, as it leads to trouble to see at night. While I am still able to see partially during daytime, since 2005 I have lost the ability to read texts with my own eyes.

This was traumatic, as I have always loved reading. Yet, it is necessary to avoid complacency, and I refused to accept that because I could not read with my own eyes, I would not be able to access knowledge. Contemporary technological advances mean that one can still study despite losing one's eyesight even if it does demand more effort. What is required is the desire to know Scripture, to experience a relationship with God through his word, and apply it in obedience, as Jesus affirmed "If you love me, you will keep my commandments."

Sometimes, I am asked whether I have sought to learn to read Braille. However, there is very little academic material available in Braille to make it worth the effort. Instead, I have sought to use audio. Where a book or material is available in an original audio format this is straightforward. However, not all audio books have the needs of the visually impaired in mind, and I often find it difficult to retrieve information that I later need. For example, if I wish to quote a phrase from a book, this requires having to listen again to lengthy sections until I find the quote I need.

If all I have is the digital text, I require assistance from my son, Paul, who is in his twenties. Paul needs to convert the book from its original format into .txt format so that he can pass this through a special software which converts the text into audio. Academic books which employ footnotes are a particular challenge as the software is not able to discern them. In these cases, I need to decide, either to exclude the footnotes and miss out on the information that they contain, or to include them, and consequently the reading process becomes disruptive and harder to follow.

Another challenge refers to the Biblical languages. The software can read transliterated Greek or Hebrew words but if they were included in Greek or Hebrew script, the software skips them. With the Greek I can work around the problem as I taught Paul to read Greek when he was in secondary school. I have also taught him to access Greek study tools, such as lexicons and interlinear texts. Hence, when I wish to critique how an author has used Greek, I can ask Paul to read the Greek text aloud and inform me what different study tools explain about the text. Nonetheless, I have not had the opportunity to teach Paul how to do the same in Hebrew.

As a result of these technological advances, I have discovered that I am reading more these days, than before I lost my eyesight. Nonetheless, I am aware of how much I am indebted to the assistance that Paul gives me, and that not all those who suffer from visual impairment will have access to such help.

Thus, it is important to affirm that the one who reads is privileged but has been given this privilege to serve and bless others. In the synagogues of the New Testament period the text was read out loud, every Sabbath, in the synagogues. The ones who read from the Scriptures did not do so solely for their own benefit, but to bless all those who had gathered to listen. This is the context behind Jesus's sermon in the Nazareth Synagogue, when he is invited to read from Scripture, and offers a messianic interpretation of the text from Isaiah, applying it to his own ministry.

The synagogue model was assimilated in the New Testament assemblies. Paul expected his epistles to be shared among the churches and read out loud to bless those gathered. Thus, he commands the church at Thessalonica, "I put you under oath before the Lord to have this letter read to all the brothers" (1 Thess. 5:27) and to the church at Colossae, "when this letter is read among you, have it also read in the church of the Laodiceans, and see that you also read the letter from Laodicea" (Col. 4:16). Paul was aware that many early Christians would not be able to read, and that even those who were able, might face difficulty accessing texts. Consequently, reading Scripture out loud became an important component of the mission of the early church.

This is the likely context behind John's affirmation, "Blessed is the one who reads aloud the words of this prophecy, and blessed are those who hear, and who keep what is written in it, for the time is near." In the Greek, the one who reads is introduced with the singular definite article, while those who listen are introduced by the article in the plural, making it clear that John is referring to an individual who reads the text out loud to a group of people.

Thus, if you have been blessed with the ability to read, I would encourage you to take the decision to read to bless others. There are many people who desire to know God's word written in Scripture, but are not able to do so, and require help. I am reminded of the testimony of an older Christian lady who was a domestic worker in a household. She was illiterate but wanted to be able to read the Bible and share it with others. She asked her bosses to help her read the verses which she was studying at her church and often these were verses with an evangelistic message such as John 3:16. Through this process she was blessed, as were her bosses who read to her.

Currently, I have access to many classical texts and contemporary secular books. Nonetheless, there is a dearth of good Christian works in audio format in Spanish. It is very difficult to have access to good Bible commentaries to help me prepare my sermons and seminary classes. Therefore, I believe there is a vast mission field through the opening of access to information and knowledge which currently remains restricted to those who can see.

I would suggest finding young Christians in churches who are able to read well to provide a good oral reading. Having received permission from authors and publishers, they could then read and record a diversity of books which would increase the access of those with visual incapacity to information. In the case of books with footnotes, these could be recorded as a separate file, so that the visually impaired reader can access their information without disrupting the flow of the text. Ideally, page numbers should be indicated, and chapters recorded as separate files. This would facilitate navigating the book and quoting from it.

God does not wish that his word remains restricted to those who can see, but rather that it should go out to all. Nor does he wish that those who have visual impairment be denied the tools which enable them to be better interpreters and expositors of his world. Thus, mission does not refer only to going to another country, it can also be done by those who stay at home and allow those with visual impairment to have access to the Bible and good Christian literature.

There are also other ways I believe that those who have the privilege of eyesight could help those who are visually impaired participate in theological conversations. Firstly, events such as theological conferences, seminars, and consultations play an important role. Yet I have found that there is very little awareness of the impact of my visual limitations and little effort to accommodate me. As I do not use a walking stick, I am often left to my own devices, unless I bring someone along to assist me. With multimedia, speakers often refer to a PowerPoint slide or a picture on the large screen, without explaining its content, leaving me unable to understand what is going on.

If I am invited to be a speaker, things can be even more difficult. Ever since I lost my eyesight preparing a sermon or presentation has required the extra effort of recording my notes as audio and learning them off by heart, as I am no longer able to rely on written notes. When I arrive at the conference it is often the case that no one has put any thought into how I am going to make my way to the platform where I will give my presentation, so that I am left to overcome an obstacle course of tables, cables, and steps. In Peru, there is the expectation that speakers will provide extensive notes and PowerPoint presentations. On more than one occasion, when I have pointed out that it would be very difficult to provide this material, the invitation has been withdrawn. Hence, I discover that my visual impairment has led to my exclusion from many theological networks.

This sense of exclusion is compounded by the fact that theological knowledge and research is usually distributed through written texts. I do not have access to an adequate computer or software to produce good written material. Some people have indicated the existence of dictation software, but these are often too expensive for the typical Peruvian pastor, and generally do not have the needs of the visually impaired in mind, requiring that one be able to see what is appearing on the screen. This means that I am left reliant on others to help me write up my research. For example, this letter is being written up by a colleague, but I am not able to have a full-time secretary to help me with long term research projects.

This became an issue when I undertook my master's studies. Fortunately, my examining board recommended that I present my thesis in oral format and submitted it to a rigorous oral examination. This satisfied the need both for academic rigour and accessibility. In the light of this experience, I would plead with seminaries, publishers, and theological journals to accept the submission of audio files, not just written texts, so that the voices of those who suffer from different forms of visual impairment are not excluded from theological conversations.

In Peru, there are over 800,000 people registered with some form of visual impairment.[1] Knowing the high levels of informality in Peru, the real number is likely to be much higher. It is my belief that among this large number there are many Christians who have much to contribute to global theological conversations. I, therefore, ask you, dear colleague, to use your God given privilege of reading with your own eyes, to ensure that the loss of our visual capacity does not lead to our voices being silenced.

In Christ,

Julio Gonzáles Ulloa.

---

[1] Consejo Nacional para la Integración de las Personas con Discapacidad, 'Se registran 801 mil personas con discapacidad visual en todo el Perú', Conadis Consejo Nacional para la Integración de las Personas con Discapacidad available online at https://www.conadisperu.gob.pe/notas-informativas/se-registran-801-mil-personas-con-discapacidad-visual-en-todo-el-peru#:~:text=Se%20registran%20801%20mil%20personas%20con%20discapacidad%20visual%20en%20todo%20el%20Per%C3%BA.&text=Encuesta%20Nacional%20Especializada%20sobre%20Discapacidad,para%20ver%2C%20aun%20usando%20anteojos., accessed 23 November 2020.

11. Ultimato: "Talking about Racism"[1]
Ziel Machado, Márcio Mendes, Terezinha Candiero, Quéfren de Moura, Ana Staut and Atilano Muradas.

Ziel Machado:
"Towards a Theology Which Leads the Church to Godly Grief"

I approach the topic of racism with humility. I come as someone willing to listen, to learn from many voices which are more prepared than I am for this debate. Theological reflection on racism must start from a position of profound pain. Therefore, this leads me to the letters that Paul wrote in prison, a pastoral theology born with the scars that come from obedience to the Lord. Paul makes some statements in his letter to the Philippians, written in approximately AD 62, which allow us to start talking about racism. In verse six of the first chapter, he declares "I am confident of this, that the one who began a good work among you will bring it to completion by the day of Jesus Christ." This word is a warning that my theological labour must be attuned with the good work that Christ has begun and will complete in us. This is not a lonely effort but one which is moved by what Christ is doing in us.

Further on, Paul states "this is my prayer, that your love may overflow more and more" (Phil.1:9). This is a good objective for our theological labour, that it results in more love. A love that allows us to grow "with knowledge and full insight", a love that would allow us to be "pure and blameless" so that we may produce "the harvest of righteousness that comes through Jesus Christ for the glory and praise of God".

I faced racism as an existential problem, long before it became a theological one. I am part of a mixed-race family; my great-grandmother Joaquina was a former slave who died when I was eight. I grew up in a family of whites and blacks. Joaquina educated her children, grandchildren, and great-grandchildren in an ideology of whitening, that is, seeking to take on a white identity. She was afraid that the law would be reversed, and her descendants would suffer the same as she and her ancestors did.

---

[1] Originally published as R. Percinoto Jr, *Para conversar na Igreja: Conversando sobre o racismo* (Viçosa: Ultimato, 2020). We are grateful to Ultimato for the permission to translate and include this material.

In my family, racism and themes associated with slavery were met with absolute silence. We noticed some depreciating and mocking comments, which later I would identify as recreational racism. As my family achieved higher social levels, I faced more and more examples of this crisis of Brazilian cordiality.

The church I grew up in, located in an impoverished urban community, was also silent about racism and other related subjects. We were concerned with filling heaven up. It was also a mixed-race church. As I grew up, studied, and became more mature, racism become a theological problem which led to the question "Why is the church silent on such a fundamental issue?"

Later I became scandalised as I realised that more than silence, there was support for racist ideology. As a young person in the 1980s, I increasingly encountered a racist discourse directed at myself and others. Thus, the theological problem of racism was reflected in three forms of behaviour that were incompatible with Christian faith: silence towards racism, attachment to racist ideology and explicit racist practice. How did my evangelical heritage reach this situation?

Since I became aware of this problem, I have gone through a process of blackening my thought, seeking to connect myself with this dimension of my roots. As I have tried to relate this process to my faith, I have sought to educate myself concerning racism and for this reason, have sought to listen to many Christian voices to help me understand my Christian perspective towards racism.

One of the challenges that theology faces is to reencounter history. We need to educate ourselves concerning racism to understand the depth of this reality and anchor our theological effort in the reality of the pain this history tells us, a pain which is still present. History should instruct our theology so that we can connect with the roots of our problems.

I make a distinction between the Christian confession of faith and the historical experience of the Christian community. These are two things which, throughout history, have not always been coherent or connected to each other. There is a difference between what the Christian faith confesses regarding human beings and the historical experience of the Christian community towards racism. This is complicated by the fact that certain forms of Christian theology have sought to justify and promote racism. Part of the challenge is to understand these discrepancies. How did the Christian faith, based on love of God and neighbour, fail to heal these social evils? Why, historically, did the Christian community become attached to a system of slavery? Why did some forms of understanding the Christian faith sustain, support, and promote segregation? These are questions with theological dimensions and historical roots which we need to engage with seriously.

Thus, I propose a theological approach which begins with self-critique. We need to review the ways that the church tried to gag God's word, and even God himself, becoming a silent accomplice of the scandal of modern slavery and all that resulted from this experience. This approach should also be humble. We need to listen, re-educate ourselves to understand what happened. We need to bring those on the margins to the centre of the conversation, those who have been silenced, those who bear the scars on their bodies and souls. We need a theology which listens attentively to God, but also to those who have been subjects of this history.

This theology should be experimental, it should lead to continuous pastoral innovation, as listening to the marginalised should lead to significant changes. We need new answers to these old problems, because so far, we have offered inadequate answers. This theology should be daring in dealing with structural racism and courageous in the alternatives it proposes

Above all, we need a theology which leads to sadness. We need to mourn. This is the sadness according to God which Paul describes: "for godly grief produces a repentance that leads to salvation and brings no regret, but worldly grief produces death" (2 Cor. 7:10). This theology should lead the church to contrition, to a deep godly grief, which leads to repentance and brings salvation. We need a grief which produces the same fruit in us as it did in Zaccheus (Lk. 19:8). When confronted with Christ, he repented, grieved, and gave half his fortune to the poor and offered fourfold restitution to those he had extorted. Such sadness could lead to a range of different responses to racism. It can encourage society to a wider practice of restitution and reparations. Nonetheless, we should not forget the need for a true encounter with Jesus Christ. In announcing the gospel, we should take people to Christ, and they should realise the implications of this encounter for all areas of our life.

We need to change the focus of our Christian practice. Generally, we have focused on the centre, the powerful, on fame and status. In the gospels we find Jesus paying attention to the reality at the margins. Who are the marginalised that we have ignored? Our theology needs to deal seriously with the pain of those our eyes cannot see.

Our theological endeavour has the responsibility of including those who have been excluded with dignity, as equals. We cannot forget that we live in a society that marginalises, excludes, and produces criminals. Such a society challenges our theological thinking. A church which is adjusted to this model of society does not listen and integrate the voices of the marginalised into its mission and is incapable of developing a theology which takes history, lives, and the pain in this world seriously. Too often, we ended up preaching a Christ who became incarnate while avoiding ourselves the challenge of incarnation.

The challenge of inclusion leads to the challenge of compassionate restoration. In the gospels we see this in Jesus, as he listens to people, pays attention to them, talks with them, and touches them. To listen, to touch and to talk are concrete models of mercy.

It is best to start small, redefining our focus, seeking to include others and assessing our pastoral models of mercy. I am hopeful that godly grief will lead to life and salvation. It is impossible to deal with racism without the appropriate sadness, as this will produce in us the willingness to restore, repair and offer restitution, to do that which is required. When theology goes hand in hand with history we can understand and educate ourselves about what has happened and is happening. We can then hear God, through his word, and hear the world and thus have a theology which is born from God's revelation in his word and incarnation in history to heal all our pain. We will have a theology which will enable us to love God above all things and our neighbour as ourselves.

Let us be united in the fight against racism, wherever it is manifested, even, as has been my experience, when it is manifest in ourselves. The Lord's grace is greater than this pain and can restore us and change our history.

Márcio Mendes: The Path of Non-Discrimination

The Brazilian National Day of Black Consciousness, celebrated on 20 November, reminds us of black resistance to slavery and racism. The date was chosen to coincide with the anniversary of the death of Zumbi dos Palmares, in 1695. It is a time to remember black resistance to slavery from the first forced transport of Africans to Brazilian soil in 1594. It is a date for Brazilians to remind themselves of the struggle for an equal, democratic, united society, free from prejudice and which loves God and keeps his commandments.

On this day, Zumbi, the warrior leader of the Palmares Quilombo[2] was captured and assassinated, having his head exposed in Recife as a means of intimidating slaves against following his footsteps. He thus became a symbol not only of black resistance in Brazil, but the struggle for human liberty.

Racism is still the clearest form of discrimination in Brazil. On television, in books, in university and workplaces blacks are still regarded and treated as inferior to whites. Racism is a crime in Brazil, and can lead to a prison sentence, but above all Brazilian society needs to develop the awareness that skin colour does not interfere in an individual's capacity or character.

Remembering the History

In the fifteenth century, blacks were already enslaved in Portugal, Spain, the Azores, Madeira Island and Cape Verde. From the sixteenth century onwards, slave ships, bearing the English flag, brought Africans to Brazil. This was justified by claiming that blacks were stronger and more docile workers in comparison to indigenous Brazilians. Therefore, some Brazilians became slave traffickers and the slave trade accounted for one third of colonial imports. Some historians estimate that forty percent of captured Africans died during the journey, of hunger, thirst, ill treatment, and shipwrecks caused by excessive freight. When the slave trade was forbidden in 1808, this transport became clandestine. When ships saw American and English navy vessels, they would cast the Africans into the sea, in chains with iron weights attached to their feet, to avoid detention and the confiscation of their vessels.

---

[2] Quilombos are communities of escaped slaves or of decedents of escaped slaves in Brazil, founded by people of African origin.

When Princess Isabel abolished slavery in 1888, this was more a political gesture than sincere concern for slaves, an attempt to buttress the monarchy as public opinion became increasingly sympathetic towards republican ideals. Although legal slavery was abolished, in real terms it continued, and many blacks faced a worse situation. Nearly all were illiterate, and when freed, were sent away without food, home, jobs, or any form of compensation. As all that they could do was work on land and in sugar mills and they ended up working on the same farms where they had been slaves, in exchange for food.

Blind ambition and the desire to accumulate wealth leads humans to oppress, despoil, discriminate, and even kill their neighbours. Nonetheless, as Christians we believe that God created humans in his image and likeness (Gen. 1:26) to have a dignified existence, free and full of hope. He has a project of love, rescue, and salvation for all who believe. For this reason, discrimination offends God and his purposes for human beings.

God created humans with reason, intelligence, and the freedom to make our choices. We are called to be prophets, voices which cry out for our society to be one of justice and peace, where all are treated as equals without discrimination. When the Bible says that we should "love one another" (Jn. 13:34), this helps us to regard the other as our equal, invited by God to enjoy eternal life and not as an object of exploitation and discrimination. This was, after all, why Jesus came. As he declares in John 10:10 "I came that they may have life and have it abundantly", may this abundance of conscience and life reach the Brazilian church and people. May God bless our nation so that we can find the path of non-discrimination.

Terezinha Candieiro:
Racism and Childhood: A Recipe for Suffering and Perpetuating Prejudice

Reflecting on racism reminds me of two significant episodes. The first was as a nine-year-old, playing with one of my cousins at the home of Mrs Josefina, a family friend. Mrs Josefina had a son, Juninho who was our age and we really enjoyed playing together. One day, as we were playing, Juninho told his mother:

"Mum, when I grow up, I want to marry Maria."

His mother instantly rebuked him saying:

"Not Maria, no way ... she is a little black girl![3] Make sure you choose a white girl to join our family."

This comment filled me with sadness, even though I did not have a clear understanding of the exact meaning of these words. That mother casually expressed a racist opinion without any awareness of the pain it would cause on the children involved. There was no shame in her words, which used biological

---

[3] Translator's note: The Portuguese term used *"pretinha"* is offensive and demeaning in Brazilian culture.

and physical characteristics to discriminate against a child. This was not simply a lack of respect but an act of racism against a young girl by an adult.

My second experience occurred on a journey to South Africa, still facing the aftermath of the apartheid regime of racial segregation. We were at a holiday resort with my eight-year-old son. We were one of the few black families at this crowded resort, as most where white. The children were playing near the swimming pool and two boys started to argue. In a harsh voice one of the boys cursed the other saying:

"You are black, you should not be here."

There was a stunned silence and the offended boy left in tears. Both sets of parents were surprised and uncomfortable with the childish argument and left the pool as soon as possible. A child had committed a racial offense against another child.

These narratives encourage us to reflect on how such prejudiced and twisted worldviews remain within our societies. We need to lead our society to reflect on what parents have taught their children through words and actions. On what are we basing the worth of a person? Should this worth be based on factors such as race, ethnicity, physical characteristics, or social class?

Like Father, Like Son ... Like Mother, Like Daughter?

Childhood is a vitally important period for personality formation, establishing relationships, and learning those principles and values which will affect how a child develops throughout life. During childhood and adolescence, children learn how to treat others and form healthy relationships. Therefore, what they learn from their families will be reproduced throughout their lives.

There are children who suffer due to racism and there are children who are taught to be prejudiced, racist and to offend those who have different physical characteristics from their own. This is a daily reality long experienced by children in diverse places and environments, including churches.

Children, especially the youngest, do not have the emotional maturity to deal with these issues, either as victims or as perpetrators of racist acts and offenses. Thus, it is necessary to reflect on how we can minimise the pain of those who suffer and avoid leading other children to commit violent racist acts. Children need the opportunity to hear and be heard. By expressing their own opinion and listening to others, they develop in a healthy manner, learning to respect and value all, free from the prejudices absorbed from a structurally racist society. Therefore, it is necessary to talk about racism with honesty and wisdom in the diverse social spaces that children interact with, such as the home, school, church, and social media.

What Is the Role of the Church in All This?

We need to critique the way the church has sought to minimise the impact of racism on children and adults. Racism is a form of violence and attacks children in a cowardly way. For this reason, it is considered a crime in Brazilian legislation and many other countries. We like to think that racism is absent from our churches, but this is not true. This behaviour goes against what God's word teaches us that "God shows no partiality" (Romans 2:11).

On one occasion, the disciples sought to stop some children from reaching Jesus (Matt. 19:13–15). Jesus confronted and rebuked his disciples for discriminating against children due to their age. He called the children, welcomed them, and hugged them. We should have a similar response when faced with situations of racism, violence and verbal abuse against any persons.

Racism is a form of aggression which humiliates the other, and therefore it is necessary to fight against it. There are many children, teenagers and adults who have scars on their souls, even their bodies, from the racist treatment they have faced in childhood or at other stages in their lives. Some are not even aware of what they have faced, and only with time understand the racist dimensions of their suffering.

The church can contribute to society by revealing Jesus' attitude towards injustice, inequality, disrespect, and discrimination. The church offers a learning environment which can provide children and adults with opportunities to interact well with others, independent of ethnic background.

May the church never reproduce nor perpetuate violent and harmful behaviours which affect human development and society in general. May our legacy for the present and future generations be to live and act according to Jesus's teaching to love God and neighbour.

Quéfren de Moura: The Bible and the Mythical Roots of Racism

Racism is a set of theories, beliefs and practices which presuppose or establish a racial or ethnic hierarchy. It is based on the right of one race, considered pure or superior, to dominate others, regarded as inferior. According to the anthropologist Kabengele Munanga, "racism is this tendency to consider that the intellectual and moral characteristics of a certain group are a direct consequence of their physical and biological characteristics".[4]

Racism is not a biological, scientific, or genetic category, but one which is socially constructed "charged with ideology ... hiding something which is not proclaimed: the relationship of power and domination".[5] According to the sociologist Clóvis Moura, "racism is an ideology deliberately set up to justify the domination of one group over another".[6] Thus, racism subjugates, humiliates,

---

[4] K. Munanga, 'Uma abordagem conceitual das noções de raça, racismo, identidade e etnia' *Universidade Federal de Minas Gerais Homepage* available online at https://www.ufmg.br/inclusaosocial/?p=59 accessed 5 May 2021.

[5] Munanga, 'Uma abordagem conceitual das noções de raça, racismo, identidade e etnia'.

[6] C. Moura, 'O racismo como arma ideológica de dominação' *Revista Principios* 34 (1994), p. 28.

mocks, pillages, denies rights and rapes, in the name of power. It is something perverse and violent and completely contrary to the values of the word of God.

Nonetheless, one of the mythical origins of racism comes from a biblical narrative, which is interpreted to teach the inferiority of blacks. This is the text of Genesis 9:20–29. After the flood Noah gets himself drunk and remains naked in his tent. The Hebrew text is unclear, but Ham, Noah's son comes and "sees" his father nakedness. In the Hebrew Bible to see nakedness can be a euphemism for an act with sexual connotations (cf. Lev. 18:6–19, 20:11) which in this situation would mean a grave dishonour to the father and his authority as family leader. In telling his brothers what happened, Ham is challenging Noah's patriarchal leadership possibly because as the youngest child he was excluded from the patriarchal succession. The other two brothers, however, seek to protect and respect their paternal figure by covering his nakedness without looking at him. When Noah finds out what happens he curses Ham, "cursed be Canaan; lowest of slaves shall he be to his brothers". Noah's curse is directed at Ham's son, thus, at his descendants and family line.

Throughout history, this narrative was used to legitimise slavery and racism, declaring that blacks came from Ham's line and thus were heirs of the curse of slavery. This interpretation lacks biblical warrant but has been used to offer a colonialist, incorrect reading to ideologically justify racism.

Racism seeks to depersonalise individuals. It excludes rather than brings together. It is opposed to God's purpose for humanity which is life in community (Gen. 2:18). Racism reifies oppression, dehumanises, and seeks homogeneity. In the Bible, this univocality is not presented as God's plan, but is a human plan of power and domination, evidenced at the tower of Babel. In this narrative we see that the desire for power leads people to gather and build a tower to raise their name and acquire fame. In response God confuses and frustrates their plans by mixing up their languages. This allows for the construction of plural identities and ethnicities.

Genesis 4 provides us with a biblical perspective on contemporary issues related to violence and racism. In this passage God enquires of Cain concerning the whereabouts of his brother Abel, in the aftermath of the first fratricide in the Bible. Cain's insolent answer is in the form of a question, "am I my brother's keeper?" (Gen. 4:9). God's answer remains elliptic in the narrative but echoes throughout Scripture and Israel's history. It is the same for Cain and each one of us. Yes! You, and every human being, are responsible for your brothers and sisters. The blood of each brother, of each sister, cries out from the earth. The pain of each little one reaches God and will be demanded of us.

In Jesus's words and acts and throughout the New Testament we can see the importance of the principles of love, compassion, solidarity, equality, and respect for one's neighbour. Jesus emphasised on many occasions that love is the foundation for existence (Matt. 5:43–44, Jn. 15:12) and Paul declares that even if all passes away, love remains (1 Cor. 13:13). This love is relational and needs to be experienced and lived with one's neighbour. This love is not just a feeling, but solidarity, welfare and social justice and leads to human dignity and equality.

In Matt. 25:31–46, Jesus refers to a future judgement, when the welcome and solidarity of each person towards those in need, those who have been exploited, who have faced hunger and thirst, who have been naked, were foreigners or homeless will be judged:

> Then the righteous will answer him, 'Lord, when was it that we saw you hungry and gave you food, or thirsty and gave you something to drink? And when was it that we saw you a stranger and welcomed you, or naked and gave you clothing? And when was it that we saw you sick or in prison and visited you?' And the king will answer them, 'Truly I tell you, just as you did it to one of the least of these who are members of my family, you did it to me.'

In Galatians 3:28 Paul writes that there "is no longer Jew or Greek, there is no longer slave or free, there is no longer male and female; for all of you are one in Christ Jesus." Paul considers those distinctions between human beings which lead to inequality and violence artificial. In Christ all these distinctions are emptied, and the Christian faith should be marked by a genuine experience of what it means to be brothers and sisters.

A just person respects and supports those who suffer and struggle so that their pain be healed. This involves not only avoiding racist practices but fighting them. It is unacceptable for Christians to ignore the existence and impact of racism as this denies our role in constructing a more equal society. If we want to be like Jesus, it is necessary to carry on his legacy, defending those who are oppressed. This is not an option or a choice, but the mission which should infuse all parts of our lives.

Ana Staut: Ethnic Diversity in the Language of the Gospel

> They sing a new song: "You are worthy to take the scroll and to open its seals, for you were slaughtered and by your blood you ransomed for God saints from every tribe and language and people and nation." Revelation 5:9

This verse reveals the diversity within creation and the kingdom of God. Not only are we created in the image and likeness of the Father, which gives us a unique cosmic value, but individually belong, thanks to Christ's sacrifice, to the promise of eternal racial reconciliation.

Denying Diversity

Race is neither a biblical nor biological concept but has been defined socially through a set of phenotypes, such as hair, facial characteristics, and skin colour. Race in this provisional sense, is that which makes me different from others, becoming part of my identity, leading to inclusion within certain urban tribes and being assigned to certain groups of social risk or privilege. Being black in Brazil is to be part of statistics concerning marginalisation, unemployment and low schooling, a legacy of a colonial slavery regime which perpetuates itself and continuously threatens social welfare.

Racism divides, and points to a failure with regards to loving one's neighbour. It is a sin. The New Testament was written in a context in which the relationship between Jews and Greeks, Gentiles and Samaritans was one of constant discrimination. Paul's epistle to the Romans, which emphasises that God does not display partiality, provides firm foundations to condemn this offence. Neither in the church nor in society can there be discrimination between blacks and whites.

The Purpose of Diversity

> Declare his glory among the nations, his marvellous works among all the peoples.
> For great is the Lord, and greatly to be praised. Psalm 96:3–4.

There are no racial criteria to achieve grace and justification, Moreover, it is in our multicoloured differences that we can glorify the Lord together. God has desired and planned ethnic diversity for his worship. In Acts 2 the Holy Spirit comes upon the church at Pentecost. Linguistic differences were transcended, as the Bible tells us that all understood the apostolic message even though they spoke different dialects. These differences were no obstacle to hearing God's word and do not thwart our salvation in Christ and our growth in faith. Likewise, contemporary racial divisions are no reason for divisions among peoples in eternity. Pentecost points to what will occur in this final racial reconciliation, diverse human beings, united as children of God.

The Redemption of Diversity

Mercy frees us from the anger, sadness and bitterness caused by the offenses we suffer. We are, then, empowered to forgive and request forgiveness, love our enemies, and reconcile ourselves, through our faith in Christ, giving glory to the one who gave us life.

"Be kind to one another, tender-hearted, forgiving one another, as God in Christ has forgiven you" (Eph. 4:32). Our willingness to forgive others, as we have been forgiven in Christ, is a necessary element to achieve reconciliation in the church. To accumulate bitterness is to deny the grace God mercifully offers us. We have peace in Christ, trusting that all the injustices of the world have already been judged, which gives us the energy to forgive those who offend us. It is important to emphasise that racist acts should still be confronted, but that evil will not lead to our personal destruction:

> Let no evil talk come out of your mouths, but only what is useful for building up, as there is need, so that your words may give grace to those who hear. And do not

grieve the Holy Spirit of God, with which you were marked with a seal for the day of redemption. Ephesians 4:29–30

Repentance is another characteristic of an environment of reconciliation. A sinful heart is the cause of much of the hurt caused by racism: pride, arrogance, perversity, apathy towards our neighbour and indifference when faced with injustice. These deficiencies within our hearts need to be transformed by the power of the Gospel. This is the same merciful word we need to bear witness to the world, caring for the present kingdom and signalling the one that will come, the body of Christ in its full diversity.

Humbling ourselves due to our sin is part of the Christian walk, deepens our relationship with our Creator and intensifies our gratitude towards Him. To repent from the sin of racism is to recognise that we have sinned against God himself.

Racial reconciliation is part of the victory on the cross. Christ died so that all sins might be forgiven and injustice cease. It is the church's responsibility to promote harmony among Christ's peoples, empowering its members and condemning discriminatory attitudes. To participate in the Christian community in this process demonstrates the truth that we are all called to glorify God, the creator of all ethnicities and nations.

The Practice of Diversity

We should seek, admire, and preserve diversity in the body of Christ. The ethnic diversity God placed in creation should be reflected in the church, announcing his eternal kingdom. To ignore this agenda, is to close one's eyes to one of the ways that the perfect beauty and glory of the Father is revealed.

There is a personal responsibility to pray for God's help and wisdom in advancing towards reconciliation. May the gospel allow individuals and churches to seek diversity, racial harmony, and fellowship between Christians in our life together: "For in the one Spirit we were all baptized into one body – Jews or Greeks, slaves or free – and we were all made to drink of one Spirit" (1 Cor. 12:13).

Atilano Muradas: Between Flowers and Prejudice

I recently visited my mother's home in a small town in Minas Gerais where I was born. Walking through the different squares, I saw that they were prepared for spring, well cared for with many flowers. My mother's yard was full of flowers and plants which she lovingly cares for and waters daily. She knew all their names, and loves to paint them, so that the walls of her home were full of paintings. Her love for plants and flowers inspired me to love floral diversity so as to have informed conversations with her.

For this reason, when I lived in Brasilia, I appreciated the beautiful gardens scattered across the city. In my travels I have learned to admire the gardens and flowers in different regions of Brazil. I have had the chance to photograph and film wonderful gardens in the United States, become enchanted with the gardens of London and Paris. Returning to Latin America, I encountered Buenos Aires' spectacular flower beds. I shared these photos and films with my mother, who sighed with every detail, especially when she saw the gardens of the English palaces. Many people love to care for their gardens as if they were part of their own family.

When we consider animals, we see the same. God really went overboard in the diversity of the animal kingdom, so that zoologists and biologists run out of names to catalogue the variety of life on earth. There are many paintings of birds on the walls of my mother's house which she has painted with exquisite skill. This diversity of plants and animals undoubtedly reflects God's glory, as the heavens do (Ps. 9).

It was God's idea to fill the earth and the heavens with these incredibly perfect and beautiful things, visible and invisible. Yet when God created humanity, he went even further, for while he called plants and animals into being with his word, in our case he used his hand and even "breathed". The wind of God came into us, his touch seals our very essence and he has made us deep and perfect beings because we are called to be stewards of his creation and govern both plants and animals.

Yet the best of God's creativity is, in my opinion, expressed in ethnic diversity. History unfolds and people emerge with intricate personalities, different shapes and sizes, varied hairstyles, eye colours and numerous shades of skin colour.

One of my grandmothers was black, married a native Brazilian and gave birth to my mother. One of my grandfathers was white, a descendant of Spanish Jews, married a Brazilian and gave birth to my father. I am black-indigenous-white-Jew-Spanish-Brazilian. I have brown skin and carry genes from the thousands of my ancestors who lived in different parts of the world. We are all like this. No one is ugly, no one is beautiful, no one is better, and no one is worse. We are all the product of ancestors who are neither ugly, beautiful, better, or worse. We are all God's creation, filled with his breath and his touch, responsible for caring for all that He has placed before us, including our neighbours.

Every human being is as different and beautiful as the flowers and animals painted by my mother. The Bible has taught me to love and appreciate all human beings beyond their shapes and colours. We need to recognise that God calls each of us by the name, just as my mother calls each of the plants in her garden. Each one is different, but my mother cares for them without discrimination, with the same kindness. Likewise, God continues to nurture and care for each one of us until the day we are called to meet him in eternity, where diversity will be even greater.

I do not understand why people make fun of one another, mocking accents, hairstyles, height, and skin colour. We all come from the same source, the same eternity, and are part of the same heavenly flowerbed where diversity is our richest and most beautiful gift. It is even better to be reminded that God is the gardener of the universe and Revelation 22:2 teaches us that in heaven there will be a square where all the saved of all nations will walk, independent of status, height, age, nation, or skin colour. We will be the flowers in this square with our different shades of skin and eye colour. Let the one who can hear, hear. Let the one who can see, admire, and give God the glory!

12. Redemption for the Land, Justice for Its People: A Cry from Peru
Rut Pérez-Saldarriaga

Lima, Peru, 2021

Dear Colleagues,

We are all affected by our environment and shaped by the different experiences which make us who we are. My name is Rut Pérez-Saldarriaga, and I am a young Peruvian woman. My family is a mixture of different Peruvian cultural groups. Although I was born in Lima, I have always felt a stronger connection with Andean culture having grown up surrounded by aunties and cousins who spoke Quechua and cooked Andean dishes. One of my aunties remained in the village where my father was born, and she would always send us fruit and delicious bread that was produced in that region. Thanks to her, we regularly ate Andean food.

I come from an evangelical family and as a child my brother, my cousins and I attended the church where my parents were married. I made many great friends at this church with whom I continue to stay in contact. This church taught me how to form true friendships, the content of Biblical narratives and what it means to serve God. When I grew up, I joined the Peruvian evangelical student movement AGEUP (Asociación de Grupos Evangélicos Universitarios del Perú), linked to the International Fellowship of Evangelical Students. Participating in AGEUP helped me increase my knowledge concerning God, my faith and Christian life. I learnt that God's mission should be carried out in a holistic, integral manner, focusing on all aspects of human life. I learnt that the gospel of Jesus Christ should be shared in a contextualised manner, meeting people where they are, connecting to their daily reality, understanding their needs, and sharing their pain. In other words, we should follow Jesus in presenting a more humane gospel.

Through AGEUP I participated in an ecological initiative called Caring for our Common Home which sought to raise awareness concerning Peru's environmental issues, offer a theological reading of the climate crisis, and rethink our prophetic responsibility with regards to our common home. We carried out Bible studies and workshops on caring for the environment in seven regions, preparing an informative newsletter containing theological reflection, Bible studies and news updates. We did not always manage to set up an environmental project in every location, yet participants would nonetheless often continue to work for climate justice in their regions. This programme came to an end in 2020 amid the Covid-19 pandemic.

Caring for our Common Home was linked to the Renew our World campaign, led in Peru by the *Asociación Paz y Esperanza*. AGEUP has been part of this campaign from its start. Its main objective is to engage churches in raising awareness and carrying out activities in favour of creation and climate justice. We encourage evangelical churches and organisations to stand alongside those most affected by environmental issues, forming links and alliances with other groups in civil society to influence political decision makers with regards to the environment and climate change. I am now directly part of the campaign team, and this has blessed my faith and my professional development. It has given me the opportunity to meet my peers from other countries, to travel and discover the reality in other continents. Hearing my Asian colleagues share how they have faced climate crises causes me sadness but reveals opportunities for common action to work for environmental rights locally and globally. Participation in this campaign allows us to place the Global South's agenda at the heart of this global movement.

This experience has encouraged me to dedicate my professional skills to environmental issues in Peru. I have thus moved out of Lima and have become part of the Technical Team for Environmental and Human Health, through which we monitor those persons, mainly women, affected by heavy metals in Peru through the extraction of natural resources such as minerals and hydrocarbons, among others.

In many nations these activities have been part of the quest for development but have brought little benefit for residents. It takes perseverance to share about these problems, especially in churches. For too long we have remained distant and alienated from this reality, ignoring the cry of those who suffer directly from the negative effects of extractive industries.

Peru's Environmental Problems

In Peru, as in other places, environmental problems do not exist in isolation. According to the Public Advocacy Office in Peru, in March 2021, most of the social conflicts in the country were caused by socio-environmental causes. We have 194 social conflicts of which 125 are socio-environmental (64.4%).[1] These, however, are only the most obvious conflicts, and there are many others which this state department does not consider. Among the most serious socio-environmental problems that we face are:

---

[1] Defensoría del Pueblo. Reporte Mensual de Conflictos sociales N° 205. Marzo, 2021.

Illegal Deforestation of the Peruvian Jungle

One of the main causes is the illegal lumber trade which cuts down trees without reforestation. This wood is sold at high prices with little concern for its origins. Illegal mining takes place in the Madre de Dios region seeking gold, destroying trees, and contaminating rivers. Forests are being razed to make way for agriculture, damaging the land, disrupting water capture and causing erosion, endangering local populations and their future crops. A terrible example is that of national and foreign companies who plant oil palms, causing irreversible damage to soil quality. Oil palms are used mainly in the food industry, but also in cosmetics, not only in Latin America but in other continents.

Deforestation involves the invasion of territories which mainly belong to indigenous and native communities. Sadly, in our country the ownership of land is not fully regulated and where rules exist, they reflect urban cultures and do not consider the collective lifestyle of indigenous communities. For many years there have been national and international campaigns for greater understanding of collective lands, yet despite laws being in place, many strategies are employed to steal the land from those who have lived on it for generations. For example, many companies sue communities and persons claiming that they are occupying lands for which they have no ownership deed. This has often occurred because the community has decided not to seek ownership deeds for land that they have occupied for centuries, or because the deeds they have been given only give them the right to use the land, rather than ownership.

Water Contamination

In Peru the Andes provide water to our lagoons, lakes and rivers, our sources of fresh water. These waters are used for human consumption, so that their contamination affects both aquatic and human life.

The mining industry is the main cause of water contamination. Although there are laws which forbid the direct disposal of liquid residue in lakes and rivers, these laws are often ignored, and many mining companies have no water treatment systems. This has caused serious health problems in adjoining populations so that there is now a national database, the *Plataforma Nacional de Afectados y Afectadas por Metales Pesados*, of those persons who have been affected by heavy metals in their bodies. Many are adults, but often represent families with sick children, some with cancer. Sadly, the Peruvian state has been negligent in caring for these people. Some have suffered for years without receiving any treatment for the presence of heavy metals in their bodies, only being given painkillers. Pressure is still being put upon the Congress and the Presidency for laws in favour of these populations.

Another cause of water contamination is the leakage of agrochemicals, especially in discarded pesticide and fertilizer containers. Many agricultural workers do not dispose these containers properly preferring to throw them into bodies of water. This is due to a lack of awareness of how this can contaminate aquatic life and their own sources of water. The problem is that the nitrogen present in fertilizers and pesticides mixes with other elements to produce nitrates which increase the number of plants in streams, rivers and lakes, a process known as eutrophication. The result is lack of light for the development of aquatic plants and the oxygenation of water, so that plants, fish, and other species all die leading to a putrefied source of water.

Another factor worth mentioning is contamination through different chemical products such as cocaine chloralhydrate and residues from textile and food industries. In these cases, products such as chlorohydric acid, nitrogenised compounds and others affect the natural acidity of the water and harm the animals that live in these regions. Humans suffer not only due to poorer water quality but also due to the damage to the fish and other aquatic animals that they eat. Hence, water contamination harms both environmental and human health.

Poor Management of Solid Residues

Peru generates nineteen thousand tonnes of residues every day, of which half are produced in Lima and Callao. Fifty-two percent of these solid residues are disposed of in sanitary dumps, which are the safest form of disposal. We have a total of fifty-six sanitary dumps located in eighteen of the twenty-four departments in Peru. Thus, there are six departments which do not have sanitary dumps where solid residues are disposed of in unauthorised rubbish dumps causing serious harm to human and environmental health. These dumps attract pests, cause disease and water contamination, and in windy regions their residues can be taken far afield.

In theory, the Environmental Ministry has been working for a better management of solid residues and the Finance Ministry has been encouraging local municipalities with training, guides, and financial support. In practice, good residue management projects are rarely properly executed due to the corruption of local authorities and the high levels of local government debt which thwart the purchase of machinery and the hiring of the workforce to carry these projects out.

Sadly, our country does not have a culture of separating waste for recycling. This has not been taught, neither at home nor at school, although gradually it has been incorporated in the educational curriculum. Often it is the children and adolescents who have been educating adults.

Harm to Biodiversity

Peru is one of the four countries in the world with the most biodiversity, due to different altitudes, the presence of the Andes mountains and climatic diversity. We are able to sow a variety of foods, and there is a diversity of animals and insects. Thus, our ancestors' diet has, since ancient times, been healthy and nutritionally diverse.

This biodiversity is under pressure from climate change and new global needs. For example, overpopulation has stimulated the demand for genetically modified seeds better adapted to adverse conditions, with shorter harvest times and better nutritional quality. In theory, there is nothing wrong with this, but in practice this is dangerous as those who produce such seeds have a market monopoly and have patented the genetic base of seeds. Thus, farmers face the danger of being sued for using seeds that they have planted for generations. There is also the risk of the homogenisation of the seeds used, harming the natural biodiversity in the region.

Another threat to biodiversity is the trafficking of wild plants and animals to cities to satisfy a market for exotic goods. This brings zoonotic diseases to places where they had never been seen before.

Social Consequences

Damage to the environment has social consequences as it affects whole communities, breaking social dynamics. For example, when the Spaniards arrived in our country, they disrupted not only Incan social laws, but also human relationships with the land. They disrupted human relationships, murdering thousands, and raping scores of women. People were enslaved and not paid for their labour. Without wishing to idealise Incan rule, there was a genuine attempt to live in harmony with nature allowing the land to rest and there was respect for times of sowing and harvest, guided by lunar and solar calendars. The Incas felt a deep connection with what they called *Pachamama* (Mother Earth) and with *Inti* (the sun) and *Quilla* (the moon). This was replaced by the colonial lust for extracting resources and exploiting the earth.

This mentality continues in many places where large companies arrive solely concerned with profiting at the expense of the environment and human life. They do not pay people wages and sometimes even withhold documentation so that their workers cannot resign. These large companies often promote parties every weekend and women, children, and persons from the LGBT community are trafficked to work as prostitutes.

Colonialism and Exploitation

In 1492 Christopher Columbus set out on his journey towards India but arrived in Latin America. These journeys are often described as journeys of "discovery", the start of the Spanish Conquest. For indigenous peoples this was the start of an invasion marked by damage to the land and denial of fundamental human rights.

The new arrivals came in an intense search for riches and goods despising indigenous peoples as beings who lacked souls, who needed to be rescued and civilised. They looked at indigenous peoples with a discriminatory gaze, characterised by hatred. This gaze led to violence, resulting in the rape of indigenous women, the assassination of many innocents, and devastation to their lands. Whole people groups were subjected and oppressed, their languages and cultures despised and repressed. A sense of cultural superiority and entitlement led new arrivals to invade lands, wrenching creation from its indigenous stewards and transforming a collective heritage into private property. This was often carried out through laws which established that all the land belonged originally to the State.

A system of slavery emerged where power became concentrated in the hands of Spanish immigrants, and in the hands of their descendants born in Latin America, known as *criollos*. These *criollos* were often conceived through rape, having a Spanish father and a native mother. Both groups oppressed those who were closer to creation subjecting, enslaving, and oppressing indigenous peoples, peasants, descendants of Africans and impoverished women. This led to a hierarchical system in which all those who did not have economic or racial power were despised, despite their deep agricultural and nutritional knowledge. Polluted by the innocent blood spilt, pillaged in the name of profit, the land joined its peoples in subjection.

When Latin American countries achieved their independence from the Spanish Crown in the nineteenth century the *criollos* took over. In other words, there was little change to the political system. Governments saw the success of the Industrial Revolution in England and Europe and sought to strengthen their new states by opening our borders to foreigners to bring economic advance and progress. They also allowed immigrants to bring their religion, if they helped improve the economy. Thus, Protestantism arrived with a social dimension setting up schools, hospitals, shelters, and other institutions. Missionaries from the United States followed the arrival of European protestants, focusing on the cities with little desire to approach rural or native populations. As in Catholicism, the assumption was that people should convert to Christianity without missionaries listening to native thoughts concerning God. There was little interest in approaching or learning from native communities. Protestantism arrived in Peru under the banner of white supremacy. Churches were run by foreigners rather than Peruvians and the focus was on individual salvation with little concern for communal interests, which were so important for indigenous communities.

This situation should remind us that we have not experienced freedom in Latin America. We have had foreign languages, lifestyles and religion imposed upon us and have had our freedom to develop our own lands denied. Sadly, this situation has not improved with time. While Latin American countries became independent, and in Peru we are preparing to celebrate two hundred years of independence, this has only benefited the *criollo* class. Their lands have received all the benefits, and they have controlled the governments. Laws continue to favour the *criollos* while women and minorities such as blacks and indigenous peoples continue in submission.

A clear example of this exploitation is in the mining activity which took place in Potosí. This was done by using the *mita* system which the Spaniards inherited from the Incas. In the Incan Empire this would involve male labour on royal construction projects, in exchange for food and shelter. *Mita* workers would work shifts and for a limited number of hours. Under Spanish rule the *mita* was used to extract minerals from Potosí and women and children were forced to work alongside men for long hours, for months on end. Their food was discounted from their payment, and they were given no protective equipment in the mines. Even today, many mining companies continue to operate by forcing their workers to work for long hours for low wages with no concern for their health.

Why touch on these subjects? We cannot talk about Latin America without analysing our recent history. The suffering of our ancestors cannot be kept silent. Their blood and suffering are etched upon our land and provide us with the strength to struggle for dignity and justice. It is sad to see how little has changed. A small minority still control most of the wealth, power and influence and take decisions at the expense of those who are least favoured. Most of our governments are immersed in institutional corruption, which has become so enshrined in our societies that those who enter politics become enslaved by this corrupt system.

A Faith-Based Response

Latin America has made important contributions towards theological reflection on themes related to land, creation, and ecology. In Latin America, the fates of creation and indigenous peoples have always been intertwined. The enslavement of indigenous people and exploitation of ecological resources were both integral aspects of the colonial project, which in many forms continues until today. Thus, in Latin America, care for creation and freedom for oppressed peoples go hand-in-hand and I would like to share some of the ideas emerging from the work we have carried out in Latin America.

What are we doing as children of God if our lands are suffering so much?
As a Christian I believe that we can no longer remain in silence when faced with socio-environmental problems. I am led to Romans 8:19–21:

> For the creation waits with eager longing for the revealing of the children of God; for the creation was subjected to futility, not of its own will but by the will of the one who subjected it, in hope that the creation itself will be set free from its bondage to decay and will obtain the freedom of the glory of the children of God

These verses leave us with an important task. Creation eagerly awaits that as children of God we do something. Creation is suffering due to greed and avarice. Crops and seeds have been damaged, yet we have chosen to remain in silence. This passage should encourage us to reveal ourselves, to raise our voice, to carry out our role as children of God. It is also important to understand that redemption in Christ is not exclusively for human beings but involves all of creation. Thus, it is meaningless to focus exclusively on individual salvation as our labour as Christians is also to seek liberty for all of creation.

Where Are We and What Are We Doing Here?

I am also led to Genesis 6-7, and the description of the ark that God orders Noah to build. Although we often imagine a boat, the ark resembles a box, or even a rectangular home. God orders Noah to take every type of food to store into the ark and pairs from every species of animal, including seven pairs of every clean animal and seven pairs of every kind of bird. They spend over forty days in this ark, on the waters, unable to leave. This ark, or home, marks a new beginning for creation. It is a form of rebirth in which different species must learn to live together again. In Jewish culture the numbers forty and seven point to changes. The ark was a symbol of the reordering of relationships between humans, between humans and other creatures, humans and the land and all living beings with the land. It is also a reordering of the relationship between the Creator and his creation. We can interpret this ark as representing the earth, our common home where we live alongside many other beings who are also God's creation. We also need to evaluate and re-order our relationships, with other living beings, with the land and with our Creator. We also need to learn to live in a more balanced and respectful way.

The Samaritan Church

We have read the passage of the good Samaritan in Luke 10:25–37 on many occasions and have probably been encouraged to imitate the Samaritan and help those who are in need. Nonetheless, I want to invite you to take a closer look at the story. It begins with a question by a teacher of the law: "who is my neighbour?" After telling the story Jesus responds with a further question: who "was a neighbour to the man who fell into the hands of the robbers?" Jesus is inviting the teacher of the law to rethink his own place. The neighbour is not the one who receives but the one who carries out the good deed. The issue is not who our neighbours are, but who are we neighbours to?

It is interesting that this teaching is given to a teacher of a law, someone who was part of the religious elite, but still lacked understanding. Thus, we can apply this question to ourselves as the church: who are we neighbours to? The Samaritan was the neighbour to a Jew, someone who was considered an enemy, someone he was seeing for the first time and had no relationship with. This text encourages us to be concerned not only for our fellow believers but to become neighbours of and to all those who suffer violence in this world, including socio-environmental violence.

Rest for the Land and Respect for Life

When we turn to Leviticus 25:1–23 we encounter the first laws that Yahweh gave Israel with regards to its future life in the promised land. The land which will welcome the people of Israel is entitled to a year of sabbatical rest, and the crops are to be consumed not only by those who work the land, but also by orphans, widows, and foreigners. Even though it was God's people who would occupy the land, human reality meant that there will still be poor and vulnerable populations who needed to be cared for.

We seemed to have ignored this text from Leviticus. We have chosen to develop our cities and lifestyles with little concern for those who are most vulnerable, or the natural resources we depend upon. We create vulnerable populations, and then claim that they are the ones responsible due to their lack of effort.

God demands that we consider the land we are settled in, and the people we share this geographical space with. We need to find a more equitable lifestyle and care for future generations as "the land is mine; with me you are but aliens and tenants" (verse 23).

What Can We Do?

As many churches and believers have not made environmental issues a priority, there is the need to develop action focused ecological theologies. This involves reviewing our current theology and the role that creation plays, so that we can decide upon our future actions.

There already are churches that are making a difference in their local communities, both by participating in environmental initiatives set up by local governments or carrying out their own interventions to protect natural habitats. This involves getting to know local and regional contexts to determine what is happening and what can be done. As it is impossible to do everything, it is important to start with what is feasible, even if this is simply raising environmental awareness among friends and family.

My family background, my university studies, and my professional career have led me to live out my Christian faith with first-hand knowledge of many of Peru's socio-environmental problems. Seeing the pain that many in my country bear and the scars that creation carries means that social and environmental issues are particularly relevant for me. I believe that as Christians the time has come for action and to say, "No more!" – no more pillaging of God's creation, including human beings made in his image: no more assassinations of indigenous leaders: no more expropriation of indigenous lands: no more appropriation and theft of indigenous culture and its artefacts; no more subjugation of whole ethnic groups in the name of modernity.

Bendiciones,

Rut Pérez-Saldarriaga.

13. The Dawn of the Brazilian Missionary Movement
Felipe Fulanetto

Introduction

Brazil is unique among South American countries for many reasons, including its evangelical heritage. French Huguenot missionaries established in Brazil the first Protestant church in the whole Americas in 1557 and became the first martyrs in 1559.[1] Brazil has more evangelicals and sends more missionaries than all other South American countries put together.

The Brazilian evangelical church has grown exponentially in the last decades, from nine percent in 1991 to twenty-two percent in 2010.[2] In the present, projections estimate fifty-nine million evangelicals representing twenty-eight percent of the population.[3] Current growth suggests that evangelicals will make up half of the Brazilian population by 2035, while more conservative estimates suggest this will happen by 2050.[4] Brazil's missionary force has also grown so that the latest research carried out by the Brazilian Association of Transcultural Missions (AMTB) estimates fifteen thousand cross-cultural Brazilian missionaries.[5] This chapter explores the reasons for the growth of the Brazilian missionary movement, its present reality and potential for the future.

---

[1] J. Mordomo, 'Unleashing the Brazilian Missionary Force', in T. Steffen & M. Barnett (eds.), *Business as mission: From impoverished to empowered,* Evangelical Missiological Series 14, (Pasadena: William Carey Library, 2006), pp. 113–114.
[2] D. Mariani and S. Ducroquet, 'A expansão evangélica no Brasil em 26 anos', *Nexo Journal Homepage* available online at https://www.nexojornal.com.br/grafico/2017/11/06/A-expans%C3%A3o-evang%C3%A9lica-no-Brasil-em-26-anos, accessed 24 October 2019.
[3] A. Medeiros, *Relatório como ouvirão 2018* (João Pessoa: Missão Juvep, 2019), p.85.
[4] This calculation is based on present statistics and future projections. Current growth is of 4.45% a year compared to population growth of 1.07%. The conservative calculation brings the evangelical growth down to 3% a year.
[5] A. Menezes et al, *Força Missionária Brasileira Transcultural*, available online at http://www.amtb.org.br/wp-content/uploads/2020/04/Forc%CC%A7a-Missiona%CC%81ria-Brasileira-Completo.pdf, accessed 10 April 2021.

The Influence of International and National Congresses

Elben César divides the evangelisation of Brazil into three periods: Catholic missions in the sixteenth, seventeenth and eighteenth centuries; Protestant missions in the nineteenth century and Pentecostal missions in the twentieth century.[6] Rather than discuss missionary arrival and evangelical growth,[7] our focus is on the different factors that stimulated the emergence of a missionary movement in Brazil, starting with some national and international congresses.

International Congresses

William Carey hoped for a global missionary conference to be held in Cape Town in 1810 with representatives from the whole world.[8] Although there were six significant meetings between 1810 and 1910, Carey's vision was only fulfilled a hundred years later, in Edinburgh, through one of the most important conferences in Christian history.

The 1910 World Missionary Conference is one of the most important conferences in Christian history and became a catalyst for the ecumenical movement which led to the formation of the World Council of Churches. However, its attempts to develop a strategic plan for cooperation in global evangelisation were contradictory and controversial. Only Africa and Asia were regarded as mission fields, excluding North America, Europe, and Latin America, despite the latter's importance for the global missionary movement. The conference lacked diversity as most participants were white, Protestant Anglo-American men, without any black Africans, only seventeen Asians and no Latin Americans. Despite these contradictions and the triumphalism of believing that the whole world would soon be Christianised, the conference is important, not so much for the proceedings themselves but their aftermath.[9]

---

[6] E. César, *História da Evangelização do Brasil: dos jesuítas aos neopentecostais* (Viçosa: Ultimato, 2000), pp. 14–15

[7] For further details see P. Sipierski, 'Missionários protestantes estrangeiros no brasil: dos primórdios ao Congresso do Panamá' in T. Carriker (ed.), *Missões e a Igreja Brasileira: Perspectivas Históricas*, São Paulo: Editora Mundo Cristão, 1993, C. Caldas, *O último missionário* (São Paulo: Mundo Cristão, 2001), pp. 20–24, F. Shalkwij, 'Índios evangélicos no Brasil Holandês' in Carriker, *Missões e a Igreja Brasileira,* and E. Smither, 'The impact of evangelical revivals on global mission: The case of North American evangelicals in Brazil in the nineteenth and twentieth centuries', *Verbum et Ecclesia* 31:1, 2010 .

[8] A.Yeh, *Polycentric Missiology: twenty-first-century mission from everyone to everywhere* (Downers Grove: IVP, 2016), pp. 7–33 and pp. 124–127. The six conferences took place in New York (1854, 1900) London (1854,1878, 1888) and Liverpool (1860).

[9] D. Bosch, *Missão Transformadora: Mudanças de Paradigma na Teologia da Missão* (São Leopoldo: Sinodal, 2002), p. 25, pp. 403–409 and A. Yeh, 'O futuro de missões é de todos para todos os lugares', *Análise Global de Lausanne* 7.1 (2018), available at www.lausanne.org/pt-br/recursos-multimidia-pt-br/agl-pt-br/2018-01-pt-br/o-futuro-de-missoes-e-de-todos-para-todos-os-lugare accessed 25 October 2019.

Dismay at the exclusion of Latin America led some participants to meet during and after the conference and decide to organise the Christian Action in Latin America Congress in Panama, in 1916 which placed Latin America on the radar of many denominational and interdenominational agencies. Although two hundred and thirty delegates attended Panama 1916, only twenty-one were Latin Americans including three Brazilian Presbyterians, Eduardo Carlos Pereira, Álvaro Reis, and Erasmo Braga. Delegates were united in believing that Edinburgh 1910 represented Protestant abandonment of the continent and encouraged the organisation of a series of congresses after Panama 1916.[10] This resulted in greater evangelical investment of money, persons, and structure in Latin America so that while there already were missionaries in Brazil in the nineteenth century, Panama 1916 led to a significant growth in the numbers sent.[11]

The Latin American Evangelisation Congresses (CLADE) were an important catalyst for the Brazilian Missionary Movement. The first congress was organised by the Billy Graham Evangelistic Association seeking to create an evangelical counterpart to the ecumenical movement represented by the Latin American Council of Churches (CLAI).[12] North American domination proved controversial and in response Latin American theologians gathered and founded the Latin American Theological Fraternity (FTL) in 1970, seeking to escape foreign control. The FTL organised the next conferences: CLADE II (1979 in Peru), CLADE III (1992 in Ecuador), CLADE IV (2000 in Ecuador) and CLADE V (2012 in Costa Rica). The first conversations on integral mission theology took place during CLADE I and were nurtured through the FTL.

The emergence of integral mission theology allowed Samuel Escobar and René Padilla, with the encouragement of John Stott, to raise the issue of the relationship between evangelism and social action at Lausanne 74 and include the social responsibility of the church in the Lausanne Pact.[13] Consequently, the 1974 International Congress for World Evangelisation, known as the Lausanne Movement, or just Lausanne, is one of the most influential on the Brazilian Missionary Movement. The Lausanne Covenant of 1974 and the Cape Town Commitment of 2014 have acquired a creedal status for many churches and missionary organisations in Brazil so that Brazilian missionary practice is shaped by integral mission theology, seeking to unite preaching and social action.[14]

The missiological and theological thinking emerging from the Lausanne and Cape Town congresses, and the tools, strategies and books published have also

---

[10] S. Tunes, *O Pregador Silencioso: Ecumenismo no jornal Expositor Cristão (1886 a 1982)* (São Bernardo: Universidade Metodista, 2009), p. 73.
[11] V. Steuernagel, *Obediência Missionária e Prática Histórica: em busca de modelos* (São Paulo: ABU, 1993), pp. 14–15.
[12] L. Longuini Neto, *O Novo Rosto da Missão os movimentos ecumênico e evangelical no protestantismo latino-americano* (Viçosa: Ultimato, 2002), pp. 153–180.
[13] Yeh, *Polycentric Missiology*, pp. 205–207.
[14] Smither, 'The impact of evangelical revivals on global missions.'

been significant. Many Brazilians have participated in events promoted by the Lausanne Movement, and have brought with them the new ideas and impetus promoted at these events.

National Congresses

Inspired by Lausanne 74 the Brazilian branch of the International Fellowship of Evangelical Students (ABUB) promoted a missionary congress in Curitiba in 1976, with the theme "Jesus Christ: Lordship, Purpose and Mission".[15] René Padilla and Samuel Escobar, who worked with the Latin American student movement, helped organise this conference, which was attended by over six hundred students, professionals, and pastors. The congress produced the Curitiba covenant, clearly influenced by the Lausanne covenant, and started the process of seeing Brazil as a sending country. Missiological thinking in Brazil was thus moving away from the single centre perspective of Edinburgh 1910 to a new polycentric reality, with mission being considered from everywhere to everywhere.

The subsequent Brazilian Evangelisation Congress (CBE) in Belo Horizonte in 1983 and the North-eastern Evangelisation Congress in 1988 helped contextualise the Lausanne Covenant's vision in Brazil and encourage sharing the gospel with all peoples.[16] Other important events include the four congresses promoted by COMIBAM (Iberian-American Missionary Cooperation) which cover Latin America, Portugal, and Spain. Eight hundred Brazilians attended the first congress in São Paulo in 1987 which encouraged churches, denominations, and interdenominational missionary agencies to develop a new vision towards reaching unreached peoples, both within and outside of Brazil.[17]

Luis Bush, who was President of COMIBAM, expressed this new polycentric attitude to mission, "in 1916, Latin America was declared a mission field. Now, in 1987, Latin America declares itself a mission force."[18] For Girón this is a "change of paradigm" from an attitude of dependence towards seeking to send missionaries.[19]

The CBE congress in 1983 and COMIBAM 87 encouraged the Brazilian Transcultural Missions Association (AMTB) to organise Brazilian Missionary

---

[15] Steuernagel, *Obediência Missionária e Prática Histórica*, p. 5.
[16] Longuini Neto, *O Novo Rosto da Missão*, pp. 77–78.
[17] O. Prado, 'The Brazil Model', *AD 2000 Homepage,* available at www.ad2000.org/gcowe95/prado.html accessed 28 October 2019. LB Ekström, *Aos Que Ainda Não Ouviram: desafios missionários rumo ao século XXI* (São Paulo: Sepal, 1998), p.89.
[18] Quoted in R. Girón, 'Desafíos contextuales y generacionales en la misión del siglo XXI', paper presented at the IV Congreso Misionero Iberoamericano COMIBAM 2017.
[19] Girón, 'Desafíos contextuales y generacionales en la misión del siglo XXI'.

Congresses (CBM).[20] The first Congress took place in 1993 in Caxambu with approximately a thousand participants and a hundred and two denominations represented.[21] This is now the main Brazilian interdenominational missionary event and eight congresses have been held in 1993, 1998, 2001, 2005, 2008, 2011, 2014 and 2017. They are currently held every three years with the 2020 congress being postponed due to the Covid-19 pandemic. The influence of the Congress can be seen in the increase of a hundred and fifty percent in the publication of mission related books during the years when the Congress is held.

Our focus has been on the events which have had the greatest interdenominational impact, although there have also been dozens of other events with a strong impact on specific denominations and individuals. These conferences and congresses do not represent the totality of the missionary movement but are of a celebration of what has been happening in different ministries. Many churches may not even be aware of these expensive events, yet their results become visible and influential with time, as can be seen with the first church council in Acts 15 and others throughout the history of the church such as Nicaea and Chalcedon.

Missionary Organisations

Writing in 1998 Bertil Ekström divided the history of mission from Brazil in two stages, through denominational structures between 1900 and 1950 and since then through interdenominational agencies.[22] A new structure, not predicted by Ekström, has emerged since the start of the twenty-first century: mission through both denominational and interdenominational institutions.

The first mission organisation to be formed in Brazil was the Brazilian Baptist World Missions Board, in 1908, which immediately started to financially support Portuguese missionaries. However, only in 1925 did the Board commission the first Brazilian missionary to Portugal and Aquiles Barbosa and new missionaries were sent in 1927, 1933 and 1937.[23] The Brazilian Presbyterian church sent a family of Portuguese nationals as missionaries in 1910. The National Mixed Missions Board was founded in 1940 and in 1944 three Brazilian missionaries were sent to Portugal.[24]

The first interdenominational agency, the Caiuá Evangelical Mission, was founded in 1928. It continues to work among indigenous peoples as does the Amazonian Evangelical Mission set up in 1948. From 1950 there is a dramatic

---

[20] LB Ekström, *Uma Análise Histórica dos Objetivos da Associação de Missões Transculturais Brasileiras e o seu Cumprimento* (São Paulo, Faculdade Teológica Batista De São Paulo, 1998), p. 5.
[21] Ekström, *Aos Que Ainda Não Ouviram*, p. 90.
[22] Ekström, *Uma Análise Histórica*, pp. 10–12.
[23] Ekström, *Uma Análise Histórica*, p. 11.
[24] R. Tucker, *Missões até os confins da terra: uma história biográfica* (São Paulo: Shedd, 2010), pp. 603–605.

growth in the emergence of new mission agencies, so that there are currently two hundred and fifty active missionary agencies recorded, not including many more of which we are unaware.[25] Until the 1970s these were mainly international agencies, led by foreigners, but from then onwards many new Brazilian missionary agencies emerged and many of the international agencies came under national leadership. This process was accompanied by church growth and an increase in the numbers of missionaries sent. For decades, interdenominational mission agencies had the missiological know-how and the decision-making power and were thus the main protagonists in mobilising, training, and sending missionaries through the Brazilian church.

The AMTB, although not itself an agency, has played a significant role as a catalyst for this missionary movement, promoting unity among missionary agencies in Brazil. Its roots are in a series of informal meetings in 1976 sponsored by *Missão Informadora do Brasil* (MIB). Subsequent meetings in 1977, 1978, 1980 and 1981 led to its official foundation in 1982. These meetings sought to bring mission leaders together to support one another, provide a forum to discuss common themes and maintain a spirit of cooperation.[26] AMTB continues to promote alliances and research throughout Brazil and currently has seven active departments and eighty-five affiliate organisations which represent twenty-five percent of the Brazilian missionary force.[27]

Nonetheless, in recent decades there has been a resurgence of denominational organizations. In various denominations, such as the Assemblies of God, The Foursquare Gospel Church, Charismatic Baptists, Charismatic Presbyterians, Wesleyans, and Nazarenes there is a trend towards opening or reorganizing agencies and taking control of work they had previously delegated to interdenominational agencies.

My own experience indicates that denominations are increasingly supporting their own projects and missionaries, meaning that they are unlikely to support those who are not part of their organization. This means that interdenominational agencies have experienced a loss of financial and human resources, leading to tension between organisations. This indicates that it is necessary to adapt to a new missiological and ecclesiastical paradigm, as we are no longer in the period where denominational agencies dominated (1900–1950) nor when interdenominational agencies were the protagonists (1950–200) but in a period where both types of agencies are active. Thus, the path forward is one of strategic partnerships, seeking unity between denominational and interdenominational agencies according to the requirements of each specific mission field. If not, both types of agencies will struggle to maintain themselves and continue their ministry.

---

[25] Menezes et al, *Força Missionária Brasileira Transcultural*, p. 21.
[26] Ekström, *Uma Análise Histórica*, p. 2.
[27] Menezes et al, *Força Missionária Brasileira Transcultural*, p. 21.

The Current Brazilian Missionary Force

This historical background allows us to better understand the Brazilian Missionary Movement in the present. This section is based on the most recent data presented by the Research Department of the AMTB and presented at the VII Brazilian Mission Congress in 2017.[28]

Two terms need to be clearly defined, "evangelical" and "missionary". We are following the Brazilian custom of treating the terms evangelical and Protestant as synonymous. The Brazilian evangelical field can be divided into three groups, 1) traditional churches such as Baptists, Presbyterians, and Methodists; 2) Pentecostals and 3) Neo-Pentecostals. The latter group refers to churches of Brazilian origin which started to emerge in the 1970s. They place a considerable stress on prosperity theology, deliverance ministries and healing. They tend to work independently of other churches and have poor relationships with other denominations.[29] Thus, for strategic and theological reasons they have not been included in this research.

The importance of defining the term "missionary" is illustrated in different estimates of the Brazilian missionary force in 2010 by Patrick Johnstone and Todd Johnson. Patrick Johnstone only counts Protestants, independents and Anglicans sent by churches and agencies, and estimates three and a half thousand missionaries.[30] Todd Johnson adopts a wider definition which includes Catholics, Orthodox and other groups and those Brazilians who have migrated for missionary purposes, independent of any church or agency. This leads to a much higher estimate at thirty-four thousand.[31]

This chapter distinguishes between three different categories of missionaries: 1) those sent by denominational or interdenominational agencies; 2) those sent by local churches with no link to agencies and independent missionaries; 3) and those with no link to agencies or local churches.[32] It counts Brazilian nationals in transcultural missionary situations, that is working in Brazil or overseas among ethnic groups which are not their own. These include those working

---

[28] Menezes et al, *Força Missionária Brasileira Transcultural*.
[29] Arguably the most well-known overseas is the Universal Church of the Kingdom of God (Igreja Universal do Reino de Deus) other churches include the Igreja Internacional da Graça de Deus, Igreja Renascer em Cristo, Comunidade Evangélica Sara Nossa Terra and Igreja do Poder de Deus.
[30] P. Johnstone, *O Futuro da Igreja Global*, (São Paulo: Cultura Cristã, 2017), pp. 225–233.
[31] T. Johnson and S. Lee, 'Da cristandade ocidental ao cristianismo mundial', in R. Winter, S. Hawthorne and S. K. Bradford, *Perspectivas no Movimento Cristão Mundial*, (São Paulo: Vida Nova, 2009), pp. 260–263. In private communication Johnson suggests that using Johnstone's leads to an estimate of nine thousand missionaries.
[32] In comparison, Moon only includes the first category of mission to estimate twenty thousand South Korean missionaries in 2013. S. Moon, *The Korean Missionary Movement: Dynamics and Trends, 1988-2013* (Pasadena: William Carey Library, 2016), p. XVII–XXIII.

among indigenous peoples, riverside communities,[33] travellers, *quilombolas,*[34] deaf persons, immigrants, refugees, and hippies. We only counted missionaries from traditional Protestant and Pentecostal churches, not including Neo-Pentecostals, Catholics, Orthodox Anglicans, other groups, or immigrants.

Research took place in three stages over a two-year period. Data was collected through interviews employing a mixture of quantitative and qualitative approaches. Over seventy percent of the data came from primary sources, those active in missions. Less than thirty percent came from trustworthy sources which are aware of missionary activities without directly participating in them. Over the three stages we acquired two thousand items of information referring to organisations, missionaries and missiological approaches. Overall, we identified two hundred and fifty missionary organisations active in Brazil or overseas. One hundred and thirty-six took part in the research and five hundred and ninety-four missionaries answered the full questionnaire. The final tally was a total of fifteen thousand transcultural Brazilian missionaries at work in Brazil and overseas.

The Profile of Brazilian Missionaries

The average age of missionaries is thirty-nine with fifty-two percent being women. Seventy percent are married, and fifty-five percent have at least one child, with the birth rate being 1.98 children per couple. Twenty-seven percent are single, of which nearly four out of five are women. Divorced and widowed individuals make up two percent and one percent of the missionary force, respectively.

Thirty-five percent have no university education, and three and a half percent only finished primary school. Just over a quarter of missionaries have postgraduate studies, and one in fifty have completed their doctoral studies. Eleven percent affirm that they received no missionary training before being sent into the field. The average term of service is ten years, with approximately half of the missionaries serving in Brazil and the rest overseas.

Twenty-two percent work among indigenous peoples, twenty-one percent among Muslims, ten percent among secularists, ten percent among animists, six percent among traditional African religions, five percent among Buddhists, five percent among Hindus, two percent among travellers and two percent among Catholics.

Missionaries are involved in a variety of ministries, and individual missionaries often participate in more than one ministry with nearly a quarter are linked with more than one missionary agency. The most popular ministries are evangelism (41.2%) and church planting and renewal (37.7%). Other significant

---

[33] This is a traditional Brazilian people group being a mixture of indigenous peoples and descendants of Portuguese and slaves, who live by the side of rivers and survive off fishing, having their own distinct culture.

[34] Descendants of African slaves who developed their own distinctive culture in refuges, distant from urban centres.

ministries include administration (30.3%), social action (26.7%), mobilisation (24.5%) theological education (24.5%), church leadership (15.3%), Bible translation (9.9%), missionary support (9,9%), and professionals in mission (8.2%).

The Profile of Missionary Organisations

The fact that sixty-nine percent of the organisations participating in the research were founded between 1981 to 2016 reflects the recent growth of Brazilian evangelicalism and its missionary force. The average age of their leadership was just under forty-six with forty-five percent of organisations having an equal number of men and women leaders, forty-four percent having a majority of male leaders and eleven percent having a majority of female leaders.

Although most Brazilian evangelicals are Pentecostal in their theology, only thirteen percent of agencies were Pentecostal, with twenty percent being independent and fifty-eight percent traditional. Eighty-three percent were interdenominational, fourteen percent denominational, one percent based in a local church and one percent set up as NGOs.

Nearly nine in ten organisations offered missionary training. Fifty-five percent prioritised training before departure to the mission field, seventy-one percent during service and twenty-six percent upon return. Most training focuses on missiology (76.3%), teamwork, (69.7%) and theology (50%). Less than four in ten agencies offer anthropological training and less than three, linguistic training, a deficit which recent research indicates impacts missionary effectiveness.[35]

Seventy-six missionary organisations sent in a financial report. They had an average yearly turnover of eighty million reais, with most funds coming from local churches and personal offerings. Less than four percent of funds came from overseas, confirming that the Brazilian missionary movement is financially independent of foreign funds. This self-sustainability is confirmed by the fact that while the financial crisis of 2016–2017 led to fundraising difficulties only one percent of missionaries were forced to return from the mission field ahead of schedule.[36] Approximately a quarter of funds was spent on administrative expenses, thirty-four percent on supporting missionaries overseas and forty-six percent on missionaries in Brazil.

Organisations consider their main difficulties finance (65.8%) and missionary recruitment (40.7%), although one area of further concern is that over half of the agencies with missionaries working in vulnerable situations had no evacuation plan.

---

[35] L. de Carvalho, *Fortalezas e debilidades do movimento missionário ibero-americano: Fase II. 2015-2016* (São Paulo: Comibam, 2016), p.14.
[36] D. Pereira, *Resultado da Pesquisa Arrecadação de Agências Missionárias* (São Paulo, Sepal & AMTB, 2019), p. 8.

Reflecting on the Present and Future

Annual Growth Rate

Reflecting on the annual growth rate of the Brazilian missionary movement requires taking into consideration the diverse methodologies employed by the different surveys of this movement. Research coordinated by Larry Kraft and Ted Limpic in 1989, 1996 and 2006, identified 1,360, 1,794 and 3,500 transcultural missionaries, respectively. AMTB's research from 2017 estimates fifteen thousand transcultural missionaries but includes missionaries with no connection to missionary agencies, such as those sent by local churches, who were not counted by Kraft and Limpic.

If we adopt a similar methodology as Kraft and Limpic, we reach an estimate of 8,299 missionaries. This means that annual growth between 1989 to 2017 was close to seven percent, with four percent between 1989 and 1996, seven percent between 1996 and 2006 and eight percent between 2006 and 2017. This overall growth is higher than the growth of the Brazilian evangelical church in this period (5.8%) and that of the Brazilian population (1.58%).

This sustained growth confirms Robert Harvey's hope, in the 1960s, that Brazil could become a missionary powerhouse.[37] Nonetheless, we are still far from reaching our full potential and it is uncertain whether the Brazilian church is ready to support the continuation of this growth. Even if future growth reduces to five percent a year, this projects thirty thousand missionaries by 2030. However, the average Brazilian Christian only contributes two reais a month to missions so that it takes approximately four thousand Brazilian evangelicals and thirteen churches to send a single missionary. Current areas of concern, such as the lack of adequate training, poor pastoral support for single missionaries, especially women, lack of support for children in the mission field, lack of effective policies for missionaries in vulnerable contexts and lack of effective support for missionaries returning from the mission field, will only increase with the continued growth in the number of missionaries.

Financial Issues

Brazil's economy became the sixth largest in the world in 2014, following a period of sustained exponential growth in the last few decades. Many Brazilians were thus able to buy their own house, a car, and many consumer goods. Nonetheless, Brazil continues to suffer from social inequality, especially in urban centres. This is reflected in the Brazilian church which has become rich and powerful, but with considerable financial differences between churches. Brazil has large mega-churches, with thousands of members and a monthly turnover of millions of reais while there are also hundreds of small churches in rented buildings and difficulties in supporting a full-time pastor.

---

[37] See Ekström, *Uma Análise Histórica,* pp. 15–16.

Adequate missionary support is correlated with remaining on the mission field.³⁸ Yet, as we have seen, the average Brazilian evangelical contributes less than two reais a month to mission so that we still depend on the widow's mite to engage in world evangelisation. Consequently, mission training centres and agencies indicate that their main difficulty is the lack of money.³⁹

New sending countries have yet to awaken to the need of developing a dynamic culture of offering for mission as can be seen in countries with centuries of missionary experience such as the United States, England, and Germany. While Brazil is ahead of most other Christian majority world countries in this area, there is still much to do.

Another important factor is the difficulty in raising support for missionaries with a more strategic role and those located at the home base. As they are not on the front line of evangelisation and church planting, there is less emotional appeal in raising their support as in the reductionist Brazilian perspective they are not real missionaries. Nonetheless, paradoxically, despite the financial difficulties involved in sending Brazilian missionaries, the reasons for premature return are not linked to lack of support.⁴⁰ Increasingly, we are facing the new reality of the return of retired missionaries to Brazil, who need to be relocated and supported. As a country still new to sending missionaries, we are still learning to deal with missionaries who are no longer active.

While the Brazilian church has left behind the paternalistic process of dependence on foreign finance, nonetheless, missionary support mainly comes from friends and family, rather than churches and organisations.⁴¹ Thus, we desire to see a church committed not only to preaching the gospel but supporting missionaries.

Poor Usage of Missionary Training Centres

Research carried out by AMTB's Missiological Education Department discovered that mission training centres had a yearly average of fourteen students. As there are fifteen thousand transcultural missionaries and more than fifty million evangelical Christians in the country, this indicates poor usage of missionary training centres.

Many large centres, able to receive hundreds of students, have little more than ten students. In private conversations course coordinators confide their difficulties in recruiting students and keeping their programmes sustainable. These centres generally employ ancient and obsolete systems, often the same as

---

[38] R. Hay et al, *Dignos de Cuidados: perspectivas globais na melhor prática de retenção missionária*, (Londrina: Descoberta, 2008), p.489.
[39] Menezes et al, *Força Missionária Brasileira Transcultural* and Pereira, *Resultado da Pesquisa Arrecadação de Agências*.
[40] Pereira, *Resultado da Pesquisa Arrecadação de Agências*.
[41] Menezes et al, *Força Missionária Brasileira Transcultural* and Pereira, *Resultado da Pesquisa Arrecadação de Agências*.

was thirty years ago. Even in a conference held in 2018, training centres showed little openness towards distance learning or hybrid methods which mix on-site and off-site learning. Possibly one advantage of the Covid-19 pandemic has been to force training centres to update and reinvent their teaching methods, otherwise they would be destined to continue to be insignificant.

The Least Evangelised Sectors

God desires that all peoples know and worship his name. Seven thousand of the thirteen thousand ethnolinguistic groups remain unreached, and in Brazil, we have seven least evangelised groups which require church attention.

1. Indigenous groups are scattered across the nation in forests and urban centres: currently there are nine hundred thousand indigenous Brazilians, divided in two hundred and twenty-eight officially recognised ethnic groups of which close to one hundred and fifteen have little or no knowledge of Jesus Christ.
2. Thirty-seven thousand communities located on the riversides in the Amazon basin: about ten thousand have no evangelical church.
3. Travellers, especially those of the Calon ethnicity: there are approximately a million Calon in Brazil, and less than one percent are Christians. Cultural and linguistic difficulties, and the prejudice displayed by Brazilian society have led to obstacles in their evangelisation. There are also nomadic, semi-nomadic and sedentary travelling communities which makes research and access to preach the gospel more complex.
4. *Sertanejos,* those who live in the remote zones of the semi-arid region in the Northeast of Brazil: despite the advance of the gospel in this region, there are still more than six thousand communities without an evangelical presence.
5. *Quilombos,* Afro-Brazilian communities which have been organised in the last two hundred years: There are approximately five thousand such communities in Brazil of which two thousand do not have an evangelical church.
6. Immigrants in Brazil, estimated at seven hundred and fifty thousand: these include Venezuelans, Cubans, Chinese, Haitians, Congolese, Syrians, and Bengalis. Many come from countries which are closed to the gospel and have their first opportunity to hear about Christ in Brazil.
7. Deaf or hearing-impaired Brazilians: this community has its own way of understanding the world and most churches are not prepared to communicate with them. There are less than one percent of believers among the ten million deaf persons in Brazil, and few ministries dedicated to this segment.

Increased Polarisation

The power of sin means that life in this world is characterised by tensions and contradictions in human relationships with God, creation, and one another.

Through God's grace, the Holy Spirit is present and active restoring these relationships. Nonetheless, we are not fully in the new creation and continue to express these tensions as can be seen in the high levels of polarisation experienced in Brazilian society and the church.

The Brazilian church has always faced theological polarisation but the impeachment of President Dilma Rousseff in 2015 led to an increase in political discussions, infecting churches with ideological debates. Churches have been divided along political and ideological lines a reality which has affected the frontline of missions.

The current context is one in which missiological debates become emotionally charged and intense. Even when these debates are illogical and lack theological foundations, they have become a part of everyday mission work. Polarisation surrounds topics such as: mission in Brazil or mission overseas; urban missions or transcultural missions; missions or evangelism; missions among the poor or business as mission; short term or long term; and preaching or social action.

One area of significant polarisation lies in the relationship between interdenominational agencies and the newly resurgent denominational agencies. To make matters even more complex, mega-churches are sending their own missionaries with no links to any agency. The reliance of interdenominational agencies on finances and human resources from churches contributes to increasing tensions. Nonetheless, rather than the end of interdenominational agencies this new situation is an opportunity for their reinvention, forging strategic partnerships with churches and denominational agencies, according to the specific needs of different mission fields. Although it is possible to find examples of unity and partnership, denominational and interdenominational agencies will struggle to support themselves and be effective without a deliberate effort to work together.

Balance between Missional and Missionary Church

The concept of a missional church presented by Darrel L. Guder in his 1998 book, *Missional Church* led to an effervescent discussion and many publications.[42] This North American concept was imported to Brazil without critical reflection, often creating more confusion than clarity especially when pastors exploit the concept of a missional church to justify their churches limiting their focus to their local contexts. However, the apostolic and pastoral responsibilities of the church are not in competition and they should work together in a cohesive and symmetric fashion. Correctly defined, a missional church is one that is both relevant in its own society and concerned with global

---

[42] D. Guder (ed.), *Missional Church: A vision for the sending of the church in North America* (Grand Rapids: Eerdmans, 1998).

missionary needs.[43] Thus, every church faces the challenge of being both missional and missionary.

The Danger of Excessive Professionalisation

The Brazilian missionary movement is full of inspirational stories of men and women who have dedicated their lives to the gospel in the face of catastrophic situations and a chronic lack of resources. Most missionaries sent in the 70s, 80s and 90s were simple people with little education who became heroes of the faith through their love for Christ.

The economic and numerical growth of Brazilian churches has changed the profile of missionaries sent and the circumstances they face. Most have access to secular studies and training. They have access to tools which previous missionaries could not even imagine. While this is all beneficial, we are in danger of being a generation with much knowledge of missions but with little practical achievement. We have well prepared missionaries who give up in adverse situations. Brazil faces a real danger of specialist and professional missionaries who lack evangelistic fervour, financial sacrifice, and long-term vision. I believe that unreached peoples will remain ignored if Christians continue to be unwilling to go to the farthest and most difficult places where these persons are located.

Develop Self-Critical Missiological Thinking

The Brazilian church has grown in numbers, strength, wealth, and knowledge. The number of missionaries we send is higher than the number we receive. This growth has accompanied Brazil's economic growth and exceeded our numerical growth. This reveals that we are progressing towards theological, ecclesiastical and missiological maturity.

Mordomo's claim that there is no Brazilian missiology,[44] must be weighed against the increasing number of missiological articles and books being published. There are already over four hundred missiological books published by Brazilians such as Analzira Nascimento, Antonia Leonora Van Der Meer, Bertil Ekström, David Mesquiati, Jairo de Oliveira, Marcos Amado, Roberto Zwetsch, Ronaldo Lidório and Valdir Steuernagel. There is also a substantial body of literature by foreign authors immersed in Brazilian culture such as Alicia Bausch Macedo, Bárbara Burns, Timoteo Carriker, Russell Shedd, Sherron George and others. Brazil already has many evangelical missiological and anthropological research centres and academic institutions offering masters and doctoral programmes in missiology. As Yeh indicates, missiology is not limited to academic research and books, and Brazil is rich in missiological thinking in the form of music, arts, preaching and congresses.[45]

---

[43] M. Goheen, *A Igreja Missional na Bíblia: luz para as nações* (São Paulo: Vida Nova, 2014)
[44] Mordomo, 'Unleashing the Brazilian Missionary Force', p. 227.
[45] Yeh, *Polycentric Missiology*, p. 209.

What is required, to become fully self-theologising,[46] is more systematic, academic, investigation of mission from a Brazilian perspective. It is important to study theology from the perspective of different cultures, and therefore to investigate how different countries understand mission.[47] While we agree with Justo González's desire that majority world theologians take the leadership in mission and theology,[48] Brazilians should not exploit this change in circumstances to suggest the superiority of Brazilian theology and missiology. Rather we should search for a truly polycentric missiology which reflects the beauty of the global community. Contextual studies are an essential steppingstone in developing a theology of mission for the whole church.[49]

It is important to emphasise that a Brazilian missiology will be different from a more regional Latin American missiology. Outsiders often make the mistake of assuming that all Latin Americans are culturally similar, but there are significant differences between countries and their cultures, and in each country, evangelical churches have their own specific characteristics. Thus, we believe it is necessary to develop a missiology which can be applied in each country, in a polycentric perspective.

The Need to Think of the New Generation

Changes of paradigms and generations cause unavoidable conflicts and tensions, yet as people come and go, it is necessary to make some concluding comments on the need for new voices in mission.

In Brazil we are facing a pastoral generational gap. In the past, most seminary students began their studies at about eighteen and started their first pastorate at twenty-two. Many are still ministering today, after thirty, forty or fifty years of serving the Lord. It was also common to see pastors' sons following their fathers into ministry. However, the current situation is different. The average age of a seminary student is between thirty and forty and very few sons are following in their fathers' footsteps. For this reason, many denominations are seeking ways to mobilise, care for and prepare new pastors.

The missionary movement is not quite in this same state, but sadly we are not far away. Between 2000 and 2010 a generational gap emerged, with little

---

[46] According to criteria suggested in P. Hiebert, *O Evangelho e a Diversidade das Culturas: um guia de antropologia missionária,*(São Paulo: Vida Nova, 2010), p.15 and Bosch, *Missão Transformadora*.
[47] So W. Dryness, *Learning about Theology from the Third World* (Grand Rapids: Zondervan, 1990), p. 86. For example, Verkuyl explores how mission is understood in Germany, Holland, England, the United States and others in his 1978 book *Contemporary Missiology*. Nonetheless, he only dedicates one paragraph to Brazil, possibly a consequence of the lack of reflection at that time. J. Verkuyl, *Contemporary Missiology: An Introduction* (Grand Rapids: Wm. B. Eerdmans 1978), p. 86.
[48] J., González, *Historia del Cristianismo: obra completa* (Miami: Editorial Unilit, 2009), p. 558.
[49] Bosch, *Missão Transformadora*, p. 592.

investment in new young leaders. However, God has been gracious and recently we have seen deliberate and cooperative actions to raise a new generation committed to mission. We can point to the Vocare movement which is mobilising young people to understand their vocation, and many are now serving as leaders of missionary organisations. In 2019 the Send event took place in Brazil, gathering one hundred and fifty thousand youth in stadiums where they were exhorted to preach the gospel to all nations, with various missionary organisations promoting follow up events. We have much to improve upon, but it is encouraging to see what has happened and what God is doing.

Conclusion

Although Brazil does not have the same ethnic and populational complexity we observe in China and India, there are similar challenges in understanding a missionary movement emerging in a country with continental dimensions and high statistical numbers. We praise the Lord for the perseverance of transcultural interdenominational agencies in the expansion of missionary work and in sharing knowhow with new initiatives. We praise the Lord for the strong involvement of denominational boards in missionary work, leading to a wave of mobilisation, training and sending of missionaries. We praise the Lord for the strategic alliances uniting churches and agencies working on behalf of the kingdom among minority groups and for the new missionary mobilisation movements such as *Perspectivas, Povos & Línguas,* Vocare and others. We praise the Lord for those in the mission field, those pastors who support missions and those thinkers engaging in missiological reflection. We praise the Lord for increasing opportunities for specialised preparation in mission, the increasing numbers of those praying for mission and, above all, the marvellous grace of Christ.

The Brazilian missionary movement proceeds with the hope and the faith that God is in control of all things, and we do not want to be outside of what he is doing in the world. Brazilian missionaries are in all continents, part of a polycentric movement proclaiming Jesus to unreached, disengaged and frontier peoples. Thus, the Brazilian missionary movement is certainly marching on!

14. Do Christians Have a Place at the Table for Muhammed? Separating the "Muhammed of Faith" from the "Muhammed of History"

Marcos Amado

A Muslim asked a Christian missionary, living among them for many years, if the Christian believed in the Koran and in Muhammed. He thought for a while, asked God for wisdom and replied, "if I believed in the Koran and in Muhammed, I would be a Muslim. As I am a Christian, I believe in the Bible and in Jesus." His questioner accepted the answer, and this allowed the dialogue to continue.

This missionary could have chosen a more tortuous path, but instead of attacking either the Koran or Muhammed, preferred to affirm his confidence in the Bible and in Jesus. He thus avoided two possible extreme positions frequently seen among Christians, including leaders, when the subject is Muhammed or the Koran: Islamophobia or Islamophilia.

Both Muhammed and Jesus are important for Muslims. At an international conference about Christian work among Muslims, a missionary shared a question that is often asked "we, Muslims, have a place at the table for Jesus. Do Christians have a place at the table for Muhammed?" When Muslims affirm that they "have a place at the table for Jesus", they are referring to the fact that Islam considers Jesus a prophet sent by God. Can we, therefore, do the same for Muhammed?

As evangelicals we believe that Jesus is the only way to the Father, and that outside of him there is neither salvation nor eternal life with God. We believe that the Bible is the only book truly inspired by God. We understand also that we cannot accept any gospel different from that revealed by our Lord Jesus. Yet Muhammed presented a gospel without the death and resurrection of Jesus. Therefore, we cannot accept Muhammed as a prophet sent by God, nor that the Koran is part of God's special revelation. Nonetheless, we should also try to discern through the lenses of the New Testament and Jesus' example, what our attitude should be towards Muhammed, the Koran and Islam. I have suggested elsewhere that it should be possible for Christians to regard Muhammed as:

A man who was a child of his own age who during his youth but also his adult life, had contact with Jews and Christians, heard their religious stories and who despite his imperfections, believed (mistakenly) that he had the divine mission to preach to the Arabs, who did not yet have the Holy Scriptures in their own language, that which already had been revealed to Jews and Christians.[1]

Many Brazilian evangelicals would probably react negatively to this suggestion. After all, we have learnt that Muhammed was violent and merciless, a false prophet influenced by evil spirits whose life and words, registered in rich detail in the Koran, inspire violent atrocities across the world.

Muhammed, the Imposter?

Various Christian scholars affirm this perspective. Since the 1970s Don Richardson, a well-known missionary and author, has released books inspiring millions of Christians across the world with their "redemptive analogies".[2] In 2003, in a sudden shift of focus, he wrote *Secrets of the Koran,* which he declares is solely based on the Koran. Richardson invites the reader to question if in truth we are talking about a book of peace or Muhammed's *Mein Kampf*.[3]

Richardson suggests that the violent verses declared by Muhammed need to be analysed according to their context, and that the events described need to be confirmed by Muslim sources.[4] According to Richardson, Muhammed caused a mini genocide, annihilating the Jews living in the city of Medina who resisted his supposedly prophetic message. At Medina Muhammed was little more than "the leader of a community of thieves, who were unwilling to earn their living honestly."[5] He enslaved girls and women, keeping some for himself and giving others to his followers, promoted female circumcision, authorised the cruel assassination of pagan Arabs in Mecca, consented to the death of poets who did not accept his leadership and forced women to become his concubines. Moreover, he condemned to the stake those Muslims who became atheists, committed child abuse by marrying a nine-year-old girl and through manipulation was able to marry his daughter-in-law, his adoptive son's wife.[6]

---

[1] M. Amado, 'Maomé e o Alcorão: uma ameaça a ser combatida? Respostas fáceis para perguntas difíceis', *Ultimato* 18 March 2019, available online at https://www.ultimato.com.br/conteudo/maome-e-o-alcorao-uma-ameaca-a-ser-combatida-respostas-faceis-para-perguntas-dificeis accessed 25 April 2021.

[2] Among the most important books translated into Portuguese which have influenced Brazilian Christians are *Lords of the Earth, Peace Child* and *Eternity in Their Hearts.*

[3] D. Richardson, *Segredos do Alcorão* (Minas Gerais: Horizontes América Latina, 2007), p. 19.

[4] Richardson, *Segredos do Alcorão*, p. 28.

[5] Richardson, *Segredos do Alcorão*, p. 37.

[6] Richardson, *Segredos do Alcorão*, ps. 35–82.

Defining Muhammed Based on Questionable Historical Texts

This incomplete list of atrocities and immoralities seems to leave a Christian with little alternative apart from a thoroughly negative assessment of Muhammed. However, most of the statements above are either found in very few details in the Koran or are only in the traditions known as Hadith.[7] These traditions are collections of Muhammed's supposed words and actions which are believed to have been faithfully transmitted orally and compiled by Muslim academics about two hundred years after the death of Islam's prophet.[8]

Muslim scholars are not unanimous concerning these traditions. Their veracity, and the trustworthiness of those transmitting the traditions orally was debated in Islam's first decades and around 850 AD, Muslim theologians belonging to the *ahl al-kalam* movement totally rejected the Hadith.[9] With time, Muslim scholars accepted the Hadith as revealed by God and its study became an important science in Muslim legal and theological studies. Nonetheless, doubts persisted:

> Virtually every one of the [Muslim scholars] who [stopped accepting] the Hadith ... insists that at one time they were devoted to the authority of the Hadith, but that an extensive study of the literature ... led them to realise that those traditions [regarded as] trustworthy simply could not be accepted as such.[10]

Many contemporary Christian, Muslim, and secular scholars who study Islamic origins do not accept the Hadith as an historical source.[11] This is due to the literary complexities of the Hadith, which are preserved in different collections, of dubious provenance, compiled by different authors.

The different collections were gathered in the eighth and ninth centuries. Among the *muhaddithun,* Muslims who dedicate themselves to the study of the Hadith, correct interpretation requires discerning which traditions have a believable "chain of transmission" to determine those which are most trustworthy. Yet, Muslim scholars do not agree among themselves which of these Hadith have an acceptable chain of transmission and thus, which are trustworthy:

---

[7] The Prophet's Sunnah comes from the Hadith. The Sunnah is considered the authoritative record of Muhammed's life, words, and character. See D. Brown, *Rethinking tradition in modern Islamic thought* (Cambridge: Cambridge University Press) position 122.

[8] It is worth remembering that the first centuries of Christian history saw the emergence of various pseudepigraphal texts such as the Gospel of Thomas, the Secret Gospel of Mark, the Gospel of Phillip, and the Shepherd of Hermas which considerably altered the profile of Jesus received from the canonical gospels. The same happened with Muhammed with the advent of the Hadith.

[9] Brown, *Rethinking tradition in modern Islamic thought,* position 144.

[10] Brown, *Rethinking tradition in modern Islamic thought,* position 641.

[11] Such scholars regard the Hadith as a useful source to understand the development of Islam and Muslim perceptions of Muhammed, and the theological development of Islam, but not as a trustworthy source concerning Muhammed's life and work.

> The Hadith collections ... have been a disputed territory since the beginnings [of Islamic history]. Some of the first collections of the Hadith suffered from a lack of a clear *isnad* which could indicate a connexion with [the prophet],[12] and were rejected by subsequent generations [of Muslims]. Later collections included complete *isnads*, but, as time went by, it became easy to fabricate such connections. Most accounts that emerged were rejected for different reasons .... There is evidence of political manipulation or even "sponsorship". Even the collections which are currently regarded as the most trustworthy were disputed by Muslim academics, both Sunnite and Shiite, at different times ... The Hadith collections were and continue to be a matter of debate in the Muslim community.[13]

In 1885, for example, the Indian Muslim scholar Chiragh Ali concluded that the Ahadith were inventions he could not trust, while in the middle of the twentieth century another Muslim academic, the Egyptian Mahmoud Abu Rayyah, suggested that the Hadith collections should be submitted to an extensive review to test their trustworthiness.[14]

There is yet another complicating factor. Due to historical and doctrinal differences, the Sunnite and Shiite communities do not use identical Hadith collections. The Shiite do not recognise the first three caliphs who led the incipient Islamic community after Muhammed's death and thus they do not accept the validity of Ahadith which depend on the testimony of these caliphs. Likewise, they do not accept any of the Ahadith which are validated by the supposed testimony of Aisha, one of Muhammed's widows and believed to be his preferred wife. In contrast, Sunnites regard Aisha as the "mother of the faithful" and she is the main contributor towards the traditions found in the Bukhari collection, which is the most treasured Sunnite Hadith collection.[15]

The challenge is that Muhammed's biography is based on the traditions not the Koran. Brown affirms that "for any incident in Muhammed's life there are probably dozens of different traditions which tell the same facts in different and incompatible ways."[16] There is even a selection of Hadith called *asbab al-nuzul* (revelatory occasions) which provide the context in which different parts of the Koran were supposedly declared by Muhammed. Without this it is almost impossible to offer a correct interpretation of the Koran's content:[17]

---

[12] *Isnad* is the list of the names of those people who formed the oral chain of transmission of one or various Ahadith.
[13] B. Power, *Challenging Islamic Traditions* (Pasadena: William Carey Library), p. 16.
[14] Power, *Challenging Islamic Traditions*, p. 19. In Arabic, Ahadith is the correct plural form of Hadith.
[15] Power, *Challenging Islamic Traditions*, explores this in more details, providing a list of the main Sunnite and Shiite collections.
[16] D. Brown, *A new introduction to Islam,* 2nd ed, (Chichester: Wiley-Blackwell, 2019) Daniel Brown is a Christian academic, author of various books about Islam and director of the Institute for the Study of Religion in the Middle East.
[17] In *Rethinking tradition in modern Islamic thought* Brown discusses in detail controversies among Muslims, especially in the Indian subcontinent and Egypt, with

The whole impressive edifice of traditional Islamic scholarship is built upon the building blocks of the Hadith. So, all this impressive enterprise is surrounded by a crucial question: how can one tell if a certain Hadith is authentic or not?[18]

Without the Hadith, the information regarding Muhammed's birth on the outskirts of Mecca is very scarce and there are no details about his infancy or youth. Although the migration (*hijra*) to Medina is of utmost importance in Islamic development, it becomes an obscure event without the Hadith. Even the details about the revelations Gabriel trusted to Muhammed are not found in the Koran but in the Hadith. Therefore, the Koran does not tell us a story it only presents information, often in a disconnected way, requiring the historical context offered by the Hadith. Thus, textual critical questions concerning the historicity of the Hadith, lead to doubts concerning Muhammed's biography, which is based on the Hadith.[19]

Historical Rigour

Should we follow Don Richardson and others and base our understanding of Islam on the dubious traditions found in the Hadith, defining Muhammed according to questionable texts which emerged two centuries after his death? There is inconsistency in the way some Christian authors only accept material from the Hadith which allows them to present Muhammed in a negative light but reject other traditions such as that a bunch of dates fell from trees at his command, or that he fed multitudes with only small portions of food in his hand.

At a conference I attended in the Middle East, Martin Accad, a Lebanese Christian academic caused great controversy with his suggestion that we should completely abandon the Hadith, separating the "Muhammed of faith" from the "Muhammed of history". We should therefore just use the Koran which according to recent research was close to completion fifty years after Muhammed's death.[20]

The challenge is that there is no chronological or thematic order to the Koran, and it is not formed by books, but by chapters (suras) which provide no reliable historical context. For example, it is the Ahadith, rather than the Koran, which support the common Muslim declaration that the violent verses in the Koran were declared in the city of Medina and those promoting peace among Jews,

---

regards to the Hadith. See also Power, *Challenging Islamic Traditions*, B. Power, *Engaging Islamic traditions: Using the Hadith in Christian ministry to Muslims* (Pasadena, California: William Carey Library, 2016) and M. Accad, *The quest for the historical Muhammad* (Beirut: Institute of Middle East Studies. 2019)

[18] Brown, *A new introduction to Islam*, p. 2544.
[19] As discussed in Accad, *The quest for the historical Muhammed*, p. 1.
[20] M. Amado, *Crítica textual e a formação do Alcorão: implicações para a interação entre cristãos e muçulmanos*. (São Paulo: Martureo – Centro de Reflexão Missiológica. 2015)

Christians, and Muslims in Mecca. In solely using the Koran to understand Muhammed we will therefore develop an image different from that imagined by contemporary Muslims, but be better able to dialogue with secular and Muslim scholars employing rigorous historical criteria.

Muhammed of the Koran

Peace and Love

What emerges when we focus solely on the Koran? We discover a religious Muhammed, not necessarily a prophet but someone with a passing knowledge of biblical stories and concepts, sometimes according to apocryphal literature or Christian and Jewish exegesis and not according to the canonical texts.

Muhammed was concerned with the practice of usury by the rich, the indebtedness of the poor and with the well-being of orphans (Sura 8.40) and with the polytheism of his countrymen. He believed in a day of resurrection and of judgement (Sura 4.87) and regarded complete submission to the will of Allah as the only way to escape the fires of hell. He believed that Gabriel announced to Mary that she would become pregnant, in the virgin birth of Jesus and his miracles. However, he did not believe that Jesus was the son of God or had been crucified, but ascended to the heavens where he is living until now.

At some point, Muhammed defended that "there should be no compulsion in religion" (Sura 2.257). After all, he saw himself as a monotheistic prophet sent by God to confirm and communicate, in Arabic, what had been transmitted through Jews and Christians (called the people of the Book in the Koran) through the Biblical prophets and the Messiah (Sura 3.3–4, 26.192–197; 46.12). For this reason, he encouraged Jews and Christians to obey the Pentateuch and the Gospel (Sura 5.68) as in this way they would achieve salvation:

> The [Muslim] believers, the Jews, the Christians, and the Sabians – all those who believe in God and the Last Day and do good – will have their rewards with their Lord. No fear for them, nor will they grieve (Sura 2.62)

> For the [Muslim] believers, the Jews, the Sabians, and the Christians– those who believe in God and the Last Day and do good deeds– there is no fear: they will not grieve. (Sura 5.69)

Muhammed also stated that if there were any doubts regarding the revelations, they should be explained by Christians and Jews "So if you [Prophet] are in doubt about what we have revealed to you, ask those who have been reading the scriptures before you." (Sura 10.94)

Muslims should therefore only argue with Christians and Jews in a loving way, as both Muslims and the people of the Book believed in the same God:

> [Believers], argue only in the best way with the People of the Book, except with those of them who act unjustly. Say, 'We believe in what was revealed to us and in

what was revealed to you; our God and your God are one [and the same]; we are devoted to Him.'(Sura 29.46)

Ambiguity

On the other hand, Muhammed sometimes changes his mind, becoming ambiguous towards Jews and Christians. On some occasions he exalts Christians at the expense of Jews, claiming that the Jews were hostile and Christians friendly (Sura 5.82). In other situations, he increases his polemical tone towards the "People of the Book", affirming that the problem was not with the sacred scriptures of the Jews and Christians, but with their disobedience, so that he instructs Muslims not to make alliances with them:

> If they had upheld the Torah and the Gospel and what was sent down to them from their Lord, they would have been given abundance from above and from below: some of them are on the right course, but many of them do evil. (Sura 5.66)

> So let the followers of the Gospel judge according to what God has sent down in it. Those who do not judge according to what God has revealed are lawbreakers. (Sura 5.47)

> You who believe, do not take the Jews and Christians as allies: they are allies only to each other. Anyone who takes them as an ally becomes one of them– God does not guide such wrongdoers– (Sura 5.51)

Violence: Persecution and War

However, Muhammed's frustration towards Jews, Christians, and all those who did not accept his message is so great that there are many violent recommendations he gives to Muslims: [21]

> Fight in God's cause against those who fight you, but do not overstep the limits: God does not love those who overstep the limits. Kill them wherever you encounter them, and drive them out from where they drove you out, (Sura 2.190, 191)

> Fight them until there is no more persecution, and worship is devoted to God. (Sura 2.193)

> So do not take them as allies until they migrate [to Medina] for God's cause. If they turn [on you], a then seize and kill them wherever you encounter them. Take none of them as an ally or supporter (Sura 4.89)

---

[21] It is important to emphasize that many of these passages do not mention Christians and Jews directly. They refer to "unbelievers", "those that fight against you", "idolaters", "hypocrites" etc. Some Muslim exegetes affirm that in these cases Muhammed is referring to the idolatrous and polytheistic Arabs who lived in the city of Mecca before it was completely conquered by Muhammed and did not accept his monotheistic message. Nonetheless, in other passages Muhammed is clearly referring to Jews and/or Christians.

Cut off the hands of thieves, whether they are man or woman, as punishment for what they have done– a deterrent from God: God is almighty and wise. (Sura 5.38)

Your Lord revealed to the angels: 'I am with you: give the believers firmness; I shall put terror into the hearts of the disbelievers– strike above their necks and strike all their fingertips.' That was because they opposed God and His Messenger, and if anyone opposes God and His Messenger, God punishes them severely. (Sura 8.12–13)

When the [four] forbidden months are over, wherever you encounter the idolaters, kill them, seize them, besiege them. (Sura 9.5)

Fight those of the People of the Book who do not [truly] believe in God and the Last Day, who do not forbid what God and His Messenger have forbidden, who do not obey the rule of justice, until they pay the tax and agree to submit. (Sura 9.29)

The Jews said, 'Ezra is the son of God,' and the Christians said, 'The Messiah is the son of God': they said this with their own mouths, repeating what earlier disbelievers had said. May God confound them! How far astray they have been led! (Sura 9.30)

You who believe, fight the disbelievers near you and let them find you standing firm be aware that God is with those who are mindful of Him. (Sura 9.123)

They swear by God that they did not, but they certainly did speak words of defiance and became defiant after having submitted; they tried to do something, though they did not achieve it, being spiteful was their only response to God and His Messenger enriching them out of His bounty. They would be better off turning back [to God]: if they turn away, God will punish them in this world and the Hereafter, and there will be no one on earth to protect or help them. (Sura 9.74)

When you meet the disbelievers in battle, strike them in the neck, (Sura 47.4)

He will not let the deeds of those who are killed for His cause come to nothing; He will guide them and put them into a good state; He will admit them into the Garden He has already made known to them. (Sura 47:4–6)

Reading such passages, one might even ask why Don Richardson even bothered to search the Hadith for justification for violence within Islam, as on their own these passages give scope for radical interpretations.

Yet how should we interpret such passages? As we see with Christian interpretations of the Bible, Muslim interpretations vary according to legal and theological positions be they secular, fundamentalist, or others.

Violent Passages in the Bible

Christian historian Philip Jenkins provocatively affirms that the typical Christian and Jews believe "that the Koran teaches war while the Bible offers a message of love, peace, and charity."[22] But will Muslims always see love, peace and

---

[22] P. Jenkins, *Laying down the sword: Why we can't ignore the Bible's violent verses* (New York: Harper Collins, 2011), p. 15.

charity when reading certain Bible passages, especially episodes from the lives of important characters such as Moses, Joshua, Samuel, David, and Elijah?

For Jenkins, with regards to violence, "any simplistic claim of the superiority of the Bible in relation to the Koran would be fundamentally wrong."[23] To support his claim he points to Psalm 137:9 which declares that blessed are those who smash Babylonian children against the stones, and the divine order to completely destroy certain cities with their animals and inhabitants (Deut. 20.16-17). He points out that the order given by God to Moses was "exemplary fulfilled" by Joshua in the conquest of Jericho and in the conquest of Ai (Josh. 6:21, 8:24–26). Jenkins also emphasises God's order to Saul through Samuel to "go, attack the Amalekites and totally destroy everything that belongs to them. Do not spare them: put to death men and women, children and infants, cattle and sheep, camels and donkeys" (1 Sam.15:3). He indicates that such narratives have been used to justify raging war for Christian purposes. While just war theorists have sought to establish limits on the use of violence "extremists have tried to restore the implacable practices of *herem*, biblical holy war, war without mercy."[24]

Reformed theologian Tremper Longman III makes a similar point, presenting a daring analogy between the extremist ideologies of Osama bin Laden and that which we see in the Old Testament especially Deuteronomy and Joshua.[25] For Longman:
1. Both ideologies believed in the idea of sacred space occupied by infidels. In the case of bin Laden, it was the presence of westerners in Saudi Arabia.
2. Both regarded their actions as a holy war blessed and sanctioned by God.
3. Both had the aim of destroying every last person, without concern for age or status.[26]

Hermeneutical Lenses

How can evangelical Christians affirm that Christianity is a religion of peace, and that Moses, Joshua, David, and others were God's holy servants in the light

---

[23] Jenkins, *Laying down the sword,* p. 15.
[24] Jenkins, *Laying down the sword,* p. 11. According to John Walton *herem* means "holy war or interdiction requiring the complete destructions of people, animals, and property as a sacrifice for Jehovah." J. Walton, 'Herem' in J. Walton, V. Matthews and M. Chavalas (eds.), *IVP Bible Background Commentary: Old Testament,* Downers Grove: IVP, 2000.
[25] T. Longman, 'The case for continuity', in S. Gundry (ed.), *Show them no mercy: four views on God and the Canaanite Genocide* (Grand Rapids: Zondervan, 1994), pp. 159-190.
[26] M. Lynch, *Joshua and violence (part 5): show them no mercy.* Retrieved from https://theologicalmisc.net/2016/04/joshua-violence-part-5-show-no-mercy/

of the violent acts narrated in these passages? This leads us to the hermeneutical issue, the theoretical study of how we interpret written texts.[27]

We interpret the biblical text according to predefined methods and techniques, so that our hermeneutical lenses lead us to certain conclusions. Evangelical Christians read Scripture taking into account its authority, the genre of different books (narrative, poetry, wisdom, prophecy, etc.) and the historical, grammatical, and cultural context. We read with New Testament lenses, affirming that Christianity is a religion of peace and that biblical characters who carried out violence did this because they lived in another time, in different historical and cultural contexts and in a different moment in salvation history. There are, however, other groups, in the past and in the present, who also consider themselves Christians and who, using other hermeneutical lenses, conclude that Scripture accepts, or even ordains the use of violence to fulfil God's will.

Could something similar happen among Muslims? It is common to find, in Saudi Arabia, Iran and other parts of the world, Muslims who, in opposition to radicals, affirm passionately that Islam is a religion of peace, despite the belligerent passages from the Koran mentioned above. As in Christianity, there are different theological schools in Islam, and most Muslims use interpretative methods and techniques which lead to the self-image of a peaceful people following the example of their prophet.[28]

Brown explains that a Muslim scholar wishing to reach the correct interpretation of a passage would first need to have profound knowledge of Arab grammar and vocabulary to avoid relying on a translation of the Koran into another language. The complexity and uncertainty regarding vocabulary would lead him to lexicography, and require studying traditional ancient Arab literature, especially poetry. The scholar would also require a comprehensive understanding of the main commentaries on the Koran. They would have to consider the context, acquiring a deep knowledge of Muhammed's life and the circumstances each passage was revealed in. This requires investigating the extensive literature describing the "occasions of revelation" to decide if a passage is intended for a general or a particular audience and if a certain commandment is limited to specific circumstances or intended for general application. Finally, he would need to compare the passage with other parallel passages in the Koran related to the same topic to determine if there are other Koranic passages which substitute, modify, or explain the passage in more detail.

---

[27] See B. Lategan, 'Hermeneutics' in D. N. Freedman (ed.), *The Anchor Yale Bible Dictionary* (New Haven: Yale University Press, 1992)

[28] Non-radical Muslim theological schools, following the hermeneutical rules established for the correct understanding of the Koran, base themselves on passages such as Suras 4.90, 5.16, 8.61 and 10.25 and the description of Allah as "the one who brings peace" (Sura 59.23) to defend that Islam is a religion of peace and that Muslims can only use violence to defend themselves from attack.

Finally, they would repeat the process for the Hadith, finding traditions which explain the objective of a passage or limit its application.[29]

Where does this lead us? What is its importance for those who sincerely desire to present Jesus to Muslims as the resurrected Lord and Saviour?

The Quest for Truth

The quest for truth should be a priority for Christian researchers, despite those forms of postmodernism that state that such a quest is useless and impossible. This requires recognising, in the words of R.C. Sproul, that "all truth is God's truth".[30] Keith Mathison, associate editor of the *Reformation Study Bible,* demonstrates that this belief was important for Augustine, Thomas Aquinas and John Calvin who affirmed "all truth comes from God; consequently, if iniquitous men affirm anything that is true and just, we cannot reject it, as it comes from God."[31]

If we pay heed to Augustine, Aquinas, Calvin and Sproul and other prominent Christians, we should not abandon the quest for the truth, wherever it may be found. Thus, with regards to Muhammed, as Christians we need to answer some difficult questions to carry out a sincere self-criticism if we wish to get close to the truth. The answers suggested, while being an exercise in extreme simplification, seek not to contradict any unnegotiable doctrine of evangelical Christian faith, while leading to a self-critical attitude towards our conventional beliefs. Hopefully, this will contribute towards peace between Christians and Muslims and facilitate witnessing to Christ among the more than one and a half billion Muslims across the world.

Simple Answers to Difficult Questions

Is it our duty, as evangelical Christians, to seek to construct healthy relationships between Christians and Muslims? Or should we always seek to emphasise the differences to prove that our religion is superior?

Yes, it is our duty. We were not called to prove the superiority of any religion, but to bear witness to a person, Jesus.

Does our perception of who Muhammed really was affect our witness among Muslims?

Yes, it does.

If we bear animosity towards Islam's prophet, does this influence our attitude towards Muslims?

---

[29] Brown, *Rethinking tradition in Islamic thought,* pos. 2329.
[30] Quoted in K. Mathison, 'All truth is God's truth: a Reformed approach to science and scripture', *Ligonier* available online at https://www.ligonier.org/blog/all-truth-gods-truth-reformed-approach-science-and-scripture/
[31] K. Mathison, 'All truth is God's truth.'

Yes, it does.

Do Christians have a place at the table for Muhammed? Is it possible to find an intermediate position without compromising the fundamentals of our faith?

There is no place at the table for Muhammed as a biblical prophet. However, we can recognise him as an influential figure in the last fourteen centuries, who, mistakenly, believed he was announcing to Arabs what had already been announced to Jews and Christians. Given the lack of historically reliable data regarding Muhammed, it would arguably be better to develop an understanding better suited to a constructive dialogue and effective Christian witness.

Are there differences between the historical Muhammed and the Muhammed of faith? If so, in our quest for truth, should we base our perception on the historical Muhammed, or the Muhammed of faith?

In dealing with Muslims, we must bear in mind the Muhammed of faith as, despite what has been argued in this article, their understanding of Muhammed is based on certain traditions from the Hadith. Nonetheless, in our own understanding we should remember that there is no historical evidence that he was the dissolute and bloodthirsty leader presented by Don Richardson and other evangelical leaders.

Textual criticism indicates that the only relatively reliable material that we have concerning Muhammed, is the Koran itself. In it, we find a very religious man, who oscillated between respect for Jews, Christians and their sacred scriptures and orders to persecute them, including the use of violence. Is Muhammed's attitude to violence that different from what we see in the Old Testament and in some of our biblical heroes?

We can see similar attitudes in biblical heroes to those of Muhammed.

If we do use the Hadith (traditions) as a source regarding who Muhammed was, despite doubts concerning the veracity and reliability of different collections, what criteria is being used when we accept as true, negative comments about Muhammed, but not those which are positive?

We need to be intellectually honest and cannot pick and choose what we prefer from the Hadith. Although the typical Muslim is heavily influenced by the Hadith, in developing an understanding of who Muhammed really was, we should turn to more reliable material.

If we can accept that certain important characters in the Old Testament used violence because they were children of their age, should we not use the same criteria with regards to Muhammed, while accepting that he is not a biblical prophet?

Yes, we can apply the same criteria.

If, despite the presence of violent passages in the Bible, we can use hermeneutical lenses which lead us to the conclusion that Christianity is a religion of peace, why is it so hard to accept that the same happens with Islam?

It is hard because we have been taught to interpret the main characters of other religions in predominantly negative ways.

The actions and beliefs of contemporary, radical Muslims are often used to deny that Islam and Muslims promote peace. At the time of Muhammed, Christians had armies and theological arguments to justify killing in the name of God. Yet it would be inaccurate to affirm that all seventh century Christians accepted violence against other humans as sanctioned by God. Why not apply the same criteria to contemporary Muslims?

The same criteria should be applied.

Is Tremper Longman III being sincere in his quest for the truth or deviating from true Christian orthodoxy in comparing bin Laden's extremist ideology and what we see in the Old Testament?

Longman is being sincere and honest. This recognition does not mean support for Bin Laden and others, but an acknowledgement that complex theological issues can be found both in the Bible and Islam.

Even today, there are radical groups which call themselves Christian and who use violence against different minorities. Does that make Christianity a violent religion? If not, why not say the same about Islam?

The presence of radical, violent extremists makes neither Christianity nor Islam violent religions.

I started this text affirming that normally Christians oscillate between Islamophobia or Islamophilia in our attitudes to Muhammed and that this defines our understanding of Muslims and Christian witness among them. May God aid us in the quest for truth and balance, and that this may help us witness to those who have yet to hear that Jesus Christ is Lord.

Index

Accad, Martin, 161
Adorno, Theodor, 57
Africa, 11, 23, 142
Albano, Fernando, 36
Ali, Chiragh, 160
Altamirano, José Antonio, 91
Alves, Rubem, 53
Amado, Marcos, 7, 154, 157, 158, 161
Amatuzzi, Mauro, 76
Amorim, Rodolfo, 43
Anabaptist, 28, 59, 66
Anderson, Allan, 3
Angelelli, Enrique, 59, 68
Aquinas, Thomas, 167
Arana, Pedro, 55
Argentina, 1, 23, 25, 58, 63, 70
Asia, 11, 23, 132, 142
Assmann, Hugo, 52
Augustine, 2, 5, 73, 74, 76, 77, 78, 79, 80, 81, 82, 83, 167
Aymara, 112
Baggio, Sandro, 24, 31
Barro, Jorge, 24
Bastos, Délnia, v, 6, 95, 106
Bauman, Zygmunt, 39
Bautista, José, 53
Bavinck, Herman, 35
Bebbington, David, 2
Beyer, Peter, 4
Bibby, Reginald, 1
Bible
   authority, 2, 10, 12, 14, 111, 157
   hermeneutics, 11, 13, 14, 16, 17, 21, 86, 123, 164, 165, 166, 168
   translation, 112, 149
bin Laden, Osama, 165, 169
Boff, Leonardo, 9
Bolivia, 10, 21, 23, 25

Bolsonaro, Jair, 6, 25
Bosch, David, 21, 27, 31, 142, 155
Brachtendorf, Johannes, 81
Braga, Erasmo, 143
Braumer, Hansjorg, 95, 98
Brazil, v, 3, 7, 22, 23, 25, 27, 30, 32, 35, 36, 37, 38, 39, 40, 43, 63, 70, 76, 102, 120, 126, 128, 141, 142, 143, 144, 150, 153, 154, 155, 156, 184
Breton, André, 68
Brinkerhoff, Merlin, 1
Brown, Daniel, 159, 160, 161, 166, 167
Brown, Peter, 77
Brueggemann, Walter, 53
Buber, Martin, 76
Buddhism, 7
Buñuel, Luis, 68
Bush, Luis, 144
Caldas, Carlos, 142
Calvin, John, 41, 83, 167
Capitalism, 23, 32, 49, 50, 51, 52, 55, 69, 86
Carey, William, 142
Carriker, Timoteo, 95, 96, 98, 100, 102, 103, 104, 109, 110, 154
Catholic Church, 4, 12, 15, 21, 26, 47, 66, 73, 91, 148
   hegemony in Latin America, 2, 14, 21, 35, 36, 58, 63
   Inquisition, 63
   progressive Catholics, 23
Cavalcanti, Robinson, 28, 56
César, Elben, 98, 142
Chesterton, Gilbert K., 71
Childhood, 121, 122
Chile, 23, 25

China, 23, 152, 156
Christianity and science, 37, 43
Christology, 20, 59
  incarnation, 11, 20, 75, 89, 119
CLADE, ix, 21, 143
Clark, Daniel, v, 1, 4, 5, 19, 27, 29, 30
Clarke, James, 1
Clawson, Michael, 20, 21
Colonialism, 85, 88, 91, 93, 124, 135, 136
  and Christianity, 15
  conquest of the Americas, 15, 35, 62, 63, 135, 136
  imperialism, 15, 16, 86, 87
  neo-colonialism, 14, 86, 90
COMIBAM, 144
Communion, 75
Comte, Auguste, 37, 57
CONEP, 2
Constantine, 61, 65, 69
Constantinianism, 5, 59, 61, 62, 63, 64, 65, 67
Costa Rica, 52, 143
Costa, Fabio, 24
Costas, Orlando, 4, 9, 14, 28
Council of Nicaea, 62, 145
Covenant, 96, 97, 102, 103, 107
Covid-19, 5, 76, 132, 145, 152
Creation, 14, 20, 36, 37, 39, 40, 41, 42, 49, 75, 78, 88, 89, 90, 97, 107, 125, 127, 128, 152
Crivella, Marcelo, 27
Croatto, Juan Severino, 103
Crusades, 62, 63
Culture, 148
  cultural mandate, 41, 42
  evangelical attitudes, v, 15, 35, 36, 37, 38, 39, 40, 88, 89
  Reformational approach, v, 5, 35, 41, 43
Cunha, Magali, 38
da Silva, Luis Inacio 'Lula', 23, 24, 25
de Almeida, Monica, 24
de Carvalho, Guilherme, 28, 41, 42, 43
de Carvalho, Levi, 149
de Santa Ana, Julio, 48
de Vaux, Roland, 105, 106, 107, 108
Deiros, Pablo, 55
Devil, 66, 95
Disability, v, 6, 111, 113, 116, 152
Domezi, Maria, 26

Donatism, 83
Dooyeweerd, Herman, 35, 36, 37, 41, 42, 43
Dualism, 36, 37, 38, 42
Ducroquet, Simon, 141
Dupont, Anthony, 81
Duriez, Colin, 42
Economy, 5, 23, 42, 45, 46, 47, 49, 50, 52, 53, 54, 55, 150, 154
Ecuador, 23, 25, 143
Ekström, Bertil, 144, 145, 146, 150, 154
El Salvador, 90
Ellul, Jacques, 53, 73, 76
Enlightenment, 57, 58, 69
Environment, 6, 50, 54, 67, 131, 132, 133, 134, 135, 137, 138
Escobar, Samuel, 4, 7, 12, 20, 21, 22, 27, 28, 31, 48, 55, 143, 144
Espoz, Renato, 55, 56
Europe, 3, 5, 11, 12, 58, 76, 142
Evangelical
  attitudes to Catholicism, 1, 2, 83
  diversity in Latin America, 2, 3, 5, 147, 153, 155
  engagement with politics, v, 3, 5, 23, 24, 27, 30, 48, 49, 57, 58, 63, 70
  global evangelicalism, 4
  Great Awakening, 11
  growth, 4, 5, 7, 12, 35, 39, 141, 142, 149, 150, 151
  identity, 1, 2, 147
  music, 2, 3, 38, 40, 154
  Reformed tradition, 5, 40
  theology, v, 1, 3, 4, 5, 9, 10, 12, 14, 17, 48, 88, 118
  unity, 2
  use of media, 38
Every-Clayton, Joyce, 108
Exclusion, 5, 6, 70, 111, 115, 116, 119
Fajardo, Alexander, 10
Fausto, Sérgio, 23
Feliciano, Marcos, 30
Ferreira, Franklin, 29, 31
France, 37
French Revolution, 58
Freston, Paul, 3, 4, 23, 30, 31
FTL, ix, 3, 4, 5, 10, 11, 12, 15, 21, 45, 46, 48, 49, 50, 54, 55, 143
Fujimori, Keiko, 25

Fukuyama, Francis, 47
Fulanetto, Felipe, vi, 3, 7, 141
Fundamentalism, 2, 11, 37, 48, 58, 82
García, Alan, 25
Gasque, Laurel, 43
Giddens, Anthony, 40
Girón, Rodolfo, 144
Globalisation, 6, 54, 58
Gnosticism, 75
Goheen, Michael, 154
Gonzáles, Julio, v, 6, 111, 116
González Ruiz, 57
González, Antonio, 55, 59, 60, 61, 62, 63, 64, 65, 66, 67, 70, 71
González, Justo, 76, 155
Grace, 20, 36, 38, 39, 62, 64, 74, 75, 77, 78, 79, 82, 83, 95, 96, 97, 99, 100, 103, 104, 120, 126, 153, 156
Guatemala, 90
Guder, Darrel, 153
Guerrero, Milton, 21
Gutiérrez Sanchez, Tomas, 2
Gutiérrez, Germán, 53
Gutiérrez, Gustavo, 1, 9, 36, 46, 50
Haiti, 90, 91, 92, 152
Hanciles, Jehu, 97
Harvey, Robert, 150
Heaney, Sharon, 47
Hiebert, Paul, 155
Hinduism, 7, 148
Hinkelammert, Franz, 47, 52, 53, 56
Hippolytus of Rome, 66
Hoffmann, Martin, 61, 63
Honduras, 90
Horkheimer, Max, 57
Hugo, John Jacob, 81
Humalla, Ollanta, 25
Ideology, 15, 30, 47, 55, 67, 69, 70, 86, 118, 123, 169
Idolatry, 51, 53, 64, 67
IFES, 21, 50
    ABUB, 144
    AGEUP, 131, 132
Inclusion, 5, 105, 106, 107, 109, 111, 119, 125
India, 156
Indigenous populations, 6, 133, 134, 135, 137, 152
Ingleby, Jonathan, 32
Integral mission, 10, 13, 19
    and justice, 14, 16, 28, 30, 31, 32, 48, 54, 67, 70, 86, 108, 121, 132
    and local churches, 26, 27
    and social transformation, 14, 26, 28
    challenges, v, 4, 5, 19, 26, 30
    contextualisation, 88
    definition, 19
    holistic approach, 4, 14, 15, 16, 19, 20, 22, 45, 131, 139
    Micah Network, 19
    roots, 4, 9, 10, 11, 12, 16, 21, 22, 26, 49, 143
    theology, v, 4, 9, 10, 11, 12, 13, 17
Inwood, M., 36
ISAL, 45, 46, 48, 50
Islam, 7, 57, 148, 157, 159, 160, 161, 167, 168
    Christian witness, 157, 167
    Hadith, 159, 160, 161, 164, 167, 168
    Islamophobia, 157, 169
    Koran, 157, 158, 159, 160, 161, 162, 164, 165, 166, 168
    Muhammed, vi, 7, 157, 158, 159, 160, 161, 162, 163, 166, 167, 168, 169
Jenkins, Phillip, 164, 165
Johnson, Todd, 147
Johnstone, Patrick, 147
Kalsbeeck, L., 43
Keppel, Giles, 57
Kidner, Derek, 95, 96, 97, 98, 99, 100
Kingdom of God, v, 9, 13, 20, 21, 28, 39, 42, 45, 46, 47, 48, 51, 53, 55, 59, 60, 61, 64, 65, 68, 70, 125
Kirkpatrick, David, 20, 22, 26, 28
Kraft, Larry, 150
Kruse, Marcos, 56
Küng, Hans, 58, 59, 62
Kuyper, Abraham, 31, 35, 38, 39, 41
Kuzynscki, Pedro Pablo, 25
L'Abri, 42, 43
Lament, 79, 86, 91, 92, 119
Lane, William, 95, 96
Lategan, Bernard, 166
Latin American social context
    polarisation, 23, 30, 32, 75, 82, 153
    poverty, 5, 10, 20, 21, 23, 28, 31, 46, 52, 89, 106, 118, 133, 139
    same-sex marriage, 30

violence, 29, 90, 138
Lausanne movement, 12, 13, 20, 27, 28
   1974 Congress for World Evangelisation, 22, 143, 144
   2010 Cape Town Commitment, 82, 143
   Committee for World Evangelisation, 22
   covenant, 4, 22, 143, 144
Lee, Sandi, 147
Lehmann, David, 26
Liberalism, 39, 51, 59
Liberation theology, 1, 3, 4, 9, 10, 11, 13, 15, 21, 29, 30, 33, 36, 45, 46, 47, 48, 50, 53, 54, 64
   Base Ecclesial Communities, 26
   use of social sciences, 9, 13, 46
Limpic, Ted, 150
Lin, Davi, v, 2, 5, 73
Livingston, George, 98
Lohfink, Norbert, 45, 51, 52
Longman III, Tremper, 165, 169
Longuini Neto, Luis, 143, 144
López, Dario, 26, 93
Luther King Jr, Martin, 59
Luther, Martin, 41, 61, 66, 73, 74, 83
Lutheranism, 66, 74
Machado, Maria, 27
Machado, Ziel, 117
Madureira, Jonas, 24, 31
Magnin, Lucas, v, 5, 57
Malafaia, Silas, 30
Mardones, José, 52
Mariani, Daniel, 141
Marion, Jean-Luc, 78
Markus, Robert, 80
Martin, Berenice, 29
Martin, David, 4
Marx, Karl, 53
Marxism, 2, 16, 21, 28, 47
Mathison, Keith, 167
McKnight, Scot, 28
Medeiros, Alisson, 141
Mendes, Márcio, 120
Méndez, Guillermo, 51
Menezes, Ademir, 141, 146, 147, 151
Merk, Frederick, 86
Metz, Johan, 69
Mexico, 1, 5, 45, 54, 85, 86, 87, 88, 89, 91, 93

Tijuana, 5, 85, 86, 87, 89, 90, 91
Migration, v, 5, 11, 85, 86, 90, 91, 92, 97, 98, 101, 102, 108, 109, 136, 148, 152
   refugees, v, 6, 93, 95, 96, 97, 98, 99, 100, 101, 102, 103, 104, 105, 106, 108, 109, 148
   trafficking, 101, 135
Miguez Bonino, José, 11, 28, 37, 48, 51
Míguez, Nestor, 54
Miranda, José, 45
Missiology, 1, 7, 10, 17, 86, 144, 154
Mission
   1910 World Missionary Conference, 142
   1916 Panama Latin America Congress, 143
   Brazilian Missionary Movement, vi, 141, 143, 147, 148, 149, 151, 155
   1976 Curitiba Congress, 144
   AMTB, 141, 144, 146, 147, 150, 151
   CBE, 144
   CBM, 145
   history, 145, 146
   contextualisation, 3, 4, 9, 10, 11, 12, 13, 14, 15, 16, 17, 19, 21, 26, 32, 33, 35, 43, 46, 58, 61, 77, 82, 85, 88, 89, 92, 93, 118, 119, 126, 131, 152
   evangelisation, 11, 12, 13, 16, 21, 88, 89, 152
   mission agencies, 5, 15, 143, 144, 145, 146, 147, 149, 150, 151, 153, 156
   mission from Latin America, 14, 17
   COMIBAM, 144
   partnership, 86, 89, 90, 92, 93, 146, 153
   Protestant missions to Latin America, 11, 14, 15, 21, 37, 86, 136, 141, 142
   religious pluralism, 7
   short-term mission teams, 5, 86, 87, 88, 89
   training, 146, 148, 149, 150, 151, 152, 154, 156
Moltmann, Jürgen, 48
Monkey Trial, 37

Moon, Steve, 147
Moore, Russell, 48
Morales, Evo, 25
Morante, Pedro, 54
Mordomo, João, 141, 154
Moro, Sérgio, 24, 25
Moura, Clóvis, 123
Moura, Quéfren, 123
Multiculturalism, 54, 57
Munanga, Kabengele, 123
Muradas, Atilano, 127
Myers, Brian, 22, 27
Nañez, Rick, 36, 37
Neves. Manuel, 46
New Calvinism, 31, 32
Nicodemos Lopes, Augusto, 24
Niebuhr, Reinhold, 48
Niebuhr, Richard, 35, 39
North America, 1, 3, 11, 37, 76, 142, 153
Novak, Michael, 47, 48, 52, 54
Núñez, Emilio, 47, 48
Ocaña, Martin, v, 5, 21, 29, 45, 49
Oliveira, David, 10, 102, 109
Oliveira, Jamierson, 96, 98, 100, 103, 104, 106, 110
Oosterbaan, Martijn, 2
Ortiz, Alejandra, v, 5, 85
Padilla, C. René, 4, 9, 13, 15, 16, 20, 21, 22, 25, 26, 27, 28, 31, 106, 108, 143, 144
Padilla, Washington, 55
Paredes, Tito, 21, 28, 33
Parker, Christian, 58
Passos, João, 3
Pentecostal, 1, 2, 3, 11, 15, 22, 26, 27, 29, 32, 35, 36, 37, 142, 147, 148, 149, 188
    Neo-Pentecostal, 3, 26, 35, 39, 147, 148
Pereira, Daniel, 149, 151
Pereira, Eduardo, 143
Pereira, Nancy, 29
Pérez-Saldarriaga, Rut, vi, 6, 131
Peru, 2, 19, 25, 26, 30, 111, 112, 115, 116, 131, 132, 133, 134
Piper, John, 31
Plato, 37, 50, 53
Pluralism, 52
Politics in Latin America
    Car Wash Investigation, 19, 24, 25

corruption, 4, 19, 23, 25, 31, 32, 133, 134, 137
democracy, 4, 25, 62, 63
dictatorship, 63, 68
Odebrecht scandal, v, 19, 23, 24, 25, 26
Pope Paul VI, 16
Portugal, 120, 144, 145
Postmodern, 39, 40
Power, Bernie, 160, 161
Prosperity theology, 3, 26, 31, 40, 47, 48, 52, 54, 60, 147
Quechua, 2, 112, 131
Racism, 6, 86, 87, 91, 105, 108, 109, 117, 118, 119, 120, 121, 122, 123, 124, 125, 126, 127, 136
Ramachandra, Vinoth, 20
Ramlow, Rodomar, 39, 41
Ramos, Ariovaldo, 25, 28, 31
Ramos, Robson, 40
Rankin, Melinda, 86, 87
Rauschenbusch, Walter, 48
Rayyah, Mahmoud Abu, 160
Reconciliation, 74, 125, 126, 127
Redemption, 14, 31, 41, 42, 52, 88, 98, 103
Reformation, 66, 70, 73, 74, 167
Reichow, Josué, v, 5, 35
Reis, Álvaro, 143
RENAS, 22
Richardson, Don, 158, 161, 164, 168
Rist, John, 77
Robert, Dana, 87
Roman Empire, 60, 61, 65, 69, 73, 77, 112
Rookmaaker, Hans, 42, 43
Rousseff, Dilma, 23, 24, 25, 153
Salinas, Daniel, 3
Sallandt, Ulrike, 22
Samuel, Vinay, 22
Sanches, Regina, v, 4, 9, 12, 13, 16
Sanneh, Lamin, 88
Schaeffer, Edith, 42
Schaeffer, Francis, 42, 43
Schwantes, Milton, 96
Sedgwick, Peter, 55
Segundo, Juan Luis, 51
Shalkwij, Franz, 142
Shea, William, 1
Sherman, Amy, 52

Sin, 12, 16, 37, 38, 39, 42, 51, 75, 79, 80, 96, 103, 104, 126, 127, 152
Sipierski, Paulo, 142
Slavery, 86, 102, 103, 104, 105, 106, 107, 108, 118, 120, 121, 124, 126, 127, 136, 137, 148
Smither, Edward, 142, 143
Social media, 2, 5, 7, 30, 75, 76, 122
Socialism, 48, 51, 64
Solalinde, José, 55
South Africa, 122
Souza, Ana, 27
Spain, 120, 144
Spiritual warfare, 3, 26
Sproul, Robert Charles, 167
Stam, Juan, 50, 95
Staut, Ana, 125
Steuernagel, Valdir, 4, 143, 144, 154
Stott, John, 4, 22, 143
Sugden, Chris, 27
Sung, Jung Mo, 46, 47, 53
Tamayo Acosta, Juan José, 57, 58, 69
Temer, Michel, 25
Theological education, 3, 31, 32, 111, 112, 114, 149, 155
Third World, 4, 15
Thompson, John, 106, 107
Timm, Alberto, 40
Tizon, Al, 21, 22, 88
Toledo, Alejandro, 25
Trinity, 76
Tucker, Ruth, 145
Tunes, Suzel, 143

Turner, Steve, 42, 43
Tutu, Desmond, 59
Ultimato, 6
United Nations, 6, 101
United States, 5, 21, 25, 52, 63, 70, 85, 86, 87, 88, 90, 91, 93
Venezuela, 5, 23, 25, 152
Verheijen, Luc, 79, 80, 191
Verkuyl, Johannes, 155
Vidales, Raúl, 51
Vílchez-Blancas, Eliseo, 21
Volf, Miroslav, 74
von Sinner, Rudolf, 37
Walls, Andrew, 93
Walraet, Pierre-Paul, 81
Waltke, Bruce, 96, 99, 100, 101
Walton, John, 165
Weigel, George, 52
Wesley, John, 59
Westmeier, Karl, 3
Wiersbe, Warren, 96, 107, 108, 109
Wolff, Hans, 105, 106, 107
Woolnough, Brian, 21, 22
World Council of Churches, 21, 142
Worldview, 3, 37, 40, 41, 42, 47
Wright, Chris, 88, 97, 98, 102, 103, 104, 105, 106, 107, 108, 110
Wright, G.E., 103
Yeh, Allen, 142, 143, 154
Zagaris, Bruce, 24
Zoom, 74
Zumbi, 120

Bibliography

Accad, Martin. *The quest for the historical Muhammad*. Beirut, Lebanon: Institute of Middle East Studies, 2019.
Aguirre Monasterio, Rafael. *Así empezó el cristianismo*. Estella: Verbo Divino, 2010.
Albano, Fernando. 'Dualismo corpo/alma na teologia pentecostal' Master of Theology thesis, 2010.
Alves, Rubem. *¿Religión, opio o instrumento de liberación?* Montevideo: Tierra Nueva, 1970.
Alves, Rubem. *Hijos del mañana*. Salamanca: Sígueme, 1976.
Alves, Rubem. *Por uma Teologia da Libertação*. São Paulo: Fonte Editorial, 2012.
Amado, Marcos. 'Maomé e o Alcorão: uma ameaça a ser combatida? Respostas fáceis para perguntas difíceis', *Ultimato* 18 March 2019, available online at https://www.ultimato.com.br/conteudo/maome-e-o-alcorao-uma-ameaca-a-ser-combatida-respostas-faceis-para-perguntas-dificeis accessed 25 April 2021.
Amado, Marcos. *Crítica textual e a formação do Alcorão: implicações para a interação entre cristãos e muçulmanos*. Martureo – Centro de Reflexão Missiológica. São Paulo, 2015.
Amatuzzi, Mauro. *Por uma psicologia humana*. Campinas, SP: Editora Alinea, 2001.
Anderson, Allan. *An Introduction to Pentecostalism*. Cambridge: Cambridge University Press, 2004.
Arana, Pedro. *Progreso, técnica y hombre*. Buenos Aires: Certeza, 1971.
Assmann, Hugo and Franz Hinkelammert. *A idolatría do Mercado. Ensaio sobre Economia e Teologia*. Sao Paulo: Vozes, 1989.
Baggio, Sandro. 'Teologia da Missão Integral em Debate'. <https://archive.fo/5xTS3> [accessed 02 February 2018]
Barthes, Roland. *El placer del texto y Lección inaugural de la cátedra de Semiología literaria del Collège de France*. México: Siglo XXI Editores, 1986.
Bastos, Delnia. 'Donde vens e para onde vais?: Ensino bíblico sobre o tema do refugiado no pentateuco' Master of Theology Thesis, Escola de Missões Transculturais do Centro Evangélico de Missões, 2018.
Bauman, Zygmunt. *Modernidade Líquida*. Rio de Janeiro: Jorge Zahar, 2001.
Bautista, José. *Crítica ética del pensamiento latinoamericano. Introducción al pensamiento crítico de Franz Hinkelammert*. La Paz: Filigrana, 2007.
Beyer, Peter. *Religion and Globalization*. London: SAGE, 1994.
Bosch, David. *Missão Transformadora: Mudanças de Paradigma na Teologia da Missão*. São Leopoldo: Sinodal, 2002.
Bosch, David. *Transforming Mission: Paradigm Shifts in the Theology of Mission*. Maryknoll: Orbis, 1991.
Boulding, Maria. *The Works of St. Augustine: A Translation for the 21st Century*. Hyde Park: New City Press, 1997.

Brachtendorf, Johannes. *Confissões de Agostinho*. Translated by Milton Camargo Mota. São Paulo: Loyola, 2008.
Braumer, Hansjorg. *Génesis 1: Comentario Esperanca*. Curitiba: Editora Esperanca, 2016.
Brown, Daniel. *A new introduction to Islam (versão eletrônica)*. Second Edition. West Sussex: Wiley-Blackwell, 2009.
Brown, Daniel. *Rethinking tradition in modern Islamic thought*. Cambridge: Cambridge University Press, 1996.
Brown, Peter. *Augustine of Hippo*. Berkeley: University of California Press, 2000.
Buber, Martin. *I and Thou*. Translated by Ronald Gregor Smith. Edinburgh: Clark, 1984.
Caldas, Carlos. *O último missionário*. São Paulo: Mundo Cristão, 2001.
Campos, Oscar. *Teología Evangélica para el Contexto Latinoamericano*. Buenos Aires: Kairós, 2004.
Carriker, Timoteo and Jamierson Oliveira J. *Biblia Missionaria de Estudo*. Barueri: Sociedade Bíblica do Brasil, 2014.
Carriker, Timoteo. *Missao Integral: Uma teología bíblica*. Sao Paulo: SEPAL, 1992.
Carvalho, Guilherme. 'A objeção reformada ao dogma da autonomia religiosa da razão.' *Revista Diálogo e Antítese* 1:1 (2009), p. 4–53.
Carvalho, Guilherme. 'O dualismo natureza/graça e a influência do humanismo secular no pensamento social cristão', in *Cosmovisão cristã e transformação: espiritualidade, razão e ordem social.*, Eds. Maurício Cunha et al. Viçosa: Ultimato, 2006, p. 123–174.
Carvalho, Guilherme. 'O senhorio de Cristo e a missão da igreja na cultura: a ideia de soberania e a sua aplicação', in *Fé cristã e cultura contemporânea: cosmovisão cristã, igreja local e transformação integral*. Eds. Rodolfo Amorim, Marcel Camargo, and Leonardo Ramos. Viçosa: Ultimato, 2009, p. 57–96.
Carvalho, Guilhermo. 'A Missão Integral na Encruzilhada: Reconsiderando a Tensão no Pensamento Teológico de Lausanne', in *Fé Crístã e Cultura Contemporánea*. Ed. Leonardo Ramos, Marcel Camargo and Rodolfo Amorim, Viçosa: Ultimato, 2009.
Castañeda, Alejandra. '¿Qué es el Programa de la Frontera Sur?'. *Boletín del Observatorio de Legislación y Política Migratoria*, COLEF-CNDH 1(February 2016).
Cavalcanti, Robinson. 'A situacao socio-economica e política da America Latina', *Boletim* Teologico 18, 1992, pp. 5-20.
César, Elben. *Cuide das raízes, espere pelos frutos: meditações diárias*. Viçosa: Ultimato, 2017.
César, Elben. *História da Evangelização do Brasil: dos jesuítas aos neopentecostais*. Viçosa: Ultimato, 2000.
Chesterton, Gilbert Keith. *Orthodoxy*. London: John Lane, 1908.
Clark, Daniel. 'Outward Mission or Serving a Ghetto: An investigation of the Missiological Impact of Brazilian Churches in West London'. PhD thesis, University of Wales Trinity Saint David, 2013.
Clarke, James. 'Friend or foe? An evangelical engaging Latin American liberation theology'. *Encounters* 27 (2007). Available online at https://encountersmissionjournal.files.wordpress.com/2011/03/friend_or_foe_27.pdf, accessed 26 April 2021.
Clawson, Michael. '*Misión Integral* and Progressive Evangelicalism: The Latin American Influence on the North American Emerging Church'. *Religions* 3 (2012), pp. 790–807.

CONFAR. 'Monseñor Enrique Angelelli: Un oído en el pueblo y otro en el evangelio', available online at http://www.confar.org.ar/descargas/textos/memoria_angelelli2015.pdf (accessed 20 April 2021).
Costas, Orlando. 'A Vida no Espírito', *Boletín Teológico* 18:21-22 (1986) p. 59.
Costas, Orlando. *Compromiso y Misión*. Costa Rica: Editorial Caribe, 1979.
Costas, Orlando. *La Iglesia y su Misión Evangelizadora*. Buenos Aires: Editorial La Aurora, 1971.
Croatto, José Severino. *Êxodo: uma hermenêutica da liberdade*. São Paulo: Paulinas, 1981.
Cunha, Carlos. *Encontros Decoloniais entre o Bem-viver e o Reino de Deus*. Campinas: Saber Criativo, 2019.
Cunha, Magali do Nascimento. *A explosão gospel: um olhar das ciências humanas sobre o cenário evangélico no Brasil*. Rio de Janeiro: Mauad X: Instituto Mysterium, 2007.
Das Neves, Manuel Gracio. *Dios resucita en la periferia. Hablar de Dios desde América Latina*. Salamanca: San Esteban, 1991.
de Almeida, Monica Arruda and Bruce Zagaris. 'Political Capture in the Petrobras Corruption Scandal: The Sad Tale of an Oil Giant', *The Fletcher Forum of World Affairs*, 39:2 (2015), pp. 87–99.
De Carvalho, Levi. *Fortalezas e debilidades do movimento missionário ibero-americano: Fase II. 2015-2016*. São Paulo: Comibam, 2016.
de Oliveira, Jairo, *Refugiados, peregrinos e forasteiros: a igreja respondendo ao desafio mundial da migração*. Londrina: Descoberta, 2017.
de Santa Ana, Julio. 'Economia e teología', in *América Latina: 500 anos de evangelizacao*. Ed. Antonio A. da Silva, Sao Paulo: Paulinas, 1990.
de Vaux, Roland. *Instituições de Israel no Antigo Testamento*. São Paulo: Editora Teológica, 2003.
Dobbelaere, Karel. 'Towards an Integrated Perspective of the Processes Related to the Descriptive Concept of Secularization' *Sociology of Religion*, 60:3, 1999, pp. 229-247.
Domezi, Maria. 'A Devoção nas CEBs: Entre o Catolicismo Tradicional Popular e a Teologia da Libertação'. PhD thesis: Pontifícia Universidade Católica de São Paulo, 2006.
Dooyeweerd, Herman. *Estado e soberania: ensaios sobre cristianismo e política*. São Paulo: Vida Nova, 2014.
Dooyeweerd, Herman. *No Crepúsculo do Pensamento: estudos sobre a pretensa autonomia da razão*. São Paulo: Hagnos, 2010.
Dooyeweerd, Herman. *Raízes da cultura ocidental: as opções cristã, secular e pagã*. São Paulo: Cultura Cristã, 2015.
Dooyeweerd, Herman. *Roots of Western Culture: Pagan, Secular and Christian Options*. Toronto: Wedge Publishing Foundation, 1979.
Dryness, William. *Learning about Theology from the Third World*. Grand Rapids: Zondervan, 1990.
Dupont, Anthony, and Pierre-Paul Walraet. "Augustine on the Heart as the Centre of Human Happiness." *Studies in Spirituality,* 25 (2015): 45-77.
Duriez, Colin. *Francis Schaeffer: an authentic life*. Nottingham: IVP, 2008.
Ekström, Leif. *Aos Que Ainda Não Ouviram: desafios missionários rumo ao século XXI*. São Paulo: Sepal, 1998.

Ekström, Leif. *Uma Análise Histórica dos Objetivos da Associação de Missões Transculturais Brasileiras e o seu Cumprimento*. São Paulo: Faculdade Teológica Batista De São Paulo, 1998.
Ellul, Jacques. *La edad de la técnica*. Barcelona: Octaedro, 2003.
Ellul, Jacques. *The Technological Society*. New York: Knopf, 1964.
Escobar, Samuel. *Diálogo entre Cristo y Marx*. Lima: AGEUP, 1967
Escobar, Samuel. *En Busca de Cristo en la América Latina*. Buenos Aires: Ediciones Kairos, 2012.
Escobar, Samuel. *La Fe Evangélica y las Teologías de la Liberación*. El Paso: Casa Bautista de Publicaciones, 1987.
Espoz, Renato. 'El testimonio de la economía en la perspectiva del cristianismo en América Latina', *Boletín Teológico* 38 (1990), pp. 101-111.
Espoz, Renato. 'La economía: una pseudo-ciencia natural', *Boletín Teológico* 34 (1989) pp. 183-206.
Espoz, Renato. 'Os cristaos frente a dependencia económica e a divida externa', *Boletim Teologico* 13 (1990), pp. 41-50.
Fajardo, Alexander and David de Oliveira. *FTL 45 anos: e as fronteiras teológicas na contemporaneidade*. São Paulo: FTL, 2016.
Fausto, Sergio. 'The Lengthy Brazilian Crisis is not yet over'. *Rice University's Baker Institute for Public Policy Issue Brief* 17 February 2017.
Ferreira, Franklin. 'Crentes no poder'. *Revista Expressão Cidadania Cristã*, 1 (2002), pp. 85-90.
Ferreira, Franklin. 'Uma Agenda para o Voto Conciente'. *Teologia Brasileira* <http://www.teologiabrasileira.com.br/teologiadet.asp?codigo=402> [accessed 01 February 2018]
Ferreira, Franklin. *Curso Vida Nova de teologia básica: Teologia sistemática*. São Paulo: Vida Nova, 2013.
Freston, Paul and Raphael Freston, 'A tão Famigerada Missao Integral', *Ultimato* 362 (2016), pp. 66–76.
Freston, Paul. 'Neo-Pentecostalism in Brazil: Problems of Definition and the Struggle for Hegemony', *Arch. De Sc. Soc. Des. Rel* 105 (1999).
Freston, Paul. 'Researching the Heartland of Pentecostalism: Latin Americans at Home and Abroad', *Fieldwork in Religion* 3:2 (2008), pp. 122–144.
Freston, Paul. *Evangelicals and Politics in Asia, Africa and Latin America*. Cambridge: Cambridge University Press, 2001.
FTL. "Declaración de Jarabacoa: os cristãos e a ação política". *Boletim Teologico 2.1*, 1984.
Gasque, Laurel. *Rookmaaker: arte e mente cristã*. Viçosa, MG: Ultimato, 2012.
Giddens, Anthony. *Modernidade e Identidade*. Rio de Janeiro: Jorge Zahar, 2002.
Girón, Rodolfo. 'Desafíos contextuales y generacionales en la misión del siglo XXI'. Paper presented at the IV Congreso Misionero Iberoamericano COMIBAM 2017.
Goheen, Michael. *A Igreja Missional na Bíblia: luz para as nações*. São Paulo: Vida Nova, 2014.
González Ruiz, José. *Dios es gratuito pero no superfluo*. Madrid: Ediciones Marova, 1970.
González, Antonio. *El evangelio de la paz y el reinado de Dios*. Buenos Aires: Kairós, 2008.
González, Antonio. *Reinado de Dios e Imperio. Ensayo de teología social*. Santander: Sal Terrae, 2003.
González, Justo L. *The Mestizo Augustine: A Theologian between Two Cultures*. Downers Grove: InterVarsity Press, 2016.

González, Justo. *Historia del Cristianismo: obra completa*. Miami: Editorial Unilit, 2009.
González, Justo. *Historia del pensamiento cristiano Tomo III*. Nashville: Editorial Caribe, 1992.
Guder, Darrel (ed.). *Missional Church: A vision for the sending of the church in North America*. Grand Rapids: Eerdmans, 1998.
Guerrero, Milton. 'El Pacto de Lausana (1974): Una Contextualización vista desde 2010'. *Integralidad* 8 (2011), pp. 5–14.
Gutiérrez, Gustavo. *A Theology of Liberation: History, Politics, and Salvation*. Revised Edition with a New Introduction. Maryknoll: Orbis, 1988.
Gutiérrez, Gustavo. *El Dios de la vida*. Lima: CEP – Instituto Bartolomé de las Casas, 1989.
Gutiérrez, Gustavo. *La fuerza histórica de los pobres*. Lima: CEP, 1979.
Hanciles, Jehu. *Beyond Christendom: Globalization, African Migration, and the Transformation of the West*. Maryknoll: Orbis, 2008.
Hay, Rob et al. *Dignos de Cuidados: perspectivas globais na melhor prática de retenção missionária*. Londrina: Descoberta, 2008.
Heaney, Sharon. *Contextual Theology for Latin America*. UK: Paternoster, 2008.
Hiebert, Paul. *O Evangelho e a Diversidade das Culturas: um guia de antropologia missionária*. São Paulo: Vida Nova, 2010.
Hinkelammert, Franz. *El asalto al poder mundial y la violencia sagrada del imperio*. San José: DEI, 2003.
Hinkelammert, Franz. 'Economia e teologia: as leis do mercado e a Fé' *Boletim Teologico* 11 (1990), pp. 43-64.
Hinkelammert, Franz. *Las armas ideológicas de la muerte*. San José: DEI, 1981.
Hinkelammert, Franz. "Teología en el acontecer de la vida", in *Itinerarios de la razón crítica. Homenaje a Franz Hinkelammert en sus 70 años*. Eds. José Duque and Germán Gutiérrez. San José: DEI, 2001.
Hoffmann, Martin. 'La Reforma, como un nuevo paradigma de la teología' *Espiga* 16 (2017), pp. 19–32.
Hugo, John Jacob. *St. Augustine on Nature, Sex and Marriage*. Chicago: Scepter, 1969.
Ingleby, Jonathan. 'Introduction', in *Carnival Kingdom*. Ed. Marijke Hoek, Jonathan Ingleby, Andy Kingston-Smith and Carol Kingston-Smith. Gloucester: Wide Margin, 2013, pp. xiii-xv.
Inwood, M. J. 'Platonism', in *The Oxford Companion to Philosophy*. Ed. Ted Honderich, Oxford: Oxford University Press, 2005.
Jenkins, Philip. *Laying down the sword: Why we can't ignore the Bible's violent verses*. New York: Harper Collins, 2011.
Johnson Todd and Sandi Lee, 'Da cristandade ocidental ao cristianismo mundial', in *Perspectivas no Movimento Cristão Mundial*. Eds. Ralph Winter, Steven Hawthorne and Kevin Bradford. São Paulo: Vida Nova, 2009.
Johnstone, Patrick. *O Futuro da Igreja Global*. São Paulo: Cultura Cristã, 2017.
Kalsbeek, L. *Contornos da filosofia cristã: a melhor e mais sucinta à Filosofia Reformada de Herman Dooyeweerd*. São Paulo: Cultura Cristã, 2015.
Keppel, Gilles. *The Revenge of God: The resurgence of Islam, Christianity and Judaism in the Modern World*. University Park: Pennsylvania State University Press, 1994.
Kidner, Derek. *Génesis: Introdução e comentario*. Sao Paulo: Mundo Cristao, 1979.
Kirkpatrick, David. 'C. René Padilla and the Origins of Integral Mission in Post-War Latin America'. *Journal of Ecclesiastical History* 67:2 (2016), pp. 351–371.
Kirkpatrick, David. 'C. René Padilla: Integral Mission and the Reshaping of Global Evangelism'. PhD thesis, University of Edinburgh, 2015.

Kruse, Marcos. 'Economo-Teología. Preliminares' *Boletim Teologico* 20 (1993), pp. 7-18.
Küng, Hans. *El cristianismo: Esencia e historia.* Madrid: Editorial Trotta 1997.
Kuyper, Abraham. *Calvinismo.* São Paulo: Cultura Cristã, 2003.
Lane, William. *Uma análise do propósito bíblico da missão.* Vicosa: CEM, 2013.
Lategan, Bernard. 'Hermeneutics', in *The Anchor Yale Bible Dictionary.* Ed. David Freedman. New Haven: Yale University Press, 1992.
Lausanne Movement. 'Cape Town Commitment'. *Lausanne Movement Homepage* available online at https://lausanne.org/content/ctcommitment#capetown accessed 2 June 2020.
Lehmann, David. 'Dissidence and conformism in religious movements: what difference, if any, separates the Catholic Charismatic Renewal and Pentecostal churches' http://www.davidlehmann.org/david-docs-pdf/Pubpap/DISSIDENCE%20AND%20CONFORMISM%20IN%20RELIGIOUS%20MOVEMENTS.pdf [accessed 12 November 2012].
Livingston George. *Comentário Bíblico Beacon. v. 1, Gênesis a Deuteronômio.* Rio de Janeiro: CPAD, 2005.
Lohfink, Norman. "Reino de Dios y economía en la Biblia", *Communio* 8 (March-April 1986), pp. 112–124.
Longman III, Tremper. 'The case for continuity', in *Show them no mercy: four views on God and the Canaanite Genocide.* Ed. Stanley Gundry. Grand Rapids: Zondervan, 1994.
Longoni, Ana y Ricardo Santoni. *De los poetas malditos al videoclip. Arte y literatura de vanguardia.* Buenos Aires: Cántaro, 1998.
Longuini Neto, Luis. *O Novo Rosto da Missão: os movimentos ecumênico e evangelical no protestantismo latino-americano.* Viçosa: Ultimato, 2002.
López, Darío. "Hechos" in *Comentario Bíblico Contemporáneo.* Buenos Aíres: Kairós, 2019.
Luther, Martin. *Pelo Evangelho de Cristo.* Porto Alegre/São Leopoldo: Ed. Concórdia/ Ed. Sinodal, 1984.
Lynch, M. 'Joshua and violence (part 5): show them no mercy'. Available online at https://theologicalmisc.net/2016/04/joshua-violence-part-5-show-no-mercy/
Machado, Maria. 'Representações e Relações de Gênero nos Grupos Pentecostais'. *Estudos Feministas* 13:2 (2005), pp. 387–396.
Machado, Maria. *Política e Religião: A Participação dos Evangélicos nas Eleições.* Rio de Janeiro: Fundação Getúlio Vargas, 2006.
Mardones, José. *Capitalismo y religión. La religión política neoconservadora.* Santander: Sal Terrae, 1991.
Mardones, José. *Postmodernidad y neoconservaduriamo. Reflexiones sobre la fe y la cultura.* Navarra: Verbo Divino.
Mariani, Daniel and Simon Ducroquet, 'A expansão evangélica no Brasil em 26 anos', *Nexo Journal Homepage,* available online at https://www.nexojornal.com.br/grafico/2017/11/06/A-expans%C3%A3o-evang%C3%A9lica-no-Brasil-em-26-anos, accessed 24 October 2019.
Marion, Jean-Luc. *In the Self's Place: The Approach of Saint Augustine.* Stanford: Stanford University Press, 2012.
Markus, Robert. *Conversion and Disenchantment in Augustine's Spiritual Career.* Villanova: Villanova University Press, 1989.
Martin, Berenice. 'Pentecostal Conversion and the Limits of the Market Metaphor'. *Exchange* 35:1 (2006), pp. 61–91.

Martin, David. 'Secularisation and the Future of Christianity'. *Journal of Contemporary Religion* 20.2 (2005).
Mathison, Keith. *'All truth is God's truth: a Reformed approach to science and scripture'*. Available online at https://www.ligonier.org/blog/all-truth-gods-truth-reformed-approach-science-and-scripture/ accessed 25 April 2021.
Mcgregor, Jock. Lecture on: *Christ and culture revisited.* Available in <http://labri ideas-library.org/do-download.asp?Lecture=1544>
McKnight, Scott. *'Evangelical Progressives: A Public Theology of Community'* <http://www.patheos.com/blogs/jesuscreed/2015/11/04/evangelical-progressives-a-public-theology-ofcommunity> [accessed 06 November 2015].
Medeiros, Alisson. *Relatório: Como Ouvirão 2018.* João Pessoa: Missão Juvep, 2019.
Méndez, Guillermo. "El sustrato teológico de la economía", *Kairós* 13 (1993).
Menezes, Ademir et al. *Força Missionária Brasileira Transcultural.* available online at http://www.amtb.org.br/wp-content/uploads/2020/04/Forc%CC%A7a-Missiona%CC%81ria-Brasileira-Completo.pdf, accessed April 10 2021.
Merk, Frederick. *Manifest Destiny and Mission in American History.* Cambridge: Harvard University Press, 1963.
Micah Network, 'Integral Mission', *Micah Network* http://www.micahnetwork.org/integral-mission [accessed 05 November 2015]
Micah Network, 'Who we are', *Micah Network* <http://www.micahnetwork.org/who-we-are> [accessed 31 January 2018] (bold in the original).
Míguez Bonino, José. "El reino de Dios y la historia", in *El reino de Dios y América Latina.* Ed. C. René Padilla, El Paso, TX: CBP, 1975, pp. 75-95.
Miguez Bonino, José. *Rostos do Protestantismo Latino-americano.* São Leopoldo: Sinodal, 2013.
Míguez, Néstor "Hacer teología latinoamericana en el tiempo de globalización", in *El silbo ecuménico del Espíritu. Homenaje a José Míguez Bonino en sus 80 años.* Ed. Guillermo Hansen. Buenos Aires: Instituto Universitario ISEDET, 2004, pp. 81-101.
Miranda, José Porfirio. *Comunismo en la Biblia.* Mexico City: Siglo XXI, 1981.
Moltmann, Jürgen. *Doutrina Ecológica da Criação.* Petrópolis: Vozes, 1993.
Moltmann, Jürgen. *God for a Secular Society. The Public Relevance of Theology.* London: SCM Press, 1999.
Moon, Steve. *The Korean Missionary Movement: Dynamics and Trends, 1988-2013.* Pasadena: William Carey Library, 2016.
Moore, Russell. *The Kingdom of Christ. The New Evangelical Perspective.* Wheaton: Crossway Books, 2004.
Morante, Pedro. *Iglesia y cultura en América Latina.* Lima: Vida y Espiritualidad, 1989.
Mordomo, João. 'Unleashing the Brazilian Missionary Force', in *Business as mission: From impoverished to empowered.* Evangelical Missiological Series 14. Ed.Tom Steffen and Mike Barnett. Pasadena: William Carey Library, 2006.
Moura, Clovis. 'O racismo como arma ideológica de dominação'. *Revista Principios* 34 (1994), pp. 28–56.
Munanga, Kabengele. 'Uma abordagem conceitual das noçôes de raça, racismo, identidade e etnia.' *Universidade Federal de Minas Gerais Homepage.* available online at https://www.ufmg.br/inclusaosocial/?p=59 accessed 5 May 2021
Myers, Bryant. 'Holistic Mission: New Frontiers', in *Holistic Mission: God's Plan for God's People.* Regnum Edinburgh 2010 series. Eds.Brian Woolnough and Wonsuk Ma. Oxford: Regnum, 2010, pp. 119–127.
Nañez, Rick. *Pentecostal de coração e mente: um chamado ao dom divino do intelecto.* São Paulo: Ed. Vida, 2007.

Nicodemos Lopes, Augusto, Jonas Madureira and Fabio Costa, 'Academia em Debate 37: Teologia da Missão Integral', available online at <https://www.youtube.com/watch?v=ng257P3XXOc> [accessed 05 November 2015]

Niebuhr, H. Richard. *Cristo e cultura*. Paz e Terra: Rio de Janeiro, 1967.

Novak, Michael. *¿En verdad liberará? Reflexiones sobre teología de la liberación*. Mexico City: Diana, 1994.

Novak, Michael. *El espíritu del capitalismo democrático*. Buenos Aires: Tres tiempos, 1983.

Novak, Michael. *El pensamiento social católico y las instituciones liberales*. San José: Libro Libre, 1992.

Novak, Michael. *Raíces evangélicas del capitalismo democrático*. San José: Libro Libre, 1989.}

Nuñez, Emilio. *Teología de la liberación: Una perspectiva evangélica*. Miami: Caribe, 1986.

Ocaña Flores, Martín "The New Apostolic Reformation and the Theology of Prosperity in Peru", in *Prosperity Theology and the Gospel*. Ed. Daniel Salinas. Peabody: Hendrickson, 2017.

Ocana Flores, Martín. 'Poder Político: Desafío para la Misión Integral en América Latina', *Integralidad* 3 (2008), pp. 19–29.

Oosterbaan, Martijn. 'Spiritual Attunement: Pentecostal Radio in the Soundscape of a Favela in Rio de Janeiro'. *Social Text* 25.3 (2008), pp. 123–145.

Pablo Deiros, edit., *Los evangélicos y el poder político en América Latina*. Buenos Aires – Grand Rapids, MI: Nueva Creación, 1986.

Padilla, C. René. 'Carta Abierta a Harold Segura'. *Fundación Kairos* <http://www.kairos.org.ar/blog/?p=997> [accessed 01 February 2018]

Padilla, C. René. 'Deus ama o estrangeiro' *Revista Ultimato* 367 (2017).

Padilla, C. René. 'Integral Mission and its Historical Development', in *Justice, Mercy and Humility*. Ed. Tim Chester. Carlisle: Paternoster, 2003, pp. 42–58.

Padilla, C. René. *Missão da Igreja: Ensaios sobre o Reino e a Igreja*. São Paulo: Temática, 1992.

Padilla, Washington. *Hacia una transformación integral*. Buenos Aires: Fraternidad Teológica Latinoamericana, 1989.

Padilla, C. René. 'The Future of the Lausanne Movement', *International Bulletin of Missionary Research* 35:2 (2011), pp. 87–88.

Paredes, Tito. 'Hipótesis de Trabajo para Comprender la Misiología de la Fraternidad Teológica Latinoamericana', *Integralidad* 16 (2014), pp. 5–12.

Paredes, Tito. 'Holistic Mission in Latin America', in *Holistic Mission: God's Plan for God's People*. Regnum Edinburgh 2010 series. Eds. Brian Woolnough and Wonsuk Ma. Oxford: Regnum, 2010, pp. 102–118.

Paredes, Tito. 'Reflexiones sobre los Desafíos y Oportunidades de Misión para las Iglesias Evangélicas Pentecostales Latinoamericanas'. *Integralidad* 4 (2008), pp. 7–14.

Parker Gumucio, Cristián. 'Pluralismo religioso y cambio de paradigma identitario en el campo político latinoamericano actual', in *Símbolos, rituales religiosos e identidades nacionales: los símbolos religiosos y los procesos de construcción política de identidades en Latinoamérica*. Ed. Aldo Almeigeiras. Buenos Aires: CLACSO, 2014.

Passos, João. 'Teogonias Urbanas: Os Pentecostais na Passagem do Rural ao Urbano', *São Paulo em Perspectiva* 14.4 (2000).

Pereira, Daniel, *Resultado da Pesquisa Arrecadação de Agências Missionárias*. São Paulo. Sepal & AMTB, 2019.
Pereira, Nancy. 'Empire and Religion: Gospel, Ecumenism and Prophecy for the 21st Century'. *The Ecumenical Review* 58:1 (2006), pp. 92–98.
Pérez, Turrent, Tomás and José de la Colina. *Buñuel por Buñuel*. Madrid: Plotediciones, 1993.
Plato. *A República*, in *Textos Básicos de Filosofia: dos Pré-socráticos a Wittgenstein*. Second edition. Ed. Danilo Marcondes, Rio de Janeiro: Jorge Zahar Editor, 2000.
Pope Paul VI. *Populorum Progressio: Encyclical of Paul VI on the development of peoples*. Vatican: Holy See, 1967. Available online at http://www.vatican.va/content/paul-vi/en/encyclicals/documents/hf_p-vi_enc_26031967_populorum.pdf. Accessed 28 April 2021.
Power, Bernie, *Challenging Islamic Traditions*. Pasadena, California: William Carey Library, 2016.
Power, Bernie. *Engaging Islamic traditions – Using the Hadith in Christian ministry to Muslims*. Pasadena, California: William Carey Library, 2016.
Prado, Oswaldo. 'The Brazil Model'. *AD 2000 Homepage*. Available at www.ad2000.org/gcowe95/prado.html. Accessed 28 October 2019.
Ramachandra, Vinoth. 'What is Integral Mission?', *Micah Network* http://www.micahnetwork.org/sites/default/files/doc/library/whatisintegralmission_imi-the-001.pdf (accessed 02 February 2018).
Ramlow, Rodomar. 'O Neocalvinismo Holandês e o Movimento de Cosmovisão Cristã'. Master of Theology Thesis, Escola Superior de Teologia, 2012.
Ramos, Ariovaldo. 'Os evangélicos descobriram o que Lula não conseguiu: para vencer é preciso mídia'. *Brasil de Fato* <https://www.brasildefato.com.br/2017/01/03/os-evangelicos-descobriram-o-que-lula-naoconseguiu-para-vencer-e-preciso-midia/> [accessed 23 April 2018]
Ramos, Robson. *Evangelização no mercado Pós-Moderno*. Viçosa: Ultimato, 2003.
Rankin, Melinda. *Twenty Years Among the Mexicans*. Cincinnati: Chase & Hall, 1875.
Reitsema, Edith. Lecture on: *The intriguing friendship between Francis Schaeffer and Hans Rookmaaker*. Available in: http://www.labri-ideas library.org/download.asp?fileID=711
RENAS, 'Histórico', *RENAS Rede Evangélica de Ação Social* http://renas.org.br/historico/ [accessed 23 April 2018]
Richardson, D. *Segredos do Alcorão*. Minas Gerais: Horizontes América Latina, 2007.
Richardson, Don. *Secrets of the Koran: Revealing insights into Islam's Holy Book*. Minneapolis: Bethany House Publishers, 2003.
Rist, John. *On Ethics, Politics and Psychology in the Twenty-first Century*. Reading Augustine. London: Bloomsbury Academic, 2018.
Robert, Dana L. *American Women in Mission*. Macon: Mercer University Press, 1998.
Rodriguez Garavito, César and Carlos Barquero Díaz. *Conflictos socioambientales en América Latina*. digital edition, Buenos Aires: Editores Argentina, 2020.
Rookmaaker, Hans. *A arte não precisa de justificativa*. Viçosa: Ultimato, 2010.
Salinas, Daniel. *Latin American Theology in the 1970s: The Golden Decade*. Religion in the Americas Series Volume 9. Leiden; Brill, 2009.
Sallandt, Ulrike. 'Ética Social: Más Allá de la Misión Integral'. *Integralidad* 3 (2007), pp. 14–19.
Samuel, Vinay. 'Mission as Transformation and the Church, in *Holistic Mission: God's Plan for God's People*. Regnum Edinburgh 2010 series. Eds.Brian Woolnough and Wonsuk Ma. Oxford: Regnum, 2010, pp. 128–136.
Sanches, Regina. *Como Fazer Teologia da Missão Integral*. São Paulo: Garimpo, 2016.

Sanches, Regina. *Introdução às Teologias Latino-americanas*. Campinas: Saber Criativo, 2019.
Sanches, Regina. *Teologia da Missão Integral*. São Paulo: Reflexão, 2009.
Sanches, Sidney. *A Teologia Evangélica Contextual*. São Paulo: Reflexão, 2010.
Samneh, Lamin. *Whose religion is Christianity? The Gospel beyond the west*. Grand Rapids: Eerdmans, 2003.
Schaeffer, Edith. *L'Abri*. Wheaton, USA: Crossway Books, 1992.
Schaeffer, Francis. *A Arte e a Bíblia*. Viçosa: Ultimato, 2010.
Schaeffer, Francis. *A morte da Razão*. São Paulo: ABU Editora, 2014.
Schuldt, Jürgen. *Civilización del desperdicio*. Lima: Universidad del Pacífico, 2013.
Schwantes, Milton. *Projetos de Esperança: meditações sobre Gênesis 1-11*. Petrópolis: Vozes; 1989.
Sedgwick, Peter. *The Market Economy and Christian Ethics*. Cambridge: Cambridge University Press 2004.
Segundo, Juan. "Capitalismo-socialismo, *crux theologica*", in *La nueva frontera de la teología en América Latina*. Ed. Rossini Gibellini. Salamanca: Sígueme, 1977.
Segundo, Juan. *Libertação da Teologia*. São Paulo: Loyola, 1978.
Shalkwij, Franz 'Índios evangélicos no Brasil Holandês', in *Missões e a Igreja Brasileira: Perspectivas Históricas*. Ed. Timoteo Carriker. São Paulo: Editora Mundo Cristão, 1993.
Shea, William. *The Lion and the Lamb: Evangelicals and Catholics in America*. New York: Oxford University Press, 2004.
Sherman, Amy. *Preferential Option. A Christian and Neoliberal Strategy for Latin America's poor*. Grand Rapids: Eerdmans, 1992.
Sinner, Rudolf von. 'Teologia Pública no Brasil', in *Teologia Pública: Reflexões sobre uma área de conhecimento e sua cidadania acadêmica*. Eds. Afonso Soares and João Décio. São Paulo: Paulinas, 2011.
Sipierski, Paulo. 'Missionários protestantes estrangeiros no brasil: dos primórdios ao Congresso do Panamá', in *Missões e a Igreja Brasileira: Perspectivas Históricas*. Ed. Timoteo Carriker. São Paulo: Editora Mundo Cristão, 1993.
Smither, Edward. 'The impact of evangelical revivals on global mission: The case of North American evangelicals in Brazil in the nineteenth and twentieth centuries'. *Verbum et Ecclesia* 31:1, 2010.
Solalinde. José. *El reino de Dios. Replanteamiento radical de la vida*. Toluca: Universidad Autónoma del Estado de México, 2016.
Souza, André. *Igreja in Concert: Padres Cantores, Midia e Marketing*. São Paulo: Annablume, 2005.
Stam, Juan. "La teología dominante y el derecho a la vida", in *Haciendo teología en América Latina. Volumen 2*. Ed.: Arthur Piedra. San José: Visión Mundial y otros, 2005.
Stam, Juan. *Profecía bíblica e missão da Igreja*. Sao Leopoldo: Sinodal and CLAI, 2003.
Steuernagel, Valdir. *Obediência Missionária e Prática Histórica: em busca de modelos*. São Paulo: ABU, 1993.
Steuernagel, Valdir. 'The Relevance and Effects of European Academic Theology on Theological Education in the Third World'. *The Evangelical Review of Theology* 27.3 (2003).
Sugden, Chris. 'Mission as Transformation: Its Journey among Evangelicals since Lausanne I', in *Holistic Mission: God's Plan for God's People*. Regnum Edinburgh 2010 series. Eds.Brian Woolnough and Wonsuk Ma. Oxford: Regnum, 2010, pp. 31–36.

Sung, Jo Mung. *Economía, tema ausente en la teología de la liberación.* San José: DEI, 1994.
Taborda, Francisco. 'Métodos Teológicos na América Latina', *Perspectiva Teológica* 19 (1987). 1987.
Tamayo Acosta, Juan José. *Otra teología es posible. Pluralismo religioso, interculturalidad y feminismo.* Barcelona: Herder, 2011.
Thompson, John. *Deuteronômio: introdução e comentario.* São Paulo: Mundo Cristão, 1982.
Timm, Alberto. 'Teologia da Prosperidade', in *Dicionário Brasileiro de Teologia.* Ed. Fernando Bortolleto Filho. São Paulo: ASTE, 2008.
Tizon, Al. 'Precursors and Tensions in Holistic Mission: An Historical Overview', in *Holistic Mission: God's Plan for God's People.* Regnum Edinburgh 2010 series. Eds.Brian Woolnough and Wonsuk Ma. Oxford: Regnum, 2010, pp. 61–76.
Tizon, Al. *Whole and Reconciled.* Grand Rapids: Baker Academic, 2018.
Tucker, Ruth. *Missões até os confins da terra: uma história biográfica.* São Paulo: Shedd, 2010.
Tunes, Suzel. *O Pregador Silencioso: Ecumenismo no jornal Expositor Cristão (1886 a 1982).* São Bernardo: Universidade Metodista, 2009.
Turner, Steve. *Imagine: a vision for Christians in the arts.* Illinois: InterVarsity Press, 2001.
UNHCR, *Manual de Proteção aos Apátridas.* Geneva: ANCUR, 2014.
UNODOC, 'UN.GIFT – Iniciativa Global da ONU contra o Tráfico de Pessoas', UNDOC Homepage available at https://www.unodc.org/lpo-brazil/pt/trafico-de-pessoas/ungift.html.
Verheijen, Melchior. *Eloquentia Pedisequa: observations sur le style des confessions de saint Augustin.* Nijmegen: Dekker & Van de Vegt, 1949.
Verkuyl, Johannes. *Contemporary Missiology: An Introduction.* Grand Rapids: Eerdmans 1978.
Vidales, Raúl. *Teología e Imperio.* San José: DEI, 1991.
Vílchez-Blancas, Eliseo. 'Signos y Condiciones de un Nuevo Contexto Misiológico'. *Integralidad* 4 (2008), pp. 27–32.
Volf, Miroslav. *Exclusion and Embrace: A Theological Exploration of Identity, Otherness, and Reconciliation.* Nashville: Abingdon Press, 1996.
Walls, Andrew F. *The Missionary Movement in Christian History.* New York: Orbis, 1996.
Waltke, Bruce. *Comentario do Antiguo Testamento: Génesis.* Sao Paulo: Cultura Crista, 2010.
Walton, John. 'Herem', in *The IVP Bible Background Commentary: Old Testament.* Eds. John Walton, Victor Matthews and Mark Chavalas. Downers Grove: IVP Academic, 2000.
Weigel, George. *Fieles y libres. Catolicismo, derechos humanos y democracia.* San José: Libro Libre, 1989.
Westmeier, Karl-Wilhelm. *Protestant Pentecostalism in Latin America: A Study in the Dynamics of Mission.* Cranbury: Fairleigh Dickinson University Press, 1999.
Wiersbe, Warren. *Comentario Bíblico Expositivo: Antigo Testamento: volume 1: Pentateuco.* Santo André: Geográfica, 2010.
Wolff, Hans. *Antropologia do Antigo Testamento.* São Paulo: Hagnos, 2008.
Woolnough, Brian. 'Good News for the Poor: Setting the Scene', in *Holistic Mission: God's Plan for God's People.* Regnum Edinburgh 2010 series. Eds.Brian Woolnough and Wonsuk Ma. Oxford: Regnum, 2010, pp. 3–16 (pp. 3-4)

Wright, Christopher. *A missão de Deus: desvendando a grande narrativa da Bíblia.* São Paulo: Vida Nova, 2014.
Wright, Christopher. *A missão do povo de Deus: uma teologia bíblica da missão da igreja.* São Paulo: Vida Nova, 2012.
Wright, Christopher. *La misión de Dios: Descubriendo el gran mensaje de la Biblia.* Buenos Aires: Certeza Unida, 2009.
Wright, Christopher. *Povo, terra e Deus: a relevância da ética do Antigo Testamento para a sociedade de hoje.* São Paulo: ABU Editora, 1991.
Wright, George. *O Deus que age.* São Paulo: Aste, 1967.
Yeh, Allen. 'O futuro de missões é de todos para todos os lugares', *Análise Global de Lausanne* 7.1 (2018), available at www.lausanne.org/pt-br/recursos-multimidia-pt-br/agl-pt-br/2018-01-pt-br/o-futuro-de-missoes-e-de-todos-para-todos-os-lugare. Accessed 25 October 2019.
Yeh, Allen. *Polycentric Missiology: twenty-first-century mission from everyone to everywhere.* Downers Grove: IVP, 2016.
Zabatiero, Julio. *Hermenêutica Contextual.* São Paulo: Garimpo, 2017.